Kenneth Numfor Ngwa
The Hermeneutics of the 'Happy' Ending
in Job 42: 7–17

Beihefte zur Zeitschrift für die alttestamentliche Wissenschaft

Herausgegeben von
John Barton · Reinhard G. Kratz
Choon-Leong Seow · Markus Witte

Band 354

Walter de Gruyter · Berlin · New York

Kenneth Numfor Ngwa

The Hermeneutics of the 'Happy' Ending in Job 42: 7–17

Walter de Gruyter · Berlin · New York

☉ Printed on acid-free paper which falls within
the guidelines of the ANSI to ensure permanence and durability.

ISBN-13: 978-3-11-018412-9
ISBN-10: 3-11-018412-5

Bibliographic information published by Die Deutsche Bibliothek

Die Deutsche Bibliothek lists this publication in the Deutsche Nationalbibliografie; detailed bibliographic data is available in the Internet at <http://dnb.ddb.de>.

© Copyright 2005 by Walter de Gruyter GmbH & Co. KG, D-10785 Berlin
All rights reserved, including those of translation into foreign languages. No part of this book may be reproduced or transmitted in any form or by any means, electronic or mechanical, including photocopy, recording, or any information storage and retrieval system, without permission in writing from the publisher.
Printed in Germany
Cover Design: Christopher Schneider, Berlin

Preface

This book is a slightly revised version of my dissertation, and I would like to acknowledge the invaluable contributions that others have made towards its realization and publication. I would like to thank my adviser and mentor, Prof. C. L. Seow, along with the other members of my dissertation committee, Profs. Patrick Miller and Dennis Olson for the personal and professional interest they have shown me both during and after my graduate work. Their patient and multiple teaching methods and mentoring have greatly shaped my thinking and writing. I would also like to express my appreciation to Dr. Albrecht Döhnert and the editorial board of *BZAW* for reading through the manuscript, providing helpful comments and accepting to publish this work.

A word of special thanks goes to the faculty members of the biblical department of Princeton Theological Seminary. Their teaching and mentoring have greatly contributed in introducing me to the world of scholarship. I cannot forget my colleagues and friends with whom I have had fruitful discussions both in and out of class over the past years. I thank especially Amy Erickson, Tom Sakon, Jacob Cherian, Nyasha Junior, Alice Yafeh, Beverly Frazier, and all those who listened to my ideas and provided helpful suggestions as I worked on the text.

A special word of thanks goes to my family for their patience and support over these past years. I would also like to express my deep appreciation to Rev and Mrs. Bame Bame whose scholarship and mentoring inspired me several years ago to embark on this journey in scholarship and service. Finally, I acknowledge and greatly appreciate the editorial and formatting assistance I received from Chris Muflam, Wilfred Ngwa, and Monika Müller. Any errors in the text remain mine.

In appreciation of their continuous support, I dedicate this work to my family.

Kenneth Numfor Ngwa

October 2005

Table of Contents

Preface v
Abbreviations ix
Introduction 1
Chapter 1: Text and Textual Analysis 9
   1.1 Text 9
   1.2 Textual Analysis 9
   1.3 Conclusion 25
Chapter 2: The Post-Canonical Life of the Text:A Selected History of
Interpretation 27
   2.1 Introduction 27
   2.2 The Versions 29
      2.2.1 11QtgJob 29
      2.2.2 The Septuagint 34
      2.2.3 Summary 42
   2.3 Early Jewish and Christian Interpretation 43
      2.3.1 Rabbinic Interpretation 43
         2.3.1.1 The Epilogue as a Text 41
         2.3.1.2 The Epilogue as a Paradigm 43
         2.3.1.3 The Testament of Job 45
      2.3.2 Early Christian Interpretation 50
      2.3.2.1 Saint Ambrose of Milan (337/339-397) 50
      2.3.2.2 John Chrysostom (347-407) 51
      2.3.2.3 Gregory the Great (540-604) 53
   2.4 Later Medieval Interpretation 58
      2.4.1 Jewish Interpretation 59
      2.4.1.1 Saadiah Gaon (882-942) 56
      2.4.1.2 Rashi (1040-1105) 58
      2.4.1.3 Maimonides (1186-1237) 58
      2.4.2 Christian Interpretation 64
      2.4.2.1 Thomas Aquinas (1224/5-1274) 61
      2.4.2.2 John Calvin (1509-1564) 63
   2.5 Historical-Critical and Literary-Critical Work on the Epilogue 71
      2.5.1 Critical Analysis 71
      2.5.2 Theological Analysis 75
      2.5.3 Interpretive Issues 76
   2.6 Summary Conclusion 79

Chapter 3: Revisiting the Epilogue 81
  3.1 Proposed Hermeneutic 82
    3.1.1 The Literary and Thematic Function of the Epilogue 83
      3.1.1.1 The Epilogue and the Prologue 80
      3.1.1.2 The Epilogue and the Human Discussion 82
      3.1.1.3 Beyond the Prologue and the Dialogue................................. 84
    3.1.2 Continuity and Discontinuity Between the Epilogue and the
          Preceding Sections 94
    3.1.3 The Comic Aspect of the Epilogue 99
  3.2 Interpreting the Epilogue... 101
    3.2.1 Divine Rebuke and Approval (42:7–9) 102
    3.2.2 The Family and Social Restoration (42:10–17) 111
      3.2.2.1 Daughters and Inheritance in the Ancient Near East 108
      3.2.2.2 Daughters and Inheritance in the Bible 109
Chapter 4: Theological Reflections on the Epilogue 118
  4.1 Re-posing the Problem of Job 120
    4.1.1 The Nature of Retribution 120
    4.1.2 The Nature of the Divine-Human Relationship 121
    4.1.3 The Reality of Human Suffering 123
  4.2 Defining the Restoration in the Epilogue.. 124
    4.2.1 Restoration Language in the Epilogue 118
  4.3 Theological Resource for Interpreting the Epilogue 127
    4.3.1 Divine Transcendence and Immanence....................................... 127
    4.3.2 Retribution and Beyond 130
  4.4 Proposed Meanings of the Epilogue 131
    4.4.1 The Master-Servant Relationship:
          Restoration As Retributive and Non-Retributive 131
    4.4.2 The Divine-Human Relationship:
          Restoration as a New Beginning 134
    4.4.3 The Reality of Suffering:
          Restoration as Possible Triumph of the Good 137
Conclusion... 143
Bibliography.. 147
Index of Scriptural and Ancient Sources.. 169
Index of Authors.. 175

Abbreviations

AB	The Anchor Bible
ABD	The Anchor Bible Dictionary. Edited by D. N. Freedman. 6 vols.
AJSL	*American Journal of Semitic Languages and Literatures*
Aq	Aquila
BET	Bibliotheca Ephemeridum Theologicarum Lovaniensium
Bib	*Biblica*
BibInt	*Biblical Interpretation*
BJS	Brown Judaica Studies
BKAT	Biblischer Kommentar: Altes Testament
BTB	*Biblical Theology Bulletin*
BZAW	*Beihefte zur Zeitschrift für die alttestamentliche Wissenschaft*
BZNF	*Biblische Zeitschrift, Neue Folge*
CAT	Commentaire de l'Ancien Testament
CBQ	*Catholic Biblical Quarterly*
CH	*Church History*
CJ	*Conservative Judaism*
CTJ	*Calvin Theological Journal*
CTU	The Cuneiform Alphabetic Texts from Ugarit, Ras Ibn Hani, and other Places. Edited by M. Dietrich, O. Loretz, and J. Sanmartin. Münster, 1995
CurTM	*Currents in Theology and Mission*
Drev	*Downside Review*
ÉBNS	Études Bibliques, Nouvelle Série
EvQ	*Evangelical Quarterly*
EvT	*Evangelische Theologie*
FAT	Forschungen zum Alten Testament
GKC	Gesenius' *Hebrew Grammar*. Edited by E. Kautzsch. Translated by A. E. Cowley. 2nd ed. Oxford, 1910.
HAR	*Hebrew Annual Review*
HAT	Handbuch zum Alten Testament
HTR	*Harvard Theological Review*
HUCA	*Hebrew Union College Annual*
IB	G. A. Buttrick, ed. *The Interpreter's Bible*. 12 Volumes. Nashville, Tenn.: Abingdon, 1982.

IBC	Interpretation: A Bible Commentary for Teaching and Preaching
ICC	International Critical Commentary
Int	*Interpretation*
ITQ	*Irish Theological Quarterly*
JAOS	*Journal of the American Oriental Society*
JBL	*Journal of Biblical Literature*
JBQ	*Jewish Bible Quarterly*
JCS	*Journal of Cuneiform Studies*
JJS	*Journal of Jewish Studies*
JNES	*Journal of Near Eastern Studies*
JR	*Journal of Religion*
JSOT	*Journal for the Study of the Old Testament*
JSOTSup	*Journal for the Study of the Old Testament Supplementary Series*
JSP	*Journal for the Study of the Pseudepigrapha*
JSS	*Journal of Semitic Studies*
JTSA	*Journal of Theology for Southern Africa*
LXX	Septuagint
MC	*Modern Churchman*
MT	Massoretic Text
MTh	*Modern Theology*
NedTT	*Nederlands theologisch tijdschrift*
NIB	Leander E. Keck, ed. *The New Interpreter's Bible*. 12 Volumes. Nashville, Tenn.: Abingdon, 1994.
NPNF[1]	Nicene and Post Nicene Fathers, First Series
OG	Old Greek
OTP	*Old Testament Pseudepigrapha*
PRSt	*Perspectives in Religious Studies*
REJ	*Révue des Études Juives*
RelSRev	*Religious Studies Review*
ResQ	*Restoration Quarterly*
RevQ	*Révue de Qumran*
RTR	*Reformed Theological Review*
SAJ	Studies in Ancient Judaism
SBLDS	Society of Biblical Literature Dissertation Series
SBLSCS	Society of Biblical Literature Septuagint and Cognate Studies
SBLSP	Society of Biblical Literature Seminar Papers
SBLSS	Society of Biblical Literature Semeia Studies
SBLTCS	Society of Biblical Literature Text-Critical Studies
SBT[2]	Studies in Biblical Theology, Second Series
SC	*Sources Chrétiennes*
SecCent	*Second Century: A Journal of Early Christian Studies*

SR	*Studies in Religion/sciences religieuses*
SSN	Studia Semitica Neerlandica
StABH	Studies in American Biblical Hermeneutics
Symm	Symmachus
Syr.	Syriac
TDNT	*Theological Dictionary of the New Testament*. Edited by G. Kittel and G. Friedrich. Translated by Geoffrey W. Bromiley. Grand Rapids, Mich.: Eerdmans, 1985
Tg.	Targum
Theod	Theodotion
ThTo	*Theology Today*
T.Job	*Testament of Job*
TRu	*Theologische Rundschau*
UF	*Ugaritische Forschungen*
VC	*Vigiliae Christianae*
Vulg.	Vulgate
VT	*Vetus Testamentum*
VTSup	*Vetus Testamentum Supplementary Series*
WBC	Word Biblical Commentary
ZAW	*Zeitschrift für die alttestamenliche Wissenschaft*
ZNW	*Zeitschrift für die neutestamentliche Wissenschaft*
ZTK	*Zeitschrift fürTheologie und Kirche*

Introduction

In the final eleven verses of the Massoretic text of Job (42:7–17), the divine rebuke of the friends in 42:7 for not speaking rightly "like my servant Job" is set against the background of the preceding sections of the book where Job and his friends debate the issue of retributive justice and the appropriate human response to the experience of suffering and evil. Still acknowledging that the source of Job's troubles was YHWH, the narrator proceeds to describe the divine blessing of Job (42:12) following the rebuke of the friends. Job regains twice as much as he lost at the beginning. The Epilogue, thus, raises at least three questions. First, how does the divine approval of Job fit with God's rebuke of Job in chapters 38–41? Second, how does the divine rebuke of the friends fit with their defense of God's righteousness in the course of the Dialogues? And third, how does the restoration square with the issue of retributive justice in the book? That is, does the restoration of Job in the Epilogue (following the divine approval of Job) not prove what the Adversary had suggested in the Prologue, namely, that the nature of the human-divine relationship is that of a "trade relationship"?[1] To the extent that these aspects of the Epilogue "look back" at, or raise interpretive questions with regards to the preceding sections, perhaps one is to make a conscious and deliberate endeavor to see in what ways the Epilogue is related to the preceding sections. That is, a significant part of the Epilogue is to be interpreted in close conjunction with the preceding sections.

Part of the interpretive challenge that presents itself to the reader, therefore, consists of creating a framework that allows one to show how the Epilogue contributes to the understanding of the book as a whole. Within this broad framework, the Epilogue functions both as the literary end to the book and as its possible ultimate interpretive context. But this interpretive challenge goes beyond just providing an interpretive framework for the book; it also seeks to explore how the various moral, ethical and religious questions

---

1 Carol A. Newsom, The Book of Job: A Contest of Moral Imaginations (Oxford: Oxford University Press, 2003), 56. Scholarly discussion on the appropriate background to the divine rebuke of the friends in the Epilogue has revolved around three main proposals: (a) that the rebuke in 42:7–9 should be interpreted in conjunction with the Prologue, particularly 2:11–13; (b) that the rebuke should be placed within the context of the Dialogues with Job's friends in the poetic section, since it is in the Dialogues that the friends formulate and express their ideas about God; and (c) that the context for interpreting the rebuke is Job's confession in 42:1–6, since Job's confession of inferiority before YHWH seems to provide a reason for the simultaneous approval of Job in the rebuke of the friends. In the present work, I will highlight the strengths and weaknesses of these arguments and propose how, together, they contribute towards a fruitful interpretation of the Epilogue.

that are raised within the book can be meaningfully appropriated. It is therefore likely that the Epilogue deals not only with issues of form but also with the content of the diverse reactions to the moral/religious crisis that Job's suffering poses.

Significant historical-critical and literary-critical work has been done to situate the Epilogue within the overall structure and content of the book. One of the results of historical-critical work is the realization that the book of Job, like many others, has a complex history of composition, with different historical and cultural experiences underlying the literary text. As will later become evident in the development of this work, this realization is true of the Epilogue. But also, the larger hermeneutical question that will be at the center of my investigation goes beyond the question of history of composition to examining the text in its final form. Therefore, while drawing upon the results and insights of historical-critical analysis, my primary focus shall be on the interpretive function of the Epilogue in its current literary form.

David Noel Freedman, in an essay on the book of Job, succinctly expresses the questions that have inspired historical-critical and literary-critical work on the book. Freedman writes:

> "The Book is one of the world's great literary works – of ancient times or any time. Its grandeur lies not only in its literary excellence but in its profound examination of foundational and perennial, agonizing and ultimate questions of human experience: the problem of suffering, especially on the part of the innocent; the general question of theodicy; the way of the world; and the boundaries of human existence, knowledge, and experience."[2]

A number of points are worth noting here. First, issues of such diverse and fundamental value to the human-divine relationship are raised and brought together within the book, thereby highlighting the multi-dimensional and multi-thematic character of the book. Second, the literary technique that the narrator uses to pose these issues is through the Adversary's probing question ("does Job fear God for nothing?" – 1:8) and the prediction that Job will openly curse God to God's face if "touched" (1:11; 2:5). The underlying assumption in the formulation of this "test" is that Job's belief system (and implicitly that of the reader) is partly shaped by economic and social conditions; the "fear of God" is not a neutral experience, but is closely linked to one's historical, cultural, and religious experience. Third, other scholars argue that the fundamental issue in the book is not human suffering, but God and belief in a personal God. Along this line, the argument focuses not so much on the general concept of suffering, but on the crisis of faith that results from the contradiction resulting from belief in a benevolent God and the experience of the harsh reality of life or the "dark side" of God.[3] Such

---

[2] David Noel Freedman, "The Book of Job," in *The Hebrew Bible and its Interpreters* (ed. William H. Propp, Baruch Halpern, and David N. Freedman; Biblical and Judaic Studies 1; Winona Lake, Ind.: Eisenbrauns, 1990), 33.

[3] See, for example, James L. Crenshaw, "Popular Questioning of the Justice of God in Ancient Israel," *ZAW* 83, no. 3 (1970): 180–195; Dermot Cox, *Man's Anger and God's*

experience of the harsh reality of life, or, as the Epilogue puts it, of "the trouble" or "evil" that YHWH brought on Job, inevitably raises questions relating to the issue of theodicy.[4] Accordingly, it is fair to say that insofar as the Epilogue constitutes the literary end of the book, it bears the theological and hermeneutical task of providing "answers" or, at least, a framework for exploring possible "answers" to the questions that arise within the development of the narrative. These questions relate not only to the form but also to the content of the book. The Epilogue is, therefore, an important part of the book, and possibly constitutes a key component in its interpretation.[5]

However, there is no reason to imagine that readers are expected to suspend their judgment about the diverse literary and theological issues in the book until the end to find "answers." Even if one were to imagine such to be the case, the likelihood is that the "answers" that readers forge at the end will be diverse and complex, often depending on the way in which the problems are posed and perceived. This diverse interpretive reality is not simply a result of the different interpretive contexts. Rather, this diversity in interpretation is to be partly attributed to the fact that the Epilogue comes after the various speeches in the poetic section, which clearly convey the sense if dialogism, open endedness, and the "unfinilizability" of meaning for

---

Silence: The Book of Job (Middlegreen: St Paul Publications, 1990), 11; R. Norman Whybray, "'Shall Not the Judge of All the Earth Do What is Just?' God's Oppression of the Innocent in the Old Testament," in *Shall Not the Judge of All the Earth Do What is Right? Studies on the Nature of God in Tribute to James L. Crenshaw* (ed. David Penchansky and Paul L. Redditt; Winona Lake, Ind.: Eisenbrauns, 2000), 1–19; Walter Brueggemann, "Texts That Linger, Not Yet Overcome," in *Shall Not the Judge of All the Earth Do What is Right? Studies on the Nature of God in Tribute to James L. Crenshaw* (ed. David Penchansky and Paul L. Redditt; Winona Lake, Ind.: Eisenbrauns, 2000), 21–41; Jean Lévêque, "Le Thème du Juste Souffrant en Mésopotamie et la Problématique du Livre de Job," in *Le Livre de Job* (Lectures de L'Écriture, Graphè 6; Paris: Presses de l'Université Charles-de-Gaulle, 1997), 11–33.

4   Although a full treatment of the problem of theodicy lies beyond the scope of the present work, a helpful portrayal of the problem of theodicy in Job is presented in Hans-Peter Müller's essay, »Theodizee? Anschlußerörterungen zum Buch Hiob,« *ZTK* 89 (1992): 249–279. On page 275, in his discussion on the theophany and its role in the book, Müller states: »Die Frage Hiobs nach einer sittlichen Weltordnung, wie sie besonders in der Weisheitsdiskussion mit den Freunden gestellt wird, scheint so zunächst durch ein außerweisheitliches Lösungsmodell beschieden: Ordnung und Sinn der Welt, die Hiob in seiner Leidensgegenwart nicht findet, sind doch von der Urzeit her ein für allemal angelegt; noch einmal soll es eine mythische Daseinsbejahung gestatten, aus den Übeln der Zeit auf eine urzeitliche Ordnungs- und Sinnstiftung zurückzugreifen, wenn es die gegenwärtige Welt nach der Norm der Urzeit zu regenerieren gilt. Gott und das Übel werden also protologisch vermittelt.«

5   See Jean Lévêque, "L'Épilogue du Livre de Job," in *Toute la Sagesse du Monde: Hommage à Maurice Gilbert s. j.* (ed. François Mies; Namur: Presses Universitaires de Namur, 2000), 37–55; Alexander Di Cella, "An Existential Interpretation of Job," *BTB* 15 (1985): 49–55; Julius B. Moster, "The Punishment of Job's Friends," *JBQ* 25, no. 4 (1997): 211–219; Samuel E. Balentine, "My Servant Job Shall Pray for You," *ThTo* 58, no. 4 (2002): 502–518; Stanley E. Porter, "The Message of the Book of Job: Job 42:7b as Key to Interpretation?" *EvQ* 63 (1991): 305–312; Geevarughese Mathew, "The Role of the Epilogue in the Book of Job," (Ph.D. diss., Drew University, 1995).

which Bakhtin argued.⁶ How, then, do the monologues of 42:7–17 engage the polyphonic character of the preceding sections of the book? This is part of the interpretive challenge with which the present work will be concerned.

Once Job is introduced (1:1–3), his religious life comes into focus. He is scrupulous about his beliefs and sanctifies his children in case they sin against God by "blessing" (that is, cursing) God in their hearts (1:5). This exceptional piety catches the attention of God. But the Adversary is not easily impressed and so poses the problem of the book: "touch him," the Adversary argues, and he "will curse you to your face" (1:11; 2:5). Job may have been concerned with his children's inner thoughts and possible sin "in their heart," but the Adversary partly shifts the location of piety from one's inner thoughts to open confession: "he will curse you to your face."⁷ Moreover, the Adversary introduces the idea of open discourse, open confession, and dialogue that has the potential to challenge any naïve assumption about Job's piety. But in introducing the possibility of debate, the Adversary is also precise as to what will demonstrate a lack of disinterested piety on Job's part. It is not that Job may curse God in his heart, but that Job will curse God to God's face. The narrator appears to have set some standard for evaluating Job's discourse and dialogue with his friends and with God.

Such a precise definition of the plot underscores at least two things in the narrative that are related to its dramatic development and eventual evaluation: (a) the reader is emotionally and intellectually drawn into the text, given the gravity of the possible sin and the challenge it poses to the otherwise morally and fairly stable framework of the divine-human relationship portrayed in the Prologue. Every word and phrase that Job utters henceforth will be subjected to careful scrutiny to determine whether it approximates in any way possible the expected reaction.⁸ The Adversary has posed the problem of religious

---

6   Mikhail Bakhtin, *Problems of Dostoevsky's Poetics* (trans. and ed. Caryl Emerson; Theory and History of Literature 8; Minneapolis: University of Minnesota Press, 1984), 166. On page 6, Bakhtin writes that Dostoevsky's work was chiefly characterized by "a plurality of independent and unmerged voices and consciousnesses, a genuine polyphony of fully valid voices." For a helpful introduction to Bakhtin's ideas of polyphony and dialogism, see Gary Saul Morson and Caryl Emerson, eds., *Mikhail Bakhtin: Creation of a Prosaics* (Stanford, Calif.: Stanford University Press, 1990), 231–268; Caryl Emerson, *The First Hundred Years of Mikhail Bakhtin* (Princeton: Princeton University Press, 1997); Sergei Averintsev, "Bakhtin, Laughter, and Christian Culture," in *Bakhtin and Religion: A Feeling for Faith* (ed. Susan M. Felch and Paul J. Contino; Evanston, Ill.: Northwestern University Press, 2001), 79–95. On the use of Bakhtin in biblical scholarship, see Dennis T. Olson, "Biblical Theology as Provisional Monologization: A Dialogue with Childs, Brueggemann and Bakhtin," *BibInt* 6 (1998): 162–180; Barbara Green, *Mikhail Bakhtin and Biblical Scholarship: An Introduction* (ed. Danna Nolan Fewell; SBLSS 38; Atlanta: Society of Biblical Literature, 2000); Carol A. Newsom, "Bakhtin, the Bible, and Dialogic Truth," *JR* 76, no. 2 (1996): 290–306; idem, *The Book of Job: A Contest of Moral Imaginations*, 3–31.

7   Newsom, *The Book of Job: A Contest of Moral Imaginations*, 55, writes that for the Adversary, "the transparency of meaning, the ostensible coherency at the heart of the moral imagination of the story is an illusion he is prepared to demystify."

8   In two instances, before the introduction of Job's friends and the ensuing dialogue with them, the narrator makes two related but unidentical evaluations of Job's reaction to the

piety in serious terms. And in initiating the context for dialogue, the Adversary has also laid down some parameters for eventual evaluation; and (b) the reader cannot theoretically come to a comprehensive perception of Job's piety until the book is finished, or better still, until Job has spoken his last word. Whether or not Job will curse God to God's face as the Adversary predicts, and the extent to which that may or may not happen, is a conclusion that the reader finally comes to only at the end, that is, only in a post-dialogue setting.

On the one hand, the reader gets involved with the characters and their expressions throughout the debate. On the other hand, once Job has finished speaking, the reader is immediately placed "outside" the various speeches as it were, and can only look back to see how they relate to the expected consequence of Job's suffering. This is the interpretive juncture where the Epilogue is situated. Structurally, it is placed outside the debate and, therefore, outside its inner dynamics, constraints, and complexities. However, through the formulation of the divine verdict and blessing of Job (42:7, 12) in a manner that conceptually relates to the preceding discussions, the interpretation of the Epilogue allows for a re-exploration or re-reading of the Prologue and the human speeches in the poetic section. At the very point where the book literarily ends, another level of its interpretation begins.

Job's last public words in the book are spoken in 42:6; his prayer in 42:10 is not spelled out but is subsumed under the friends' response to God. This means that the entire human debate is set between 1:21 and 42:6, and the Epilogue paints a post-debate scenario. In his work on Job, Michael Cheney describes monologue and dialogues (or "debate speech" as Cheney calls it) as sub-genres, and argues that monologues are only monologues insofar as they exhibit features tending towards the interactive discourse in the debate speech.[9] Significantly, the text of 42: 7–17 is a combination of alternating monologues by God and the narrator about Job, his friends and their preceding debate. Dialogue as experienced in the preceding prose and poetic sections is implied at best.[10] The hermeneutic that governs the Epilogue may,

---

suffering that came on him and his household (1:22; 2:10). Thus, even for the omniscient narrator, there is not just one single overarching evaluation of Job, but rather a "process" of provisional evaluations that evolves and changes with the nature of the context and circumstances. One might as well assume that this process does not end with the introduction of the friends; on the contrary, it gets more complex and open.

9 See, Michael Cheney, *Dust, Wind and Agony: Character, Speech and Genre in Job* (Coniectanea Biblica 36; Lund: Almqvist & Wiksell, 1994), 137–138. On the basis of comparative analysis with ancient Near Eastern texts, Cheney provides four models of analyzing monologues: a) Dialogic monologues involving two or more literary entities that portray different aspects of a single character; b) pure monologues, not subsumed under a broader category; c) denouement monologues that bring literary works to a climax or conclusion; and d) exchange of monologues that represent a plurality of voices speaking to the same issue or theme.

10 It is possible that the Adversary and Job's wife who represent the potential and reality of challenge in the Prologue serve only as "foils" for the major characters, since their views are "rebuked" and ultimately do not modify the outcome of the story. But this may not necessarily be the case, given that these characters are further developed in

therefore, be partly described as *hindsight hermeneutics* – that is, a hermeneutic that is at once deeply involved in the plurality of issues raised in the preceding sections of the book and, in fact, an extension of those issues, but also "outside" the discussion and, therefore, not limited to or constrained by the specificity of the language that sets the story in motion and the diversity and urgency of the discussion. This inside-outside character of the Epilogue invites the reader to re-read the text from the perspective of both an insider and an outsider, as both participant and evaluator.[11] Accordingly, the Epilogue is to be interpreted in conjunction with what the narrator refers to as Job's "former" life (42:12), that is, the preceding sections of the book.[12]

An important hermeneutical clue from the text that lends itself to this interpretive strategy is the narrator's assessment of the Epilogue in which God is said to have blessed Job's latter days "more than" the former. From this literary and theological context described as "more than" before, the Epilogue as a post-dialogue, post-tragic scenario invites and legitimizes critical (self) evaluation that recognizes the enduring nature and forcefulness of the crisis and destruction that could result from unequal arrangements of power structures depicted in the moral worldview of the Prologue. But as a 'happy ending' the Epilogue also provides an interpretive context that goes beyond a critique of the reality of evil and beyond a discussion on the various responses to such experience of evil to proposing models of the divine-human and human-human relationships that seek greater accountability, survival, success, and healing for the interpretive community and creation as a whole. My reading of the Epilogue as a "happy" ending is geared towards that objective.

This work is divided into four parts. In chapter one, I exegete the Epilogue, paying particular attention to the idiomatic expressions that are used, including the divine anger against the friends, the divine response to

---

later works such as the LXX and the *Testament of Job*. Whether or not Job's wife and the Adversary are "foils" for Job is a decision that the reader has to make.

11 Bakhtin, *Problems of Dostoevsky's Poetics*, 166, writes: "Dostoevsky ... was by no means a stranger to cramped and one-sided seriousness, to dogmatism, even to eschatology. But these ideas ... once introduced into the novel, become there merely one of the embodied voices of an unfinalized and open dialogue." In the case of the book of Job, the monologues in 42: 7–17 are set in conversation with the debate in the Dialogues and Prologue.

12 A similar methodology has been effectively used, within the context of intertextuality, by Patricia T. Willey, *Remember the Former Things: The Recollection of Previous Texts in Second Isaiah* (ed. Michael V. Fox and E. Elizabeth Johnson; SBLDS 161; Atlanta: Scholars, 1997); idem, "The Rhetoric of Recollection," in *Congress Volume: Olso 1998* (ed. André Lemaire and M. Sæbø; VTSup 80; Leiden: Brill, 2000), 71–78. Other essays in the same volume on the different aspects of intertextuality, the ways in which it relates to unity and diversity in texts, and the caution with which it should be used include: Kirsten Nielsen, "Intertextuality and Hebrew Bible," 17–31; John Barton, "Intertextuality and the 'Final Form' of the Text," 33–37; Michael Fishbane, "Types of Intertextuality," 39–44; Antoon Schoors, "(Mis)use of Intertextuality in Qoheleth Exegesis," 45–59; Jean Louis Ska, "Genèse XVIII 6 – Intertextualité et Interprétation: 'Tout Fait Farine au Bon Moulin'," 61–70.

Job's prayer, and the restoration of Job's possessions. I argue that the rebuke of the friends (which is situated after God's words to Job from the whirlwind) parallels God's rebuke of Job in the theophany, and should be interpreted in light of the preceding Prologue and discussion between Job and his friends. The prepositional phrase אלי in 42:7 could mean "to me" or "concerning me." In fact, I argue that it means both, and corresponds to the Prologue where Job speaks "about"[13] God and the Dialogue where he speaks "to" and "about" God. Also, although the formulation of the rebuke of Job's friends and approval of Job is largely consonant with the doctrine of retribution in Deuteronomic theology, the divine response to Job's prayer where God "lifts" Job's face (a sign of divine favor) contains a unique element of divine freedom and, therefore, transcends any strict concept of retribution.

The second chapter is a selected history of interpretation, and focuses on some of the versions (LXX-Job and 11QtgJob) and a number of Jewish and Christian scholars from the early rabbinic and patristic period to the modern period. That is, this selective survey examines some of the scholars who are representative of the major interpretive schools and ideas in the ancient, medieval, and modern periods. In the process, the survey highlights the tension between the divine rebuke of the friends and the approval of Job. It also highlights some of the interpretive moves (including the use of allegory) employed in reading and appropriating the text, where Job symbolized national experience for Jewish scholars and the church for Christian scholars. I argue that in the versions as well as other scholarly writings, there is an underlying tension between divine rebuke *and* approval that is applied to Job and implicitly to the friends.

Building on my exegesis of the text and the selected survey of its history of interpretation, the third chapter provides a re-reading of the text. I propose that a fruitful hermeneutic for interpreting the Epilogue should combine *both* the resonance and the dissonance between the Epilogue and the preceding sections. This hermeneutic is suggested by the fact that the Epilogue is set within a literary and theological context that the narrator describes as "more than" the former (42:12). First, through an analysis of a number of literary and thematic features, I show that the Epilogue is both at resonance and dissonance with the prose Prologue and the poetic Dialogue. Second, I show that in the narrative form and content of the Epilogue, one finds a significant combination of this resonance-dissonance dynamic. And third, I argue that in this combination of resonance and dissonance, the Epilogue partly transcends the Prologue and Dialogue. From this hermeneutical standpoint, the polyphonic character of the book is not just the goal or objective of the reading and interpretive process but also its starting point. That is, the

---

13 It is possible that Job's initial response in 1:21 after the first round of attack may not only be a confession "about/concerning" God, but also "towards" God. This implied speech "towards" God may underlie the need for the narrator's evaluation that Job did not sin, since the Adversary had predicted that Job would curse God "to your face."

interpretive process initiated by the Epilogue is one in which the polyphonic character of the book demonstrated in the preceding sections is already established. It is through the integration of the resonances and dissonances between the Epilogue and the preceding sections that the narrator brings the book to an end.

The final chapter explores some theological implications of my reading of the text. I argue that the language of restoration is quite pervasive in the biblical material, but also very contextual. Because of the reference to Job's former life, one is perhaps to reexamine the beginning of the book. Accordingly, the Epilogue can be read as a new beginning. Because of the literary transition that places the Epilogue in conjunction with God's words to Job from the whirlwind, I argue that the Epilogue should be read in close conjunction with the theophanic context. That is, it is the theophany-epilogue continuum that becomes the context for the new beginning. Within this new beginning, the experience of divine transcendence manifested in the divine rebuke of Job in the theophany and divine immanence as represented in the "cultic" experience (42:8–9) are brought together. Also, the concept of retribution and its limitations are equally brought together and used as theological resources for describing the human-divine relationship and dealing with the reality of trouble in the world. Consequently, even though the Adversary posed the issue of retribution in either-or terms, and even though the Dialogue largely proceeds along the same lines, the Epilogue reposes the issue in a way that the concept is no longer to be understood along such lines of either-or; rather, it is now one of both-and.

The various voices in the preceding sections of the book that contribute towards the various formulations of the nature of the divine-human relationship are no longer viewed and interpreted as competing alternatives propositions or worldviews. Rather, they become complementary possibilities for defining the complex and dynamic nature of the relationship between God and humankind, and responding to the reality of trouble in the world.

Chapter 1: Text and Textual Analysis

1.1 Text

⁷After the Lord spoke these words to Job, the Lord said to Eliphaz the Temanite, "My anger is kindled against you and your two friends for you have not spoken rightly to/about me like my servant Job. ⁸Now therefore, take seven bulls and seven rams and go to my servant Job and offer a sacrifice for yourselves. My servant Job will pray for you. Only, I will grant his request (and) not deal with you outrageously, for you have not spoken rightly to/about me as my servant Job." ⁹Then Eliphaz the Temanite and Bildad the Shuhite and¹⁴ Zophar the Naamathite went and did as the Lord had spoken to them, and the Lord showed favor to Job. ¹⁰Then the Lord turned Job's fortunes when he prayed for his friends, and the Lord increased all that Job had to double. ¹¹All his brothers and sisters and former acquaintances came to him and ate bread with him in his house. They consoled and comforted him for all the trouble that the Lord had brought upon him. Each gave him a *Qesitah* and a gold ring. ¹² The Lord blessed Job's latter life more than his former. He had fourteen thousand sheep, six thousand camels, one thousand yoke of oxen, and one thousand she-asses. ¹³He had seven sons and three daughters. ¹⁴He named the first *Yemimah*, the second's name was *Qeziah*, and the name of the third was *Qeren-Happuk*. ¹⁵There was not found women in all the land as beautiful as Job's daughters. Their father gave inheritance to them among their brothers. ¹⁶ Job lived one hundred and forty years after this, and he saw his children and his children's children to the fourth generation. ¹⁷Then Job died old and advanced in years.

1.2 Textual Analysis

The Epilogue is partly set within the context of God's response to the discourse between Job and his friends on the nature of religious piety and retribution. The adverb (אחר) in 42:7 that makes the transition from the poetic section to the prose Epilogue has the sense of temporal sequence,

---

14 The missing wāw in the MT can be explained as a haplography resulting from the graphic similarity between the *yōd* of חישוי and the expected *wāw* before צפר. All the versions have the conjunction.

probably meaning, "immediately after."¹⁵ Therefore, it situates the Epilogue "after" God's interaction with Job from the whirlwind. Although some scholars propose that this adverb should be read as a compound conjunction ("after that"),¹⁶ its sense of a temporal sequence within an on-going discussion is significant. Read in the sense of temporal sequence, the adverb preserves the aspect of continuity and discontinuity between the Epilogue and the divine speeches to Job. That is, in the present context, the expression ויהי אחר is used as a transitional statement (cf. Gen 37:9; 40:1). It is after God has spoken הדברים האלה אל־איוב ("these words to Job") that God begins to speak to the friends. LXX has, πάντα τὰ ῥήματα ταῦτα ("all these words"), which, I shall later argue, constitutes part of a harmonistic tendency of the Greek translator. In any case, the transitional character of this phrase suggests that God's address to the friends parallels God's words to Job in the theophany, where Job is rebuked for speaking without knowledge (38:2; 42:3). A theophany-epilogue continuum begins to emerge as a possible interpretive context for the Epilogue.

Just as God's opening address to Job from the whirlwind was a rebuke, so too God's word to the friends is a rebuke. God says to Eliphaz: "My anger is kindled against you and your two friends" (חרה אפי בך ובשני רעיך). The LXX has ἥμαρτες σὺ καὶ οἱ δύο φίλοι σου ("you and your two friends have sinned/failed.") The root ἁμαρτάνω retroverts to a number of Hebrew words, including חטא, חנף and רשע. This rendering of the Hebrew text by the LXX anticipates the last part of v. 9 (absent in the MT) where LXX mentions that God "loosed" the friends' sins because of Job. This reading, which (as we shall later see) is at resonance with 11QtgJob and replaces the anthropomorphic idiom about the divine anger, may be a result of the translator/author's sensitivity about the divine character in the Hellenistic context.¹⁷ Alternatively, and more significantly given the resonance of LXX

---

15 See, Dennis G. Pardee, "The Preposition in Ugaritic," *UF* 8 (1976): 251-252; idem, "More on the Preposition in Ugaritic," *UF* 11 (1980): 868; Bruce K. Waltke and M. O'Connor, *An Introduction to Biblical Hebrew Syntax* (Winona Lake, Ind.: Eisenbrauns, 1990), 192.
16 See, Samuel R. Driver and George B. Gray, *A Critical and Exegetical Commentary on the Book of Job Together with a New Translation* (ICC 18; Edinburgh: T&T Clark, 1958), 348; Edouard Dhorme, *A Commentary on the Book of Job* (trans. Harold Knight; New York: Thomas Nelson, 1967), 648; Otto Zöckler, *The Book of Job: A Commentary* (New York: Scribner, 1874), 630; Carl Brockelmann, *Hebräische Syntax* (Neukirchen: Moers, 1956), 143; Francis Brown, Samuel R. Driver, and Charles A. Briggs, eds., *The Brown-Driver-Briggs Hebrew and English Lexicon with an Appendix Containing the Biblical Aramaic Coded with the Numbering System from Strong's Exhaustive Concordance of the Bible* (Peabody, Mass.: Hendrickson, 1997), 29–30. One should note that the adverb can either have complementary particles (e.g., אחרי כן in 3:1 and the late form אחרי זאת in 42:16 or stand on its own as in 21:3. See, Hans Strauss, *Hiob 19:1–42:17* (BKAT 16/2; Neukirchen-Vluyn: Neukirchener Verlag, 2000), 392–393. The MT is corroborated by the versions (Syr., Vulg., LXX, and rabbinic Tg.).
17 So, Duck-Woo Nam, *Talking about God: Job 42:7 – 9 and the Nature of God in the Book of Job* (ed. Hemchand Gossai; Studies in Biblical Literature 49; New York: Peter Lang, 2003), 14.

with 11QtgJob, the reading may be a genuine literary and artistic feature of the Greek translator that corresponds to his "inner logic" of anticipating LXX 42:9 (where the friends are said to have sinned) and justifying the need for a sacrifice in 42:8 (see Job 1:5 where LXX describes the offering as sin offering).[18]

The idiom, חרה אף...ב, is used in the Bible to express either human or divine anger against another person. It is commonly used in the Deuteronomistic history to express divine anger against Israel and her kings, but it also occurs elsewhere in the MT. In the work of the Deuteronomistic Historian, it often initiates narrative transitions.[19] The use of the expression in the Epilogue where the Deuteronomistic theology of retribution remains a significant factor further underscores the role of 42:7 as a transitional phrase.

God rebukes the friends because they have not spoken rightly to/about God (לא דברתם אלי נכונה). LXX renders the prepositional phrase אלי with ἐνώπιόν μου – "before me" or "in my presence"; so too is Syr.'s ܩܕܡܝ ("before me"); Vulg.'s *coram me* "before me." The rabbinic Tg. has לותי, which should be understood within the context of the idiom מלל...לות – "to talk to." However, the Syriac and the rabbinic Tg. have ܡܠܠ...ܥܡ / מלל...עם in 42:7a, suggesting that both versions may have sensed a slight nuance in the meaning of the prepositional phrase in 42:7b. In fact, the word לות does carry the broader sense of "concerning." Here in 42:7b, the Syr. drops the idiom completely, reading "before me" which is perhaps interpretive, and, like the LXX, simply places the friends in God's presence without emphasizing whether the friends are rebuked for not speaking rightly "to God" or "concerning God."[20] This reading of the versions, that simply places the friends in God's presence, further underscores the association of the Epilogue with the divine manifestation from the whirlwind.

The issue, however, is not just the association of the Epilogue with the theophany, but also determining the nature of the formulation of the divine rebuke. In other words, it is important to determine the meaning of the prepositional phrase that partly shapes the rebuke, since God rebukes the friends for not speaking rightly "to/about me," אלי. The preposition אל has

---

18 See the detailed comparative analysis of the LXX and 11QtgJob renderings of the MT under the concept of intercession and forgiveness by Bernd Janowski, »Sündenvergebung 'um Hiobs willen' Fürbitte und Vergebung in 11QtgJob 38: 2f. und Hi 42: 9f. LXX,« *ZNW* 73 (1982): 253–259.

19 See Deut 6:15; 7:4; 11:17; 29:26; 31:14; Jos 7:1; 23:16; Judg 2:14, 20; 3:8; 6:39; 10:7; 2 Sam 24:1; 2 Kg 13:3. For an analysis of the structural function of this expression and its use in the context of narrative transitions in the work of the Deuteronomist, see Dennis J. McCarthy, "The Wrath of YHWH and the Structural Unity of the Deuteronomistic History," in *Essays in Old Testament Ethics* (ed. James L. Crenshaw and John T. Willis; New York: Ktav, 1974), 97–110. See also, Nam, *Talking About God*, 20–21.

20 For detailed analyses of the translation techniques employed by the Peshitta of Job, see Heidi M. Szpek, *Translation Technique in the Peshitta to Job: A Model for Evaluating a Text with Documentation from the Peshitta to Job* (ed. Michael V. Fox and E. Elizabeth Johnson; SBLDS 137; Atlanta: Scholars Press, 1993), 243–248.

the basic sense of "to" as has been argued by Budde, Saadiah, and Rickie Moore among others.²¹ This is indeed its meaning when used with the verb דבר in 2:13; 4:2; 5:8; 13:3; 42:7a; and 42:9. It is, therefore, likely that the same basic meaning is conveyed here (42:7b).

That having been said, one should not discount the possibility of the preposition meaning "concerning," given that the prepositions אל and על are sometimes used interchangeably. In 1:11, for example, we have על פניך ("to your face") where one would expect אל פניך as in 2:5. Accordingly, Dhorme argues that אלי here does not mean "to me" but "concerning me." Similarly, Driver and Gray draw attention to 1 Sam 3:12 and 1Kg 16:12 to argue that אלי here is really used for the more conventional עלי.²² Equally important is the fact that, when used with words that depict verbal communication, אל sometimes carries the sense of "concerning" or "with regard to" (e.g., Gen 20:2; Is 23:11; 29:22; 37:21, 33; Ezr 19:4; 1 Sam 4:19; 2 Sam 7:19; Ps 2:7; 69:27). Finally, one should note the use of the preposition in conjunction with נכון in the expression ושבתם אלי אל נכון ("and return to me according to what is certain" – 1 Sam 23:23). Therefore, the use of נכונה together with the qualifying phrase, "like my servant Job," allows the prepositional phrase אלי to take a broader sense beyond its basic and fundamental sense, since Job sometimes speaks "to" and other times "about" God.

Accordingly, the context for interpreting this rebuke is that of the Prologue and the poetic debate. Two things are, therefore, worth noting. First, a theophany-epilogue continuum, suggested by the transitional phrase in 42:7a, provides the immediate literary and theological springboard for interpreting the rebuke. And second, the framing of the rebuke in 42:7b, however, moves

---

21   Karl F. R. Budde, *Das Buch Hiob* (Göttingen: Vandenhoeck & Ruprecht, 1913), 272. Budde justifies his reading »zu mir« by stating that human speech has God for its hearer, and is directed toward God. Saadiah Ben Joseph Al-Fayyūmī, *The Book of Theodicy: Translation and Commentary on the Book of Job* (ed. Leon Nemoy, Judah Goldin, and Isadore Twersky; trans. L. E. Goodman; Yale Judaica Series 25; New Haven: Yale University Press, 1988), 412; Rickie D. Moore, "Raw Prayer and Refined Theology: 'You have not Spoken Straight to Me as My Servant Job Has,'" in *The Spirit and the Mind: Essays in Informed Pentecostalism to Honor Dr. Donald N. Bowdie Presented on his 65th Birthday* (ed. Terry L. Cross and Emerson B. Powery; New York: University Press of America, 2000), 40–41. Moore translates: "you have not spoken straight to me, as my servant Job has," and explains that the prepositional phrase אלי conveys the idea that Job's "*straight* speaking was *right*, and that the *right* speaking was *straight*."

22   Dhorme, *Book of Job*, 648; Driver and Gray, *Book of Job*, 348. So too, Nam, *Talking About God*, 13, who translates, "you have not spoken about me constructively." The broader sense of the preposition in this text is implied from the interchangeability of the prepositions and also from the overall context as a result of two factors: (a) the reference to Job as "my servant" places the text in conversation with the Prologue where he is equally referred to as "my servant" (1:8; 2:3). But in the Prologue, Job does not explicitly speak "to" God; rather he largely speaks "about" God; and (b) the function of נכונה in the rebuke makes the issue more than just the direct speech to God; it broadens the nature of the rebuke, since the verb כון is used elsewhere only in the Dialogues where God is both spoken to and spoken about. The rebuke thus bears on the preceding discussion between Job and his friends in the Dialogues as well as Job's remarks to/about God in the Prologue.

beyond the theophany-epilogue context and touches on the preceding prose Prologue and poetic Dialogue. Within the context of this interpretive strategy, rebuke *and* approval emerge as two dimensions of the divine response to Job and implicitly to the friends as well.

The friends are rebuked for not speaking "rightly" or "what is firm" (נכונה). The root כון occurs 14 times in Job.²³ Its basic meaning has to do with being firm or established, although נכונה also occurs in Ps 5:10 where it denotes a moral quality of rightness that is lacking from the mouths of oppressors. It can, therefore, be understood as objective "truth." However, the phrase, נכונה (אלי) דברתם (לא) also echoes the idiomatic expression דבר...כון ("a firm word"/ "speak firmly") used in two other instances in the Bible: Gen 41:32 and Deut 13:15 (repeated with slight variation in Deut 17:4). The first is used to describe God's actions to humans while the second is used to describe humankind's actions about God. In Gen 41:32 Joseph interprets Pharaoh's two dreams as essentially saying the same thing, namely, that there will be seven years of plenty in the land, and that these good years will be followed by seven years of devastating drought that will completely obliterate any memory of the good years. Joseph then concludes that the doubling of the dream to Pharaoh means that, "the matter/word is firmly established from God" (נכון הדבר מעם האלהים). The idiom thus carries the sense of certainty or inevitability, without any apparent concern over the moral implications of God's action or character. In Deut 13:15//17:4, Moses instructs the Israelites that if someone should tell them to worship and serve other gods, they should "seek, probe, and ask properly" and "if it is true, a firm word" (הנה אמת נכון הדבר), then they should stone such a person. In this context, the firm word is a result of the triple investigation of seeking, probing, and asking; it goes beyond rumors or presumptions and seeks to establish the fact of the moment. It also has a moral value since it is used together with אמת – truth.

In the context of Job 42:7, the idiom is used to describe human words to/about God, and so corresponds with the text of Deut 13:15. Accordingly, the lack of truthfulness or certainty in the friends' words may be a result of their failure to go beyond their personal and traditional presumptions about Job's experience to include the "inquiry of the moment" or the validity and credibility of new experience. The friends are then contrasted with Job. They have not spoken rightly "like my servant Job" (כעבדי איוב). Several manuscripts read the preposition ב instead of כ, which may be a result of confusion due to the graphic similarity between the two prepositions. However, the preposition ב may also be an interpretive clue that plays against the background of the theophany and attempts to harmonize with the rebuke of Job in the theophany, as we shall argue below under the history of interpretation. This designation of Job as God's "servant" is already made

---

23 See 8:8; 11:13; 12:5; 15:23, 35; 18:12; 21:8; 27:16, 17; 28:27; 31:15; 38:41; 42: 7, 8.

known in the Prologue (1:8; 2:3) and is now used four times in this section of the Epilogue. This characterization places Job among the faithful elite in the MT. It is a characterization that draws upon what God freely promises and does to/because of God's servant (e.g., Abraham – Gen 26:24; Isaac – Gen 24:14; Jacob – Ezek 28:25; 37:25; David – 2 Sam 7:5; 2 Kg 19:34; 20:6;) and what such individuals do in response to God's call and mission (e.g., Moses – Num 12:7; Jos 1:2; Isaiah – Is 20:3; the suffering servant – Is 42:1, 19; 44:1). Here, the reference is to what Job has said "to/about" God.

Following the divine rebuke of the friends is the divine demand for a sacrifice and prayer to avert possible punishment. A new phase of the friends' relationship with God is initiated. God says, "but now" (ועתה– 42:8). As Wolfgang Schneider argues, this adverb belongs to a group of syntactic signs that initiate transitional phrases within a dialogue.[24] Accordingly, the adverb is partly used here in a disjunctive manner and echoes the adverbial phrase, ועתה, in 42:5 (cf. Gen 22:11). Just as Job's perception of God partially changed with the theophany (42:5), so too the friends' relationship with God will experience a new dimension within the context of this encounter with God. The friends are to take animals for themselves and "go to" (ולכו אל) Job. The Syr.'s ܐܙܠ ܠܘܬ and the rabbinic Tg. (אזל לות) follow the MT closely, even though this particular rendering in the Syr. may also be suggestive, since it includes not just the idea of "going to" but also of "going with."[25]

The friends are to "offer a sacrifice for yourselves" (והעליתם עולה בעדכם). Both LXX and Syr. make Job the subject of the action: "and he will offer." This is probably to harmonize with Job's religion in 1:5. However, Aq., rabbinic Tg., Theod., and Symm. corroborate the MT, thereby preserving the dissonance between this text and the Prologue where Job offers sacrifices for those who may have sinned against God. Job, on his part, "will pray for" (יתפלל...על) the friends. The variant form of this expression in v.10, יתפלל...בעד is more frequently used.[26] In the present context, both

---

24 Wolfgang Schneider, *Grammatik des Biblischen Hebräisch* (Munich: Claudius, 1974), 261.
25 While the expression in Aramaic likely means "to go to," the Syriac idiom is worth noting because it can mean either "to go with" or "to draw near." By using this idiom (instead of precise forms like ܐܙܠ...ܠ – "to go to" or ܐܙܠ...ܥܡ – "to go with"), the Syriac appears to preserve two aspects of the text in which the friends "go to" Job for prayers and Job also appears to "go with" them to the altar. Accordingly, what the reader finds out only later (namely, Job's participation) is hinted at and held together much earlier in the Syriac. Perhaps the expression preserves both the distinction between Job and his friends (as they go to him for prayers) and the cooperation between them (as they go with Job to the altar).
26 See 1 Sam 7:5; 12:19, 23; Deut 9:20; Jer 7:17; 11:14; 14:11; 29:7; 42:2, 20; Num 21:7; Gen 20:7. For a historical-critical discussion on these variant expressions about Job's prayer, see Avi Hurvitz, "Date of the Prose-Tale of Job Linguistically Reconsidered," *HTR* 67 (1974): 23 n. 25; K. Kautzsch, *Das sogannante Volksbuch von Hiob und der Ursprung von Hiob cap. I. II. XLII, 7 –17: ein Beitrag zur Frage nach der Integrität des Buches Hiob* (Tübingen: Mohr, 1900), 7; Shalom Spiegel, "Noah, Danel, and Job: Touching on Canaanite Relics in the Legends of the Jews," in *Louis Ginzberg Jubilee*

expressions about Job's prayer complete the "cultic" requirements on behalf of the friends; they offer a sacrifice on their own behalf and Job prays for them.

In the second part of 42:8, God states what the divine response to Job's prayer will be. God says, "but his face I will lift" (כי אם־פניו אשא). The conditional word (אם) here has been variously treated. Bernhard Duhm proposes the accusative marker את instead of אם,[27] and Dhorme proposes to replace אם with אז, yielding כי־אז – "then," "from that moment," "in that case" – which we find in Job 11:15; 22:26.[28] However, the conjunction can be understood in a limiting sense as is the case in Gen 15:4 where we have the expression לא יירשך זה כי־אם אשר יצא ממעך ("This one shall not inherit you, but the one that comes out from your internal organs"); and again in Gen 28:17 where one reads: המקום הזה אין זה כי אם־בית אלהים ("This place is nothing but the house of God.") As these examples indicate, the compound conjunction contrasts a negative clause within the sentence. That is, just as כי אם contrasts לא יירשך זה in Gen 15:4 and אין זה המקום הזה in Gen 28:17, so in Job 42:8 it contrasts the expression לבלתי עשות עמכם נבלה. Accordingly, it is possible that the expression כי אם־פניו אשא לבלתי עשות עמכם נבלה can be read: "but/only I will lift his face and not deal with you outrageously." Job's prayer will constitute part of the process that ultimately prevents God from acting in an exceptional manner.

Alternatively, what we have here is similar to the construction in Jer 26:15 where the two conjunctions retain their basic meanings and correspond to different parts of the clauses within the sentence. We read: אך ידע תדעו כי אם־ממתים אתם אתי: "but know for sure that if you kill me." The conjunction כי ("that/when") corresponds to the first part of the clause and אם ("if") corresponds to the second part, both creating a cause-effect phrase. Accordingly, the expression about God's response to Job's prayer (ואיוב עבדי יתפלל עליכם כי אם־פניו אשא לבלתי עשות עמכם נבלה) would mean, "my servant Job will pray for you (so) that, if I lift his face, I will not do to you an outrage." In this sense, the phrase is conditional and the reader must wait until the next verse to be sure that the prayer was indeed offered and answered. Therefore, even though Job prays to prevent God from acting in an outrageous manner, the ultimate decision lies with God. As we shall later argue, this constitutes part of the paradoxical cultic experience in which frail humans relate with the sovereign God.

To better understand the use of the idiom (נשא פנים) here, it is important to briefly examine its use elsewhere.[29] The idiom is variously used in the Bible to refer either to action on one's own behalf or on behalf of others. It is

---

Volume on the Occasion of his Seventieth Birthday (New York: American Academy for Jewish Research, 1945), 324–326.
27 Bernhard Duhm, *Das Buch Hiob: Erklärt* (Freiburg: Mohr, 1897), 205.
28 Dhorme, *The Book of Job*, 649.
29 For a detailed discussion of the biblical use of this idiom, see Mayer I. Gruber, "The Many Faces of Hebrew נשא פנים ›lift up the face‹," *ZAW* 95 (1983): 252–260.

used to refer to one's sense of good conscience and freedom from guilt (2 Sam 2:22; Job 11:15; see also the slightly variant form in Job 10:15 where we have "to lift the head"); it may also just mean, "to look up" as in 2 Kg 9:32. God can lift God's face upon humans as a sign of blessing, confirming the words of blessing pronounced by the priest (Num 6:26). When used to refer to the face of another person, it often depicts an act of granting a request (Gen 19:21; 1 Sam 25:35) or showing favor to another (Gen 32:21; Mal 1:8, 9). Nominal forms of the idiom mean "honorable one" or "eminent one" (Is 3:3; 9:14; Job 22:8).

In other contexts, dealing with issues of social justice, this idiom may carry a negative connotation. Thus, for example, God is said to be One who does not "lift the face" of a human; that is, God does not show favor to humans (Deut 10:17); so too, as part of Israel's justice system, no one is to "lift the face" of another, not even of the poor (Lev 19:15; Mal 2:9). God rebukes judges for being unfair, for 'lifting the face' of the wicked (Ps 82:2), and this translates once again into Israel's social justice system (Prov 6:35; 18:5). In the book of Job, the idiom is used mostly in the negative sense. Job accuses his friends of speaking deceitfully on God's behalf and showing partiality to God ("lifting God's face" – Job 13:7–8). Because they do that, Job warns, God will rebuke them (Job 13:10). Later on, Elihu equally argues that, as part of God's just reign in the world, God does not "lift the face" of princes (Job 34:19).

When humans pray (פלל), laying the circumstance before God for consideration, God is said or is exhorted to "hear" (שמע – 1 Kg 8:28, 29, 45, 49; 2 Chron 6: 35, 39; Neh 1:6, etc), "turn to" (פנה אל – 1 Kg 8:28; Ps 102:18) the prayer, "be attentive" (קשב – Neh 1:11; 2 Chron 6:40; Ps 61:2) or "incline to the voice of" (קשב בקול – Ps 66:19) prayer, and "take/receive" (לקח – Ps 6:10) the prayer. One of these traditional renderings of the divine response to prayer is preserved in 11QtgJob where the text reads, "and God listened to the voice of Job" (ושמע אלהא בקולה די איוב) The use of the expression נשא פנים to refer to God's response to Job's prayer is, therefore, unique. Given the negative connotations associated with נשא פנים in Job, its use in 42:8 constitutes part of the theological dissonance between the Epilogue and the preceding section. Rashi, however, points out that the idiom is used in Gen 19:21 to refer to the angels granting Lot's request not to destroy the city.[30]

God's threat against the friends is described in terms of what God will not do: לבלתי עשות עמכם נבלה ("I will not deal with you outrageously.") LXX has, "I will not destroy you," a rendering that is consistent with the use

---

30 Rashi, *The Book of Job* (trans. and ed. with commentary by A. J. Rosenberg; Judaica Books of the Hagiographa: The Holy Writings; New York: Judaica, 1989), 238. Apparently, within the context of prayer and the cult, the negative sense of favoritism sometimes associated with the idiom is eliminated.

of the root נבל.³¹ The idiom עשׂה...נבל is also used to describe gross misconduct, including sexual misconduct (Gen 34:7; Judg 19:23; 20:6; 2 Sam 13:12; Deut 22:21), speaking deceitfully in God's name (Jer 29:23), or other inappropriate action (Jos 7:15; 1 Sam 25:25). Some scholars render the phrase, "so that I will not treat you according to your folly," attributing the folly to the friends.³² However, there is no reason to depart from the natural construal of the Hebrew idiom, "to do X with someone," where the X characterizes the action of the subject.³³ As I shall later argue, this idiom about God possibly acting in a "outrageous" manner and the idiom about God lifting Job's face both express the component of the divine-human relationship that transcends strict retribution.

The idiom here recalls Job's rebuke of his wife in 2:9 where we find another idiom דבר...נבל. Although we have "to do an outrage" here rather than "to speak an outrage" in 2:9, we find that in Jer 29:23 the idea of "doing an outrage" is depicted as an act of verbal discourse: יען אשר עשׂו נבלה בישראל וידברו דבר בשמי שקר ("because they have done an outrage in Israel ... and have spoken a false word in my name." Therefore, it is possible to link the idiom in 42:8 to that in 2:9. Its basic meaning has to do with acting outside the norm, and the key here is determining exactly what the theological norm is. The expression is perhaps analogous to, and the antithesis of another idiom, "to show favor to X" (עשׂה חסד עם X – Hos 6:8) or "to do good" (טב עשׂה עם – Ps 86:17).³⁴ This analogy between עשׂה נבלה עם X and עשׂה חסד עם X works to the extent that in many instances where the idiom "to show faithfulness" is used, it either anticipates or is in response to some act of kindness itself. That is, there is a sense of reciprocity or even retribution involved in the use of the idiom (e.g., Gen 21:23; Jos 2:12; Judg 1:24; 8:35; 1 Sam 15:6; 20:8; 2 Sam 2:5, 6; 3:8; 9:1, 2, 7; 10:2; 1 Kg 2:7). Accordingly, when God rebukes the friends, the threat can be interpreted within the context of retributive justice.

In other instances, however, there is no immediate sense of reciprocity involved (Gen 20:13; 24:12, 14; 40:14; 2 Sam 15:20). Thus, unlike the instances in which showing kindness to someone either anticipates or reciprocates some good gesture on the part of that person, the biblical idiom "to do an outrage" that is used in the divine rebuke is nowhere else used as a

---

31 See, Wolfgang M. W. Roth, "NBL," *VT* 10 (1960): 394–409. Similarly, Anthony Phillips, "NEBALAH: A Term for Serious Disorderly and Unruly Conduct," *VT* 25, no. 2 (1975): 238, describes the term as referring to "extreme acts of disorder or unruliness which themselves result in a dangerous breakdown in order, and the end of an existing relationship."
32 See, John E. Hartley, *The Book of Job* (Grand Rapids, Mich.: Eerdmans, 1988), 538; Gustavo Gutiérrez, *On Job: God-talk and the Suffering of the Innocent* (trans. Matthew J. O'Connell; New York: Orbis, 1987), 12.
33 See, Gerald Janzen, *Job* (ed. James Luther Mays, Patrick D. Miller, and J. Achtemeier, IBC 18; Atlanta: John Knox, 1985), 265.
34 Naphtali H. Tur-Sinai, *The Book of Job: A New Commentary* (Jerusalem: Kiryath Sepher, 1957), 580; Wolfgang Roth, "NBL," 408; Janzen, *Job*, 265.

response to some prior inappropriate act; rather, the expression itself normally describes the unruly, unconventional act. Thus, although in true retributive fashion God threatens the friends for not speaking rightly, paradoxically the threatened response is itself not exactly retributive; retribution is both affirmed (in the formulation of the divine anger) and apparently surpassed (in the threatened sanction).

The formulation of the divine anger, the threat of punishment, and the proposed divine response to Job's prayer all combine to both affirm and surpass the doctrine of retribution. Once the doctrine is expressed in the formulation of the divine anger, the threat and response to prayer express a sense of double divine flexibility with regards to the law. On the one hand, God can act in an outrageous manner; on the other, God can show favor (which in this case turns out to be a positive act). Therefore, the divine rebuke of the friends and the "cultic" requirements to avert punishment set the stage for what may ultimately constitute a dynamic of rebuke *and* approval within the narrative. In the next verse, the focus shifts to the friends. They obey and do just as the Lord commanded them (42:9). The expression, ויעשׂו כאשׁר דבר אליהם יהוה, suggests faithfulness or loyalty on their part (Gen 27:19; Exod 1:17). As a result, God "lifts Job's face." The fact that God answers Job's prayers confirms the possibility already expressed in the previous verse (that is, if one reads כי אם־פניו אשׂא as a conditional phrase); it equally confirms the fact that Job prayed (42:10). Accordingly, the expression describes not just the friends' actions but also implicitly Job's, and the divine favor manifested in God's lifting of Job's face also extends to the friends. Job and his friends are closely linked here. At this point, LXX adds that God "loosed" the friends' sin because of Job (καὶ ἔλυσεν τὴν ἁμαρτίαν αὐτοῖς διὰ Ιωβ). This is consistent with LXX's perception of the divine charge against the friends in v.7 as sin. This reading is supported by 11QtgJob, which states that God listened to the voice of Job and forgave them their sins for his sake (ושמע אלהא בקולה די איוב ושבק חטאיהון בדילה).[35]

The Lord turned Job's fortunes (ויהוה שׁב את־שׁבית איוב) as part of the divine response to the "cultic" activity (42:10). The expression about the restoration of fortunes with an individual as the genitival object of שׁבית is a *hapax*. The closest one comes to this is in Jer 30:18 where the genitival construction has as object the tent of Jacob. The object is more often the nation or the land (Jer 33:7, 11; Num 21:29) or Zion and her people (Ps 126:1, 5). Therefore, the primary issue in the interpretation of this clause is determining whether the noun שׁבית comes from the middle weak שׁוב or from the III-Hē שׁבה, and ultimately whether it relates to Job's material

---

35 See Ezek 14:13, where there was a tradition according to which Job could effectively intercede on behalf of others for their sins. See further analysis under History of Interpretation.

possession only or also to his larger experience of suffering.[36] The Syr. (*šbyt*) and the rabbinic Tg. (*glwt*) read a derivative of the root שבה, thus interpreting the noun as "captivity" and "exile" respectively. LXX translates that the Lord "prospered" Job, with the root αὐξάνω – "to make grow," or "to increase."[37] Vulg. has *conversus est ad poenitentiam*, probably reading שוב. From the versions, it is clear that the translators were not unanimous on whether to interpret the text as a derivative of שוב or שבה. This lack of consensus is equally evident in other scholarly treatment of the expression. On the one hand, Erwin Preuschen and Eberhard Baumann have argued that the expression is derived from שבה, and that it refers to the reversal of some form of captivity.[38] On the other hand, Ernst L. Dietrich has argued that the expression is derived from שוב, and was closely related to material restoration.[39]

There are four possible idiomatic expressions that could result from the consonantal text, all of which may have originally been written defectively. These include שב שבות,[40] שב שבית,[41] שב שיבת,[42] and finally השב שבות/שבית.[43] In an Aramaic inscription from Sefire (3.24) we have the expression, השבו אלהם שבית אבי ("the gods restored the fortunes of my [father's house."]) The form השבו...שבית clearly indicates that one is dealing with the middle weak verb.[44] Driver and Gray argue that what we have in 42:10 is of the pattern ריב...ריב or נקם...נקם; that is, from the same root.[45] Accordingly, the idea is something like "to turn the turning," that is, restore the fortunes of someone (Hos 6:11; Am 9:14).

Linguistically, however, the MT שבית may also reflect an original III-Hē as evidenced by שבית in Num 21:29, which clearly expresses the idea of captivity and may be part of the tradition that influenced the Syr. and rabbinic Tg. readings. Dhorme follows this reading and argues that by alliteration שב

---

36 Part of this problem is indicated in the Massoretic text, where the *Kĕtîb* is שבית and the *Qĕrê* is שבות. This is further compounded by the inconsistent use of the *Kĕtîb-Qĕrê* relative to this expression in the MT, thus making it difficult to resolve the issue on etymological grounds. For a list of the various interchangeable uses of the *Kĕtîb-Qĕrê* of שבית and שבות, see R. Borger, »Zu שוב שבות/ית,« *ZAW* 66 (1954): 315–316.
37 The root αὐξάνω retroverts to a number of Hebrew verbs including פרה, גדל, פרץ, and פרה. Accordingly, LXX may be harmonizing with 1:10 where Job's possessions "burst forth" (פרץ) in the land. The Greek verb in 1:10 is ποίεω but it also retroverts to פרץ.
38 See, Erwin Preuschen, »Die Bedeutung von שוב שבות im Alten Testamente: Eine alte Controverse,« *ZAW* 15 (1895): 1–74 especially pages 21, 22, and 72; Eberhard Baumann, »שבות שוב: Eine exegetische Untersuchung,« *ZAW* 47 (1929): 17–44.
39 See Ernst L. Dietrich, שוב שבות: *Die endzeitliche Wiederherstellung bei den Propheten*. (BZAW 40; Giessen: Töpelmann,1925).
40 Ps 14:7 = 53:7; Hos 6:11; Zep 3:20; Jer 30:3, 18; 48:47; Ezek 29:14; Am 9:14; Deut 30:3.
41 Ezek 16:53; Ps 126:4; Zep 2:7.
42 Ps 126:1.
43 Jer 32:44; 33:26.
44 See, Joseph A. Fitzmyer, *The Aramaic Inscriptions of Sefire* (rev. ed.; Rome: Editrice Pontificio Instituto Biblico, 1995), 160.
45 Driver and Gray, *The Book of Job*, 349.

or הָשִׁיב have been joined to שְׁבִית or שְׁבוּת to connote, "to bring back what has been taken away" with particular reference to the captives of Israel. This expression became proverbial and came to be used in the sense of "to restore matters; to put things once more on a firm footing."[46]

After detailed analyses of the expression in the MT, William Holladay and John Bracke have noted the different uses of the expression to describe material restoration as well as restoration from captivity or exile. But they have also maintained that although contextual nuances have to be considered in the interpretation of the expression, it does carry an overall sense of reversal or turning.[47] Bracke identifies a model of restoration in the expression whose primary characteristic is God's reversal of God's judgment. Holladay, on his part, examines the use of the expression in the covenantal relationship between YHWH and Israel, in which Israel turns to God in repentance and God turns to Israel and restores the people.[48]

The root שׁוּב that describes God's action to Job in 42:10 occurs several times in the book of Job.[49] Though its basic sense of "turn back" or "return" is maintained, the different literary contexts show significant nuances that warrant further examination. Of importance is its use in the sense of stopping an ongoing action, particularly injustice (6:29) or restraining God from acting in a particular manner (9:12, 13; 11:10; 23:13). It is also used in the sense of restoring what has been lost (20:10), for example, human righteousness (33:26). Therefore, the verb is used in a double manner to express both the idea of preventing or stopping something that is ongoing, as well as restoring what has been lost. Both meanings can be understood in the present context. In its preventive sense, the verb depicts the end of Job's painful experience; in its restorative sense, it describes Job's material blessing.

More specifically, within the context of the idiom, the double sense of the expression שָׁב שְׁבִית / שָׁב שְׁבוּת is clearly depicted in its biblical usage. For example, in Jer 29:14, שָׁב שְׁבִית is used to describe God's gathering of God's people from exile, and in Zeph 2:7 the description of the return from exile includes mention of fortunes. The same is true of שָׁב שְׁבוּת. Its use in Ps 14:7 = 53:7, for example, is intended to counteract the experience of political and moral oppression, hence the parallelism with יְשׁוּעָה in Ps 14:7. Elsewhere, the expression is used in Jer 48:47 as a reversal of the experience of captivity described in Jer 48:46 (see its use in Deut 30:3 as a reversal of casting Israel into exile in 29:27). It is, therefore, likely that the expression carries both an immaterial as well as a material sense. Accordingly, it may depict both the end of Job's painful experience as well as a restoration of his material

---

46 Dhorme, *The Book of Job*, 650.
47 John M. Bracke, "Šûb šěbût: A Reappraisal," *ZAW* 97 (1985): 233–244; William L. Holladay, *The Root Šûbh in the Old Testament, With Particular Reference to the Usage in Covenantal Contexts* (Leiden: Brill, 1958).
48 Bracke, "Šûb šěbût," 233, 239; Holladay, *The Root Šûbh*, 110–115, 144–157.
49 See 1:21; 6:29; 7:7, 10; 9:12, 13, 18; 10:9, 16, 21; 11:10; 13:22; 15:22; 17:10; 20:2, 10; 22:23; 23:13; 31:14; 32:14; 33:5, 25, 26, 32; 34:15; 35:4; 39:4, 12; 40:4.

blessing.⁵⁰ Although these two dimensions are related, they are not identical and do not always or necessarily result one from another as the book of Job itself amply demonstrates.

As I have argued concerning the lifting of Job's face, there is likely an element of divine freedom involved in the divine action. This free divine act is reflected in 11QtgJob which states that it was in "mercy" (רחמין) that God returned (תוב) to Job. A similar idea is expressed in Zech 1:16 where God promises to return to Jerusalem with/in mercy: שבתי לירושלם ברחמים. Moreover, God restores Job's fortunes at the time of his praying (בהתפללו – 42:10). That is, the use of the preposition ב together with the infinitive of פלל here probably does not only suggests the idea of cause and effect,⁵¹ but also of simultaneity; it is at the time of Job's intercession that his restoration practically begins.⁵²

Job is said to have prayed for his friends (רעהו). The MT רעהו looks like a singular, and that is how the versions take it. One expects the plural form רעיו, which occurs in 32:3. However, רעהו occurs in Job 12:4 and 16:21, where the literary contexts suggest that one should translate as plural and singular respectively. See in this connection the meaning of רעהו in 1 Sam 30:26 where it certainly carries the sense of a plural "friends." David Freedman has argued that there are a number of instances in Job (over fifty cases) where there are contractions of the diphthongs ($aw > ō$ and $ay > ē$) without any orthographic representation of the consonants. Job 42:10, Freedman argues, is probably one such instance where there was the contraction of the plural -ay diphthong before the addition of the suffix, resulting in a defective spelling of the text. Accordingly, the MT is explained as follows: *riʻayhū > *rīʻēhū > rēʻēhū – "his friends."⁵³

The restoration of Job's fortunes at the time of his prayer moves the debate beyond the notion of strict retribution, since we already know that God's manner of responding to Job's prayer will be one of showing favor to Job. Thus, although Job is right and his friends are rebuked, his restoration is nevertheless an act of divine favor that assumes but also transcends the law of retributive justice.

This aspect of divine freedom is further suggested by the next phrase in which the Lord increased all that Job had to double (ויסף יהוה את־כל־ אשר לאיוב למשנה –42:10). The idea of God "adding" or "increasing" Job's possession here may suggest that Job has already been the object of divine

---

50   See Jer 30:17–18, where the expression "to turn the turnings" parallels the idea of God bringing physical healing.
51   See, Dhorme, *The Book of Job*, 649–650, who translates: "The Yahweh rehabilitated the position of Job because he interceded for his friends."
52   Other examples of the use of the preposition in the temporal sense together with infinitives include Prov 17:17; Ps 46:2; 109:13.
53   See, David Noel Freedman, "The Orthographic Peculiarities in the Book of Job," in *Poetry and Orthography* (ed. John R. Huddlestan; vol. 2 of *Divine Commitment and Human Obligation: Selected Writings of David Noel Freedman* ed. John R. Huddlestan; Grand Rapids, Mich.: Eerdmans, 1997), 44–60, especially page 53.

favor. That is, the idea suggests continuity with some previous action (Job 27:1; 29:1; 36:1). Even though this may take the reader back to the beginning of the story, the idea of God adding may also recall the meaning of the idiom about God lifting Job's face (42:9), which could refer to intangible things such as honor and dignity. In addition to such favor, God now provides Job with material benefits. The restoration of "all that Job had" (כל־אשר לאיוב) recalls "all that belongs to him" (כל־אשר לו) in 1:10, 12 and כל־אשר לאיש ("all that a person has") in 2:4. While the expression in 1:10, 12 refers to the destruction of Job's property and servants, that in 2:4 refers to the attack on his body that caused him to sit in the dung. Thus, the destruction starts with material loss and progresses to immaterial loss (pain as depicted in chapter 29). Here in the Epilogue, the order is reversed; the restoration begins with Job's face being lifted to a position of honor, and then his property is restored to double. Material possession is not at the forefront of the divine-human relationship. But neither is it absent from the relationship.

The next verse (42:11) describes the gathering of an enlarged human assembly to console and comfort Job as well as to present him with gifts. This immediately resonates with the context of the Prologue, prompting the LXX to make three significant moves that reveal an attempt to harmonize the Epilogue with the Prologue and tone down the theological difficulties in the text. First, for MT "then all his brother and sisters and former acquaintances came to him,"[54] LXX states that all his brothers and sisters "heard all that had happened to him." This harmonizes with 2:11 where the friends hear about all the evil that had come upon Job. Second, for MT "and they ate bread with him," LXX adds καὶ πίοντες (and drank), thereby harmonizing with the description of the festivities in the Prologue where Job's children eat and drink (1:4). Third, for MT "and they consoled and comforted him for all the trouble that the Lord had brought on him," LXX has "and they marveled at all that the Lord had brought upon him," leaving out any mention of the word trouble/evil.[55] As shall later be argued, these differences between the Epilogue and the Prologue constitute part of the uniqueness of the Epilogue and should, therefore, not be easily harmonized.

As an act of hospitality, the visitors present gifts to Job: some form of legal tender referred to as קשיטה, which elsewhere is used to acquire inheritance (חלק) – cf. Gen 33:19; Jos 24:32. The versions have "ewe/lamb"

---

54 The group of brothers and sisters and former acquaintances here is perhaps in response to Job's depiction of his troubles in terms of his alienation from his brothers and acquaintances in the Dialogues (see 19: 13–14).

55 This appears to be both a theological and a literary move. In 2:11 where the MT speaks of "all the evil" that came upon him, the LXX does indeed have τὰ κακὰ πάντα, the point being that in 2:11 the subject of the act of bringing evil upon Job is unmentioned or implicitly associated with the Adversary. Here in 42:11, however, the narrator makes it clear that it is the Lord acting, and the LXX appears unwilling to ascribe evil to God. For further analyses of LXX translation techniques, see Homer Heater, *A Septuagint Translation Technique in the Book of Job* (Washington, D. C.: Catholic Biblical Association, 1982).

for קְשִׂיטָה in MT. However, in Gen 33:19 Tg. Onqelos has "young lamb", Tg. Pseudo Jonathan has "pearl", and Tg. Neofiti has "piece of money."[56] Symm. has νόμισμα – "a coin." These various readings of קְשִׂיטָה probably reflect a period of transition from trade by barter to the use of coins, when a young lamb was the equivalent of a coin.[57] The friends also give Job a ring of gold (נֶזֶם זָהָב אֶחָד), which the LXX translates as "four coins of unmarked gold," a reading that is difficult to explain. In any case, the human assembly contributes to Job's restoration.

Following the gifts, the narrator states that the Lord blessed the latter part of Job more than his former (42:12). The expression about the doubling of Job's possession in v.10b is now spelled out in concrete terms. However, within this context of the doubling of all that Job lost in the Prologue, his children remain seven (שִׁבְעָנָה). With the exception of the rabbinic Tg., the versions have seven sons. The Targum has ארבסר (14); so too Dhorme who argues that the MT is a dual form of שִׁבְעָה, and cites 1 Chron 25:5 where Heman had fourteen sons and three daughters. Dhorme further argues, on the basis of the dual form in *ān* (attested in Arabic, Akkadian, and Aramaic), that one should see here a dual of seven to which is added the feminine ending of the cardinal numbers.[58] Rashi interpreted the number of children as 14,[59] and one may suppose that given the influence of Arabic on Jewish exegesis during the medieval period in general and on Rashi in particular, he was influenced by the dual form in Arabic. Referencing the Baal cycle (52.64),[60] N. Sarna argues that what we have here is the equivalent of the old Ugaritic form שִׁבְעָנִי. That is, what we have is *šb'* "seven" + adverbial *ny*.[61]

The Hebrew adverbial ני is used elsewhere to express completeness (Gen 42:36; Prov 31:29; 1Kg 7:37).[62] As I shall later argue, the fact that Job's

---

56 See, Celine Mangan, "The Targum of Job Translated with a Critical Introduction, Apparatus, and Notes," in *The Aramaic Bible: The Targums* (ed. Kevin Cathcart, Michael Maher, and Martin MacNamara; Collegeville, Minn.: Liturgical Press, 1991), 15:12.
57 See, Daniel Sperber, "Notes on the Kesitah," *RÉJ* 127 (1968): 265–268.
58 Dhorme, *The Book of Job*, 651–652.
59 See, Rashi, *Job*, 239.
60 See, *CTU* 1.4.
61 Nahum Sarna, "Epic Substratum in the Prose of Job," in *JBL* 75 (1957): 18. The adverbial *ny* is attested in Ugaritic and used as a dual suffix in verb forms. See Cyrus H. Gordon, *Textbook of Ugaritic Grammar* (Rome: Editrice Pontificio Instituto Biblico, 1998), 102, for a list of words with the adverbial *ny*. In Ugaritic, dual and plural noun forms generally end in *êma* or *êmi*. See Josef Tropper, *Ugaritische Grammatik* (Münster: Ugarit-Verlag, 2000), 289–290. Similarly, although there are remnants of the –*ayin* dual form in Aramaic, the dual is largely identical with the plural forms. See Franz Rosenthal, *A Grammar of Biblical Aramaic* 6th rev. ed. (ed. Werner Diem and Franz Rosenthal; Porta Linguarum Orientalium, Neue Serie 5; Wiesbaden: Harrassowitz, 1995), 28. Some masculine plural absolute nouns in Aramaic end in *ān* (Dan 2:22; 7:8; Est 6:9). Other absolute noun forms that end in *ān* refer to abstract nouns (cf. Dan 7:12). Accordingly, it is possible that given the transition from *ayin* to *în* in Aramaic dual forms and the doubling of Job's possessions in the Epilogue, the rabbinic Tg. misreads the Hebrew as a dual.
62 Tur-Sinai, *Job*, 581.

children remain seven further underscores the dissonance between the Epilogue and the Prologue. Furthermore, given the fact that the supposed death of Job's children in the Prologue is not explicitly spelled out but only implied, the current number of seven in the Epilogue may be playing on the tension between family loss and survival within the narrative. This survival motif is perhaps hinted at by the focus on Job's children in the next verses.

Job's daughters are now named. The first is named *Yemimah*. A number of scholars connect this name to the Arabic *yumaymat* ("dove").[63] The description of the daughters as beautiful in v.15 coheres with the understanding of turtledove, since turtledove is elsewhere associated with beauty (cf. Song of Songs 2:14).[64] The second daughter's name, *Qeziah*, refers to an aromatic plant used with myrrh (Exod 30:24; Ezek 23:19; Ps 45:9).[65] The third daughter's was *Qeren-Happuk*, and her name is once more associated with beauty (2 Kg 9:30; Jer 4:30; Is 54:11; 1Chron 29:2).[66] Their beauty is then described in exceptional terms. The narrator states that נמצא[67] לא ("there was not found") women in the land as beautiful as Job's daughters. This exceptional beauty is then closely followed by the observation that they received inheritance from their father.

For a moment, the focus is on Job's daughters and Job the protagonist of the story is known as "their father." Their general description here recalls the characterization of Job at the start of the book. Just as Job is named, his property listed, and he is said to be greater than all the sons of the east (1:1–3), so in the Epilogue Job's daughters are named (v.14), described as more beautiful than the women in all the land, and said to have inheritance (v.15).

After this (אחרי זאת),[68] Job lives for a hundred and forty years, long enough to see his children to the fourth generation before dying old and advanced in years.[69] This verse brings Job's life to its natural end.

---

63 Dhorme, *The Book of Job*, 652; Marvin H. Pope, *Job: Introduction, Translation, and Notes* (ed. William F. Albright and David N. Freedman; AB 15; New York: Doubleday, 1965), 352; Driver and Gray, *The Book of Job*, 256.

64 The dove was, however, also associated with being silly (cf. Hos 7:11). The present literary context privileges the sense of beauty associated with the dove. For a brief overview of the uses and symbolism of the dove in ancient Israel, see V. Møller-Christensen and K. E. Jordt Jørgensen, *Encyclopedia of Bible Creatures* (Philadelphia: Fortress, 1965), 132–137.

65 Gordon interprets the name as "bow" and argues that, "the shapeliness of a bow made it appropriate for a girl's name." See Cyrus H. Gordon, *Ugaritic Textbook*, 479; Sarna, "Epic Substratum in the Prose of Job," 24. Marvin Pope, *Job*, 353, however, points out that despite the curvature of a bow, it would be a rather odd name for girls.

66 Brown, Driver, and Briggs, *Hebrew and English Lexicon*, 902.

67 Two late manuscripts have the plural form נמצאו to correspond with the plural number of girls. This is likely harmonistic. A singular impersonal passive form of the Niphal can correspond to a plural subject. See GKC, 387–388. The versions have a singular verb form.

68 LXX has "after the affliction." As shall become evident later, this is part of the Greek translator's attempt to clarify the text.

69 LXX has an extended version with an appendix on Job's expected resurrection and genealogy. See next chapter on the History of Interpretation.

1.3 Conclusion

The Epilogue follows God's address to Job from the whirlwind and Job's response. The Epilogue itself opens with God's rebuke of the friends (42:7), "after" the Lord had spoken to Job from the whirlwind. I have argued that the adverb "after" serves as a transitional phrase, preserving the element of continuity and discontinuity between the Epilogue and the theophany. The transitory character of 42:7 is further strengthened by the idiom about the divine anger, which in Deuteronomistic theology often occurs in transitional phrases. A theophany-epilogue continuum begins to emerge as a possible interpretive context for reading the Epilogue. Within this interpretive context, the prepositional phrase אלי can be read as "to me" or "concerning me." In fact, both senses should be discerned here. Some of the versions (Vulg., LXX, and Syr.) simply place the friends and Job in God's presence ("before me" or "in my presence") without emphasizing whether the friends are rebuked for not speaking rightly "to" God or "concerning" God. This rendering of the Hebrew text further underscores the hermeneutical connection between the Epilogue and the theophany.

In the rebuke of the friends for not speaking rightly "to/concerning" God, the complementary part of the rebuke, "like my servant Job," portrays Job as a righteous individual in contrast with the friends. On the one hand, based on my analysis of the idiom about speaking a "firm word," the rebuke of the friends is interpreted as one of deficiency rather than corruption. On the other hand, based on the comparative aspect of the rebuke where the friends are contrasted with Job, the rebuke is perceived as having a moral quality. In fact, LXX-Job and 11QtgJob state that the friends "sinned" against God, and only on the merits of Job's intercession were they spared. In the larger context of the theophany-epilogue continuum, this rebuke of the friends for not speaking rightly like Job creates tension with God's overall rebuke of Job from the whirlwind and Job's later admission to having spoken without knowledge. Also, Job's prayer in the Epilogue is subsumed under the obedience of the friends who go and offer a sacrifice on their own behalf. I have suggested that even though Job is contrasted with his friends in the rebuke, they all come together at the altar. The expression, "they did just as God commanded them" in 42:9 describes not only the friends but also Job. Therefore, one could discern here an implicit approval of the friends, since they are equally important in the cultic activity. Within the overall framework of the theophany-epilogue, there is both rebuke and approval that constitute a two-dimensional divine response to the human discussion in the Dialogues.

When the friends go and offer the sacrifice in obedience to the divine command (LXX and Syr., in attempt to harmonize the Epilogue and the Prologue, state that it is Job who offers the sacrifice on their behalf), God "lifts Job's face," that is, answers his prayer and spares the friends: God does not deal with the friends in an outrageous manner. Contrary to much of traditional religion represented by the friends, God can act "outrageously," that is, outside of the norms. This is a lesson that the friends learn in the rebuke and at the altar. On the other hand, contrary to Job and Elihu who argued against "lifting the face" of others (showing favor), the Epilogue portrays YHWH as doing precisely that. The divine favor shown to Job in answer to his prayer also benefits the friends. In the formulation of the divine threat and response to the human activity at the altar, retribution is both affirmed and surpassed. After a larger human assembly gathers around him to show their grief and console him (42:11), Job is then restored whatever he lost in the Prologue; every numbered possession of his is doubled, with the exception of his children. The fact that the children remain ten creates dissonance with the "doubling" motif in this context. The importance of this dissonance is that the Epilogue does not simply replicate the Prologue, but rather draws from the Prologue and then transcends it. It is within the context of this "more than" perspective of the Epilogue that Job's daughters receive inheritance from him together with their brothers, and Job's lifespan is apparently also doubled as he lives to see his children to the fourth generation before dying in a ripe old age. This "more than" perspective, which provides the interpretive context for the different readings in some of the versions, including the idea that the friends were rebuked for not speaking the truth "against" Job, will be further explored in the next chapter under a survey of the history of interpretation.

Chapter 2: The Post-Canonical Life of the Text: A Selected History of Interpretation

2.1 Introduction

The canonization of the Hebrew text brought a significant dimension of stability and finality to the process of the production of biblical texts. Yet, an examination of the translation (and interpretation) of biblical texts indicates that even with "stabilization," these texts still remained multivalent, capable of being significantly modified. Partly as a result of the wide semantic range of words and expressions, and the complex and diverse concerns of the translators' contexts, the possibilities of expanding, abridging, and transforming texts have remained very real. An examination of the biblical texts reveals that the canon itself is a combination of text and interpretation.[70] This suggests that for both the canonical text and its later interpretation, it is possible to speak of an on-going dynamic between textual stability and changeability or adaptability, closure and openness, tradition and transmission.[71]

---

[70] See, Emanuel Tov, "History and Significance of a Standard Text of the Hebrew Bible," in *Hebrew Bible, Old Testament: The History of its Interpretation*. Part 1 *Antiquity*. Vol. 1 *From the Beginnings to the Middle Ages (until 1300)* in Co-operation with Chris Brekelmans and Menahem Haran (ed. Magne Sæbø; Göttingen: Vandenhoeck & Ruprecht, 1996), 49–66. Theoretically, the sense of "finality" associated with canonization explains the reason why biblical exegetes and interpreters refer to translations of canonical texts and versions as "faithful" or "free" renderings, or "expansions," or "transformations" of the canonized text.

[71] See, James A. Sanders, "Stability and Fluidity in Text and Canon," in *Tradition of the Text: Studies Offered to Dominique Barthélemy in Celebration of his 70th Birthday* (ed. Gerald J. Norton and Stephen Pisano; Göttingen: Vandenhoeck & Ruprecht, 1991), 208: "The very fact that a story or poem was repeated in a time and space beyond its inception meant that it was adaptable and relevant to more than one situation; but if it did not have a recognizable measure of stability, or sameness, it was not, by definition, a repetition/recitation or even an allusion, but a new composition." On closure and openness of the text, see John Barton, "The Significance of the Fixed Text," in *The Hebrew Bible, Old Testament: The History of its Interpretation*. Part 1 *Antiquity*. Vol. 1 *From the Beginnings to the Middle Ages (until 1300) in Co-operation with Chris Brekelmans and Menahem Haran* (ed. Magne Sæbø; Göttingen: Vandenhoeck & Ruprecht, 1996), 67–83; on tradition and transmission, see Michael Fishbane, "Inner Biblical Exegesis," in Magne Sæbø ed., *The Hebrew Bible, Old Testament: The History of its Interpretation*. Part 1 *Antiquity*. Vol. 1 *From the Beginnings to the Middle Ages (until 1300) in Co-operation with Chris Brekelmans and Menahem Haran* (ed. Magne Sæbø; Göttingen: Vandenhoeck & Ruprecht, 1996), 33–48.

The art of creating, transmitting, and interpreting texts operates within certain literary and thematic guidelines. In his study of rabbinic writing, for example, Jacob Neusner identifies three indicators that governed the writing and establishment of documentary texts. These include (a) rhetoric, which deals with particular language and syntax as well as sentence structure; (b) logic, which deals with the logical coherence and development of thought; and (c) topic, which deals with the particular agenda, differentiating what belongs to the work and what does not.[72] But in addition to this, Neusner also identifies what he calls the "extra-and non-documentary" writing, which refers to compositions that do not strictly follow or that even ignore the three indicators of documentary works. Such works, Neusner argues, play the role of illustrations or amplifications of particular issues.[73] As a result, one finds that there are varying degrees to which translations of texts either resemble or differ from the original texts. In fact, one might even argue that in some instances (e.g., LXX-Job) there was both translation and composition, again reflecting the dynamic of the stability and changeability of texts.[74]

Because of the complexity of the content of the book of Job, the many and discordant voices expressed in it, and the changing views of some of the characters within the narrative, the interpretation of Job has often moved beyond the literary context of the Hebrew text. Readers and interpreters, coming to the book from different historical moments, have found in it, as in many other books, not the conclusive finished product of the complex divine-human relationship, but the vital building blocks of that relationship.[75] David Brown thus argues that throughout much, if not most, of subsequent Jewish and Christian history Job has in fact functioned less as a text with a specific meaning and more as a handle for investigating alternative responses.[76]

---

72 Jacob Neusner, *Texts Without Boundaries: Protocols of Non-Documentary Writing in the Rabbinic Canon* (ed. Jacob Neusner; Studies in Judaism 3; New York: University Press of America, 2002). On pages xx–xxi, Neusner writes: "Each document, without exception, differs from all others in how it combines the possibilities. These three indicators (rhetoric, logic and topic) join together in a unique combination to characterize a given document, so that that particular combination governs in no other."
73 Neusner, *Texts Without Boundaries*, xxii.
74 See, Claude E. Cox, "Methodological Issues in the Exegesis of LXX Job," in *Sixth Congress of the International Organization for Septuagint and Cognate Studies* (ed. Claude E. Cox; SBLSCS 23; Atlanta, GA: Scholars Press, 1987), 81–83.
75 Spiegel, "Noah, Danel, and Job," 325, notes that in the development of the Joban legend, the author likely retains the form of the ancient narrative, even when he transcends it in spirit, and the audience likely found the recurrence of the familiar in the new enjoyable. Similarly, Jean-Marie Delmaire, "Les Principaux Courants de l'Exégèse Juive sur Job," in *Le Livre de Job* (Lectures de l'Écriture, Graphè 6; Paris: Presses de l'Université Charles-de-Gaulle, 1997), 59, writes about the book: "Par le contraste entre le cadre et la longue partie poétique, il fait naître des discordances ou des contradictions qui demandent aussi explication. Il n'est donc pas étonnant que ce livre ait suscité des nombreux commentaires dont la plupart restent loin de la force du texte de départ."
76 David Brown, *Discipleship and Imagination: Christian Tradition and Truth* (Oxford: Oxford University Press, 2000), 177. For a study of Job that not only involves exegetical analyses but also a survey of its history of interpretation, see Wolf-Dieter

However, my focus shall mainly be on the Epilogue and how it has been interpreted as part of the entire story.

Part of the stability-adaptability dynamic of interpretation comes from the interaction between the present and the past. The hermeneutical value of this endeavor is recommended in the book of Job itself. As Bildad argues, part of the process of interpretation consists of learning from past generations (8:8). Accordingly, I shall begin by focusing on some of the versions (particularly LXX-Job and 11QtgJob). Then I shall examine other significant writings within Jewish and Christian circles in the rabbinic and patristic period, the medieval period, and finally the modern period. It should be emphasized that this is not intended to be an exhaustive survey (for that would clearly be impossible to do), but rather representative of some of the major interpretive currents that have helped in shaping the understanding of the Epilogue of Job.

2.2 The Versions

Of the versions, 11QtgJob and LXX-Job offer the most interesting readings. The others (Syr., rabbinic Tg., and Vulg.) follow the Hebrew text fairly closely, and shall not be treated in detail here.

2.2.1   11QtgJob

The discovery and publication of the Targum of the book of Job in Cave 11 in Qumran[77] led to comparative analyses with the rabbinic Targum already known and the Septuagint. More importantly, it also led to an examination of the relationship between the Qumran text and the Massoretic text.[78] Because

---

Syring, *Hiob und sein Anwalt: Die Prosatexte des Hiobbuches und ihre Rolle in seiner Redaktions- und Rezeptionsgeschichte* (BZAW 336; Berlin: Walter de Gruyter, 2004).

77   The text was discovered by Bedouin in 1956, acquired by the *Palestine Archaeological Museum*, and later on published by J. P. M. van der Ploeg and A. S. van der Woude, *Le Targum de Job de la Grotte XI de Qumran* (Leiden: Brill, 1971).

78   Among the several studies, one should note Stephen A. Kaufman, "The Job Targum from Qumran," *JAOS* 93 (1973): 317–327; Francis J. Marrow, "11Q Targum and the Massoretic Text," *RevQ* 8, no. 2 (1973): 253–256; R. Weiss, "Further Notes on the Qumran Targum to Job," *JSS* 19 (1974): 13–18; John Gray, "The Massoretic Text of the Book of Job, the Targum and the Septuagint Version in the Light of the Qumran Targum," *ZAW* 86 (1974): 331–350; Emile Puech and Florentino García-Martínez, "Remarques sur la Colonne 38 de 11Q Tg Job," *RevQ* 9, no. 3 (1978): 401–407; Takamitsu Muraoka, "Notes on the Old Targum of Job from Qumran Cave XI," *RevQ* 9, no. 1 (1977): 117–125; Bruce Zuckerman, "The Date of 11Q Targum Job: A Palaeographic Consideration of its Vorlage," *JSP* 10 (1987): 57–78; idem, "Two examples of editorial Modification in 11QtgJob," in *Biblical and Near Eastern Studies. Essays in Honor of William Sanford LaSor* (ed. Gary A. Tuttle; Michgan: Eerdmans, 1978), 269–273; David Shepherd, "Before Bomberg: The Case of the Targum of Job in the Rabbinic Bible and the Solger Codex (MS Nürnberg)," *Bib* 79 (1998): 360–380; idem, "Will the Real Targum Please Stand Up? Translation and Coordination in the Ancient Aramaic Versions of Job," *JJS* 51 (2000): 88–116; Jean Margain, "11QtgJob et la langue Targumique: à propos de la Particule BDYL," *RevQ* 13 (1988): 525–528;

of extensive damage, however, only less than a fifth of the text has survived. Still, what has survived is significant because of its resonance and dissonance with the MT. In terms of literary structure, 11QtgJob is largely similar to the MT even in those instances where there has been debate in modern scholarship.[79] In many instances, it closely resembles the MT in content as well. On the other hand, 11QtgJob is sometimes longer and sometimes shorter than its equivalent in the MT, and still in other instances the author appears to modify the MT for theological and ethical reasons.[80]

Given that in some instances where 11QtgJob differs from the MT, it closely resembles LXX-Job (e.g., the depiction of the friends as sinners), some scholars have suggested that 11QtgJob and LXX-Job could very well have belonged to an exegetical tradition.[81] However, it has been equally argued that careful examination of these two versions reveals significant differences between them that may very well be an indication of a significant level of their independence.[82] Although it is possible to trace the development or the thought progression of an author or idea within a single narrative, it is less clear how one can conclusively determine and isolate the single *Vorlage*

John C. Lübbe, "Describing the Translation Process of 11QtgJob: a Question of Method," *RevQ* 13 (1988): 583–593.

79   For example, 11QtgJob corroborates the structure of the Dialogues in the Third cycle where Bildad's speech is very short, Zophar does not speak, and part of Job's speech in chapter 27 sounds more like Bildad's. For a detailed study of the structure of the Qumran texts of Job (4QtgJob and 11QtgJob) and their relationship to the Allepo and Leningrad Codices as well as the MT, see Ernst Kutsch, »Die Textgliederung im hebräischen Ijobbuch sowie in 4QTgJob und in 11QTgJob,« *BZNF* 27 (1983): 221–228. Markus Witte has studied the third cycle of speeches (in their present form) within the overall context of the poetic section. Witte argues that the poetic section was written in three stages. The first is referred to as the *Niedrigkeitsredaktion* related to "low" anthropology; the second is called the *Majestätsredaktion* related to God's hidden and creative majesty, and the third is the *Gerechtigkeitsredaktion* related to divine justice. Job's speech in chapter 27 belongs to the last two stages of the redaction process. See, Markus Witte, »Die dritte Rede Bildads (Hiob 25) und die Redaktionsgeschichte des Hiobbuches,« in *The Book of Job* ed. William A. Beuken (BETL 114; Leuven: Leuven University Press, 1994), 349–355. A more detailed analysis is provided in Markus Witte, *Vom Leiden zur Lehre. Der dritte Redegang (Hiob 21–27) und die Redaktionsgeschichte des Hiobbuches* (BZAW 230; Berlin: Walter de Gruyter, 1994) where Witte also surveys the previous interpretive models used in attempt to understand the third cycle of speeches.

80   Such ethical and theological concerns include an emphasis on the sovereignty of God and an attempt to portray Job as a righteous sufferer. For a list of these differences between the Qumran text and the MT, see B. Jongeling, C. J. Labuschagne, and A. S. van der Woude, *Aramaic Texts from Qumran* (Leiden: Brill, 1976), 7–8.

81   Van der Ploeg and van de Woude, *Le Targum de Job*, 7: "Les Septante et le targum de 11Q sont quelquefois d'accord sur certains détails, ce qui prouve, non une dépendance littéraire, mais une tradition exégétique commune." So too, Puech and García-Martínez, "Remarques," 407.

82   Zuckerman, "The Date of 11QTargum Job," 74–75, writes: "the *Vorlage* of 11QTargum Job and the original autograph itself were probably nearly contemporaneous documents; indeed, it is even possible that our translator was also the copyist of his *Vorlage*." On the LXX, Annette Y. Reed, "Job as Jobab: The Interpretation of Job in LXX Job 42:17b–e," *JBL* 120, no. 1 (2001): 38, writes: "LXX Job appendix was not translated from Aramaic, but rather composed in Greek."

or multiple *Vorlagen* that lay behind any given text. How is one to determine and differentiate, for example, an author's innovation (freedom) from the author's conscious use of a different *Vorlage* at any one given instance? In the absence of definitive and clear-cut guidelines for such decisions, it is perhaps more fruitful to speak of the author's freedom within an exegetical tradition or within different exegetical traditions and redactions. That is, at any given moment, an author could be modifying a particular *Vorlage* or using a different one or combining two or more secondary redactions, or expanding one while at the same time reproducing two others verbatim. The process of compilation and composition was complex, this being especially true given the fluidity of the text immediately prior to and following canonization.[83]

The surviving text of the Epilogue in 11QtgJob is notably shorter than the MT, consisting only of about three verses, 9b–11. Verses 7–9a are damaged and verses 12–17 are lacking. Verse 11 ends in the middle of the line, this being the style that the author uses in the Dialogues to make transitions from one speaker to another. The space after v. 11 is large enough to contain a text that is the equivalent of the MT. Thus, the question is whether the translator/author knew vv. 12–17.[84] If he did not, then that portion of the MT may simply be a late addition.[85] On the other hand, if he knew vv. 12–17, then one should assume that they are simply lost through damage.[86] That portion of the account is found in all the other versions and later rabbinic writings. It is, therefore, likely that the author knew that section of the

---

[83] See, John Gray, "The Massoretic Text of the Book of Job," 335; Annette Reed, "Job as Jobab," 32; Harry Y. Gamble, *Books and Readers in the Early Church: A History of Early Christian Texts* (New Haven: Yale University Press, 1995), 74; Zuckerman, "The Date of 11Q Targum," 63, writes: "we cannot say for sure exactly what the translator of the cave 11 Targum of Job used for his *Vorlage* – whether he had access to more than one manuscript of Job, more than one recension of Job, or even Job in translation as well as in an original Hebrew version (or versions). Close analysis suggests, however, that the targumist essentially relied on a single Hebrew manuscript, not identical with, but largely conforming to a tradition in line with that which the Massoretes employed in producing their manuscripts of Job in the medieval times."

[84] Van der Ploeg and van der Woude, *Le Targum de Job*, 7, note this point and suggest that it could very well be that vv. 12–17 were unknown to the author, although they also mention that theoretically vv. 12–17 could very well fit in the remaining space on the scroll.

[85] John Gray, "The Massoretic Text of the Book of Job," 335, writes: "the rather naïve reference to the material restitution of Job, which has always offended spiritual susceptibilities, may be omitted for theological reasons ... but it may indicate that the book as the translator of the Qumran Targum knew it in the 2nd century B.C. ended at 42:11, the Epilogue from 42:12 being a late Midrashic expansion."

[86] Puech and García-Martínez, *Remarques sur la Colonne XXXVIII*, 404–407, have presented the argument in favor of this position. On the basis of new photos with better contrasts, these authors have argued that vv.12–17 were indeed part of the text. They proceed to reconstruct v.12, which partly reads "And God blessed Job afterwards," without the MT's "more than his former." However, Kutsch, »Die Textgliederung,« 227, argues that since the narrator of the Qumran text leaves out Job's sisters in 42:11, it is probable that he also left out the portion on their inheritance in 42:13–15, although it is difficult to determine whether 42:16–17 were also left out.

Epilogue and, treating it as a transition in the narrative, started it on a new line.[87]

The surviving text reads:

אלהא ושמע אלהא בקלה די איוב ושבק להון חטאיהון בדילה
ותב אלהא לאיוב ברחמין ויהב לה חד תרין בכל די הוא לה
ואתון[88] לות איוב כל רחמוהי וכל אחוהי וכל ידעוהי
ואכלו עמה לחם בביתה ונחמוהי על כל באישתה די היתי
אלהא עלוהי
ויהבו לה גבר אמרה חדה וגבר קדש חד די דהב

("God; and God listened to the voice of Job, and forgave their sins because of him. Then God turned to Job in mercy and gave him twice as much as he had. Then came to Job all his friends, all his brothers, and all who knew him, and they ate bread with him in his house and comforted him for all the trouble that God brought on him. And each person gave him a ewe-lamb and a gold ring.")

Even a cursory look at the text indicates that its content is broadly similar to that of the MT: (a) Job is depicted as a righteous individual who effectively intervenes on behalf of his friends; (b) God restores Job, doubling all that he earlier had; (c) there is a human assembly that gathers to console Job because of the troubles sent by God; and (d) these individuals present gifts to Job. Yet, in spite of these broad resonances with the MT, scholars have identified differences that are generally characterized as additions, subtractions, and substitutions.[89] Careful examination of the text shows that this is true of the Epilogue. One finds the following: (a) the omission of the expression about Job's prayer ("when he prayed for them"), the omission of "YHWH added" in the expression, "the Lord added and gave to Job twice as much,"[90] the omission of Job's "sisters" in the group that comes to comfort him, no description of Job's acquaintances as "former," and no mention of the "grief" shown by the human assembly; (b) additions such as the mention of God forgiving the friends' sins because of Job, perhaps already implicit in the MT; the addition of "all his friends" (כל רחמוהי) in the group that comes to comfort Job; and (c) the substitution that God listened to Job's voice (in place of the idiom that God "lifted Job's face"), and that God turned to Job in

---

87 This would correspond to the Massoretic *setumah* of the MT at the end of v.11. For detailed analysis of the use of the *setumah* and the *petuhah* in the Hebrew text and its relationship to the structure of the Qumran text, see Kutsch, »Die Textgliederung,« 221–227.

88 The first editors read ואתין here, but given the occasional confusion resulting from the graphic similarity between *wāws* and *yōds*, one should probably read ואתון. See Michael Sokoloff, *The Targum to Job From Qumran Cave XI* (Jerusalem: Bar-Ilan University Press, 1974), 168.

89 See, Shepherd, "Will the Real Targum," 89–90; Van der Ploeg and van der Woude, *Le Targum de Job*, 7.

90 David Shepherd, *Targum and Translation: A Reconsideration of the Qumran Aramaic Version of Job* (ed. W. J. van Bekkum et al.; SSN 45; Assen: Royal Gorcum, 2004), 55, 66–69, argues that these omissions are likely a result of the translator viewing them as redundant.

mercy (in place of God restoring Job's fortunes in the MT). Taken as a whole, these literary features in the Qumran text reveal both its resonance and dissonance with the MT. The interpreter's task, therefore, is not just to determine the hermeneutical value of the differences but ultimately how, in conjunction with the resonances, they impact the overall understanding of the text.

Although it is difficult to carry out a thorough assessment of the dynamic between the Epilogue of the Qumran text and its preceding sections due to the damaged nature of the scroll, an examination of the text will give us a fair idea of the author's portrayal of Job in the Epilogue. Even without knowing the precise formulation of the divine rebuke of the friends, the contrast between them and Job is clear: v. 9b presents them as "sinners" on whose behalf Job efficaciously intercedes; they are forgiven "because of Job." In response to the prayer, God "listened to the voice of Job," an expression that we have already shown to be a more traditional rendering of the divine response to prayer. In col. 6.8 (MT, 22:8) where the nominal form of the idiom נשא פנים is used, the surviving word is [א]פוהי, suggesting that the idiom was probably used elsewhere in the text. Therefore, its substitution here in the Epilogue is perhaps an attempt to avoid the negative connotations of unfairness and favoritism associated with the idiom, especially because it is used with God as subject and humankind as the object.[91]

God is then portrayed as "turning to Job in mercy," an expression that is a modification of the MT ("the Lord restored the fortunes of Job"). God's attribute of mercy (רחמין) here linguistically and thematically anticipates the coming of Job's friends (רחמוהי) to comfort him. Thus, although Job's friends sinned against God, they eventually become part of the experience of God's mercy towards Job in the restoration.[92] To anticipate what I shall develop in greater detail later, it is worth noting that in rabbinic thought, two very important aspects of the divine character were justice and mercy. Divine mercy was even personified and, according to Rabbi Akiba, was extended to those who were righteous sufferers. Thus, as an act of divine justice, Job is approved and restored because he is righteous. But since the divine attributes of justice and mercy are distinct yet closely related, the Qumran text also develops the idea of divine mercy shown to Job.

---

91 For an analysis of the Hebrew idiom, see textual analysis on 42:8. In Aramaic, the negative connotations sometimes associated with the idiom are equally expressed in the way it is used. It carries the idea of being favorable to people, an attitude that is forbidden especially within the judicial system. The rabbinic Targum consistently renders the idiom נסב...אף throughout the book of Job. In Lev 19:15 and Deut 10:17; 28:50 where the idiom is used in the injunction not to favor humans in judicial matters, both Targum Onkelos to Leviticus and Targum Onkelos to Deuteronomy render it נסב...אף.

92 See Solomon's exilic prayer where the idea of God listening (שמע) to prayers and forgiving is repeatedly expressed (1Kg 8: 36, 39, 49–50). In the course of the prayer, appeal is made to God to be gracious to Israel so that Israel's captors will be merciful/friendly (רחם) to Israel (1 Kg 8:50 x2). In 1 Kg 8:34 God is called upon to hear, forgive, and restore (שוב).

In summary, Job is portrayed as a righteous person who has been cast (or has cast himself) to "dust and ashes" (42:6) and therefore in need of restoration. Alternatively, then, the traditional rendering of the divine response to Job's prayer is more about emphasizing God's appropriate and gracious response to Job and less about avoiding the negative connotations of the idiom involving unjust favoritism. In its resonance with the MT, 11QtgJob appears to emphasize the fact that Job is a righteous individual. But it also introduces another factor in the text: that of divine mercy. The Epilogue of 11QtgJob is therefore as much, if not much more, about God's mercy as it is about Job's righteousness.

2.2.2 The Septuagint

An examination of Joseph Ziegler's critical edition to the Septuagint of Job reveals that the present form of the text is a result of at least two levels of composition that do not necessarily reflect different *Vorlagen*. The first is the Old Greek (OG) that, although following the MT closely in some instances, is also significantly different from the MT. Large parts of the MT are left out and others are expanded. In its final form, the OG is considerably shorter than the MT.[93] The second level of redaction is literalistic, being Origen's interpolation of Theodotion's version of what had not been translated in the earlier version, and which Origen marked with asterisks. An examination of Origen's use of Theodotion, however, reveals a more complex process of composition.[94]

Various reasons have been proposed for the difference between the OG and the MT, some of which include (a) omissions because of the translator's inability to understand or translate difficult texts,[95] (b) the translator's desire to avoid anthropomorphisms regarding divine action and theological

---

[93] Some of the most vigorous arguments in support of the significant degree to which the LXX faithfully renders the MT have been presented by Harry M. Orlinsky in a series of articles on "Studies in the Septuagint of the Book of Job," *HUCA* 28 (1957): 53–74; 29 (1958): 229–271; 30 (1959): 153–167; 32 (1961): 239–268; 33 (1962): 119–151; 35 (1964): 57–78; 36 (1965): 37–47. Orlinsky, however, also talked about the additions and subtractions in the OG. See, Orlinsky, "Studies," (1957): 53. See also G. Buchanan Gray, "The Additions in the Ancient Greek Version of Job," *Expositor* 19 (1931): 422–438; Heater, *Translation Technique*, 1-2; Dhorme, *The Book of Job*, cc–cciii, equally notes these differences and concludes that the translator may have increasingly curtailed his text as he progressed due to fatigue.

[94] Some of the material in the OG was not found in the MT as noted by Origen himself in his letter to Africanus. See M. Harl and N. de Lange, eds., *Origène, Philocalie, 1–20 sur les Écritures et la Lettre à Africanus sur l'Histoire de Suzanne* (SC 302; Paris: Cerf, 1983), 528. See also Claude Cox, "Origen's Use of Theodotion in the Elihu Speeches," *SecCent* 3 (1983): 89–98; Peter John Gentry, *The Asterisked Materials in the Greek Job* (ed. Leonard J. Greenspoon; SBLSCS 38; Atlanta: Scholars, 1995), 1–6.

[95] See Pope, *Job*, xliv.

language that may be offensive to God,[96] and (c) stylistic variations.[97] In a study on the translation technique employed by the Greek translator, Homer Heater argues for "a practice of the Greek translator that goes beyond the matter of style." Heater calls this the "anaphoric technique" that refers to the art of "interpolating material from some other part of the Septuagint, although usually from within Job itself, into the passage with which he is working"; a technique that involves "the interpolation or adaptation of words or phrases from other passages of Scripture where the underlying idea is the same or similar."[98] Given the significant influence of the Greek translator in the production of the text, it is impossible to isolate any single literary device as the major guideline for the translator or author. Accordingly, the Greek text is to a significant measure the creation of the translator, although it is also significantly similar to the Hebrew text.[99]

Two parts of the Epilogue are marked with an asterisk (42: 8e // 42:8b in the MT and 42:16 c–e // 42: 16b–17 in the MT), both of which are a faithful rendering of the Hebrew text. The addendum in 17:b–e, which has no parallel in the MT and in fact in none of the other versions, is unmarked. It is part of the pre-hexaplaric Sahidic version[100] and Theodotion.[101] The appendix reads:

17aα γέγραπται δὲ αὐτὸν πάλιν ἀναστήσεσθαι μεθ' ὧν ὁ Κύριος ἀνίστησιν.
17bα Οὗτος ἑρμηνεύεται ἐκ τῆς Συριακῆς βίβλου ἐν μὲν γῇ κατοικῶν τῇ Αὐσίτιδι ἐπὶ τοῖς ὁρίοις τῆς Ἰδουμαίας καὶ Ἀραβίας, προϋπῆρχεν δὲ αὐτῷ ὄνομα Ἰωβάβ·
17cα λαβὼν δὲ γυναῖκα Ἀράβισσαν γεννᾷ υἱὸν, ᾧ ὄνομα Ἐννών, ἦν δὲ αὐτὸς πατρὸς μὲν Ζάρε, τῶν Ἡσαῦ υἱῶν υἱός, μητρὸς δὲ Βοσόρρας, ὥστε εἶναι αὐτὸν πέμπτον ἀπὸ Ἀβραάμ.
17dα καὶ οὗτοι οἱ βασιλεῖς οἱ βασιλεύσαντες ἐν Ἐδώμ, ἧς καὶ αὐτὸς ἦρξε χώρας· πρῶτος Βαλὰκ ὁ τοῦ Βεώρ, καὶ ὄνομα τῇ πόλει αὐτοῦ Δενναβά· μετὰ δὲ Βαλὰκ Ἰωβὰβ ὁ

---

96 See Henry S. Gehman, "The Theological Approach of the Greek Translator of Job 1–15," *JBL* 68 (1949): 231–240; Donald H. Gard, "The Concept of Job's Character According to the Greek Translator of the Hebrew Text," *JBL* 72 (1953): 182–186; Dhorme, *The Book of Job*, cxcvii.
97 See Orlinsky, "Studies," (1961): 240.
98 Heater, *Translation Technique*, 6.
99 N. Fernández Marcos, "The Septuagint Reading of the Book of Job," in *The Book of Job* (ed. W. A. M. Beuken; BETL 114; Leuven: Leuven University Press, 1994), 265: "The Greek reader had before him a new book, if not re-written, at least re-created in Greek; a book more understandable than the original Hebrew, a narrative that translated to the linguistic system and religious universe of the Hellenistic period yet did not lose too much of the force, vigour and drama of the previous readings." For a study of such innovative writing elsewhere in the Bible, see Kristin de Troyer, *Rewriting the Sacred Text: What the Old Greek Texts Tell us About the Literary Growth of the Bible* (ed. James R. Adair; SBLTCS 4; Atlanta: Society of Biblical Literature, 2003).
100 See, Dhorme, *The Book of Job*, cci n. 8.
101 In his letter to Africanus, Origen mentions that the appendix is neither in the Hebrew text nor in Aquila's version. But he also mentions that it is found in Theodotions's and the Seventy's version. See, Harl and de Lange, *Africanus*, 528.

καλούμενος Ἰώβ· μετὰ δὲ τοῦτον Ἀσὸμ ὁ ὑπάρχων
ἡγεμὼν ἐκ τῆς Θαιμανίτιδος χώρας· μετὰ δὲ τοῦτον
Ἀδὰδ υἱὸς Βαρὰδ ὁ ἐκκόψας Μαδιὰμ ἐν τῷ πεδίῳ
Μωάβ, καὶ ὄνομα τῇ πόλει αὐτοῦ Γεθάιμ.

17ea οἱ δὲ ἐλθόντες πρὸς αὐτὸν φίλοι· Ἐλιφὰζ τῶν Ἡσαῦ
υἱῶν Θαιμανῶν βασιλεύς, Βαλδὰδ ὁ Σαυχαίων
τύραννος, Σωφὰρ ὁ Μιναίων βασιλεύς.

("And it is written that he will rise with those whom the Lord raises. This [man] is interpreted from an Aramaic book as living in the land of Uz, on the boarders of Edom and Arabia, and he previously bore the name Jobab. After taking for himself an Arabian wife, he bore a son whose name was Ennon. But he himself was the son of his father Zare, from among the sons of Esau, and of his mother Bosorra, so that he was the fifth from Abraham. These are the kings who reigned in Edom, the land over which he also ruled: first was Balak, son of Boer, and the name of his city was Dennaba; and after Balak was Jobab, who was called Job; and after him was Hasom, who governed from the country of Thaiman; and after him was Hadad, the son of Barad, who destroyed Midian in the country of Moab, and the name of his city was Gethaim. The friends who came to him were Eliphaz, one of the sons of Esau, the king of the Thaimanites, Baldad the tyrant of the Sauchites, Sophar the king of the Midianites.")

The entire Greek text of the Epilogue is both similar to and different from the MT. For purposes of analysis, I shall examine it under three themes: additions, subtractions, and explanations.

There are a number of additions in the text, some minor and others major. A minor addition, for example, is the use of "all" in the expression "all these words" in place of "these words" in the MT (42:7). More significantly elsewhere, in 42:11 Job's brothers and sisters "heard all that had happened to him," came and ate "and drank" and "wondered at all that had happened to him." These additions appear to be harmonistic.[102] Further signs of harmonization are evident in the text. The reference to Job as "this [man]" in 42:17b is rather surprising, but in conjunction with his name in v.16 and the mention of his land, Uz, the expression ("this man") harmonizes rather well with Job 1:1 where we equally have the name "Job," the land "Uz," and the demonstrative phrase "that man" used in the introduction of the story. Perhaps, Job is being reintroduced to the audience precisely for the purpose of linking him to the Jewish lineage that appears later in the addendum. Also, the reference to Job's friends as kings harmonizes with the characterization of the friends in the Prologue of LXX-Job (2:11) as kings. The rest of the

---

[102] The addition of "all" in 42:7 may be an attempt to harmonize with 42:11 where we have "*all* that had happened," "*all* who had known him before," and "*all* that the Lord had brought upon him." On the other hand, Dhorme has suggested the dependence of 42:11 on 2:11. Homer Heater goes further to suggest that the harmonization is not just between 42:11 and 2:11, but also with 2:10 and 1:22. Thus, the demonstrative ההיא in 2:11a is not translated in the Greek because it is absent in 42:11e; also, πρὸς αὐτόν ("to him") is added in 2:11b to agree with 42:11b. Then "all that had happened to him" in 42:11b is borrowed from 2:10d, where it is inserted from 1:22a. See Heater, *Translation Technique*, 130.

material dealing with Job's reign in Edom is partly culled from the Greek text of Gen 36:32–35 which very closely resembles the MT. As in the Greek version of the Epilogue, Job is identified as the son of Zare, but the translator mistakes geographical Bozrah for Job's mother. Even more compelling are the expressions, "these were the kings who reigned in Edom" and "Adad, the son of Barad, who destroyed Median in the plain of Moab; and the name of the city was Gethaim," which are exactly identical with what we have in the text of Gen 36.[103] According to Heater's anaphoric technique, the translator is combing material from the book of Job and from elsewhere to create his text.

The combination of material from elsewhere to constitute the Epilogue raises the question of the significance of the "Syriac book" to which the addendum refers, especially given that the material in the addendum does not appear in the Peshitta, the Qumran text, or the Rabbinic Targums.[104] Furthermore, as Reed and Heater have shown, the writer is more dependent on other Greek texts than on Aramaic sources. Accordingly, Reed cautions against placing too much significance on this "Syriac" source, arguing that the demonstrative οὗτος probably refers to Job as an individual rather than to the entire text that follows the demonstrative. The idea then is that it is Job who is interpreted from an Aramaic text as living in the land of Uz, not that the entire text of LXX Job is translated from an Aramaic source.[105] It is difficult to conclusively determine what the Aramaic "source" and its exact function were.

I shall now turn to the omissions in the text. The major omission here is the idea that the trouble that came upon Job was brought by God. As I have argued above, this omission is likely part of the theological view of the translator who does not see God as the source of evil or trouble. That is, in 2:11 where the source of the "evil" that came upon Job is not specified and may implicitly be attributed to the Adversary, LXX-Job does mention the word "evil." Here in the Epilogue where the narrator of the Hebrew text states that the "evil" came from God, LXX-Job drops it.

Together with the additions and subtractions in the text, the major interpretive moves of the translator are evident in his apparent desire to clarify the text and render it as unambiguous as possible. This is evident in his rendering of the MT "after this" with "after the affliction" in 42:16. The more significant clarifications occur, however, in the areas dealing with Job's approval (42:7–9) and his place within the community of God's people (LXX, 42:16b–17), and I shall now turn to such clarifications.

In the section dealing with Job's approval, the three idiomatic expressions about (a) God's anger against the friends, (b) God's resulting threat, and (c)

---

103 See, Gray, *Additions*, 432.
104 Gentry, *Asterisked Material*, 536 n.2 notes, however, that in Targum Pseudo-Jonathan we do find in Gen 36:12 that Eliphaz is Job's friend.
105 Reed, "Job as Jobab," 36–37. Reed concludes: "Although the appendix may have referred to an Aramaic source for some of its information about Job, we must reject the tempting suggestion that the LXX Job appendix simply represents a Greek translation from an equivalent Aramaic *Vorlage*."

God's response to Job's prayers are rephrased. Thus, instead of "my anger is kindled against you and your two friends" we have "you and your two friends have sinned." Also, instead of "not to do an outrageous thing to you" we have "not to destroy you." Finally, instead of "God lifted Job's face" we have "God forgave their sin for the sake of Job." On the first idiom, it is worth noting that since the translator repeatedly uses this anthropomorphism elsewhere, it is likely that the change here is not an attempt to avoid the anthropomorphisms.[106] Rather, this is probably an instance where the translator decides to spell out clearly what the divine anger expressed in the MT practically means – a move that logically prepares the reader for the need to make an offering in the next verse (see 1:5 where Job offers sacrifices because of the possible sin of his children).[107] The logic of the literary context, where a sacrifice is needed on behalf of the friends, probably led the translator to understand and render the idiom about the divine anger against the friends as an accusation over their sin.

The logically coherent Deuteronomistic pattern of sin, threat/punishment, and redemption is then carried through to the other two idiomatic expressions – hence, the author's rendering of the next idiom ("to do an outrage") with the idea of God threatening to destroy the friends. Because Job is the one interceding, he apparently does not need the divine favors which the expression "and God lifted the face of Job" in the MT suggests.[108] Therefore, in place of this expression which the Greek renders faithfully elsewhere in the book, and in order to complete his logical pattern, the author states that God forgave the sins of the friends for the sake of Job. What is implicit, subtle, and nuanced in the MT has been rendered in clear and unambiguous terms. Without necessarily contradicting the sense of the MT, the Greek translator has succeeded in suppressing the ambiguity of the idiomatic expressions here. Job's righteousness has been demonstrated not only by his ability to speak rightly in the presence of God even though under pain and pressure, but also by his ability to effectively intercede on behalf of his friends and save them from divine destruction. The impression one gets is that Job is a righteous individual who has distinguished himself from his friends, and only through his intervention can they be spared.

Even though this image of Job emerges from the text, the picture is slightly but significantly different when the relationship between Job, his friends, and God is cast within the broader context of the theophany. This is suggested by two details in the text. These are (a) the Greek translator's treatment of the prepositional phrase, אלי (to/about me) and (b) his treatment

---

106 The anger (אף) of God is repeatedly rendered ὀργῇ in 9:5, 13; 14:13 and 20:23. In fact, the fury of God's anger (חרון אף) that comes as judgment upon the wicked is faithfully rendered θυμὸν ὀργῆς in 20:23.

107 Orlinsky, "Studies in the Septuagint," (1958): 258, writes: "Our translator sometimes rendered a Hebrew word or expression by a Greek word or expression having slightly or even an entirely different meaning, because contextually, philosophically or logically a literal reproduction was felt by him to be impossible or absurd."

108 The idiom, "to lift the face," is accurately rendered by the Greek in 13:10; 22:8; and 34:19.

of the comparative preposition כ in the expression כעבדי ("like my servant"). In 42:7 אלי is rendered "before me," which simply places Job and the friends in the presence (presumably the theophany) of God. The friends have not spoken the truth in God's presence "like my servant Job" (ὥσπερ ὁ θεράπων μου Ἰώβ). But in 42:8, the divine threat to destroy the friends is predicated on their not having spoken the truth κατὰ τοῦ θεράποντός μου Ἰώβ ("against/according to my servant Job"). Given the use of ὥσπερ ὁ θεράπων μου Ἰώβ in 42:7, one may infer that the *lectio difficilior* here is "against my servant Job," which would suggest that Job also faltered.[109]

With the prepositional phrase "to/concerning me" now dropped, the issue is plainly between Job and his friends, although still in the presence of God. Two possible interpretations emerge here. First, the truth that the friends are supposed to have spoken in God's presence "like Job" (42:7) is the same truth that they failed to speak "against Job" (42:8). This would underscore the tension between approval and rebuke, especially given the fact that the Epilogue is closely connected to the theophany where Job has been rebuked. Accordingly, the friends' sin does not so much carry the sense of a moral flaw in their theological articulation as it connotes their falling short of the divine expectation; it is a sin of deficiency.[110] On the other hand, since Job has been rebuked in the theophany, the *lectio difficilior* in 42:8 is to read "according to my servant." In this second sense, the friends' sin has a moral implication since they are contrasted with Job. Overall, one senses the tension between divine rebuke and approval.

I shall now examine the section dealing with Job's expected resurrection and place within the lineage of Israel's patriarch Abraham (42:16–17). Only part of the narrative dealing with Job's lifespan is preserved in the OG; the mention of Job seeing his children to the fourth generation and then dying full of age is omitted. This is, however, restored by Origen. The reason for the suppression of the information about Job's death and his children in the OG is difficult to determine with certainty.[111]

The narrator states that Job will be raised "as it is written." The question becomes what text or texts serve(s) as the source of this claim? And associated with this, what possible theological function does this addition have?

---

109 If that is the case, then this interpretation will resonate with Job 42:6 where LXX refers to Job as saying, "I have counted myself vile."
110 The meaning of ἥμαρτες does indeed include the idea of falling short of the mark. See Henry George Liddell, *An Intermediate Greek-English Lexicon Founded Upon the seventh edition of Liddell and Scott's Greek-English Lexicon* (Oxford: Clarendon, 2000), 41.
111 Gard, "Concept of Job's Character," 185–86, notes that the Greek translator grants Job everlasting life through a resurrection, but equally notes that "the hermeneutical method followed in G is a broad and general one which is not bound by fixed rules or by a rigid system." Perhaps what one has here is a hesitation to associate righteous persons with death, as is also the case in the *Testament of Abraham*. Alternatively in the present context, the narrator may be more interested in linking Job's lineage backwards to the patriarchs than forwards to his descendants.

There are a number of instances where LXX agrees with the MT in asserting the finality of death. For example, in 7:9b the Hebrew text states that humans descend to Sheol and do not come back up, and the Greek renders it faithfully: "if a person descends to Hades, he will ascend no more." According to some of the rabbis, this clearly indicated that Job had denied the concept of the resurrection (cf. Baba Bathra 16a). Even more significant is the rendering of 14:12 where ἀνιστήμι δε is used. Following the Hebrew, the Greek has ἄνθρωπος δὲ κοιμηθεὶς οὐ μήν ἀναστῇ ("a person lies down and does not rise.") Accordingly, it is held that there is no concept of a future life in Job.[112] In this light, the narrator of the appendix in 42:17 may be responding to this denial of the resurrection in the book.

However, this still leaves unanswered the reason for the expression, "as it is written." Accordingly, some scholars argue that there is indeed a concept of a future life and in fact of a resurrection in the Greek translation. Concerning the idea of a general future life, one finds that in 14:14 where the Hebrew reads, "if a person dies, will he live?" the Greek omits the interrogative, thereby changing the question into an affirmation: "if a person dies he will live." Thus, where the Hebrew raises the question of a future life, the Greek affirms it.[113] As for the idea of resurrection, the use of ἀνιστήμι in 19:26 may be suggestive.[114] In his study of this text, P. Tremblay argues, on a syntactical basis, that the unusual fact that the Greek uses ἀνιστήμι followed by a direct object (τό δέρμα μου) may very well be intended to express the idea of a resurrection.[115] Thus, if the Greek translator understood these texts to be referring to the resurrection, then that would explain the expression, "as it is written" in 42:17. But even with this, there is nothing in 19:25–26 or 14:14 that describes Job's resurrection as forming a part of a broader general resurrection.[116] Thus, on the whole, the Greek translation sometimes portrays Job as affirming a future life and at other times as denying it. This is particularly evident in 14:12–14 where Job expresses the finality of death but then goes on (in the Greek version) to maintain that there is indeed a future life.

This discrepancy may very well be part of the reason why the appendix is added, namely, the struggle over whether and to what extent Job expected to

---

112 Marcos, "Septuagint Reading," 264; Orlinsky, "Studies," (1961): 242, writes: "Any other concept of afterlife would have made the writing of the book superfluous, for then the solution of the central problem in the Book, viz., why does the principle of *quid pro quo* fail so often to operate, would have been: in the world to come the righteous will receive their just reward and the wicked will suffer their deserved desert .... That is why, naturally, the Book ends with Job receiving his twofold reward in this world."
113 See, Gard, "Concept of a Future Life," 139; Gehman, "Theological Concept," 238.
114 Dhorme, *The Book of Job*, 284, notes that this particular verse is translated in various ways in the versions. The verb ἀνιστήμι is used to translate the Hebrew קום in several instances in Job (e. g., 1:20; 7:4; 14:12; 16:8; 19:18, 25/6; 24:22; 27:7). In many of these instances, with the exception of 14:12 and 19:25/6, the context or antecedent and contrasting idea does not have to do with death. Therefore, even in the LXX, the idea of a probable resurrection is significantly limited to a few texts.
115 P. Hervé Tremblay, *Job 19, 25–27 Dans la Septante et Chez les Pères Grecs: Unanimité d'une Tradition* (ÉBNS 47; Paris: Gabalda, 2002), 197.
116 Gray, "Additions," 431.

be raised and, even if he did, whether he should be considered part of God's community of faithful worshippers, in this case the Jewish community. The Hellenistic context where the final editing of the Greek text of Job in general and the Epilogue in particular took place[117] provides the appropriate theological background for a developed concept of a general resurrection that the narrator here assumes.[118] It also provides a historical background for the contact between the Jewish and the foreign culture, resulting in the "love-hate" relationship between Israel and Esau/Edom.[119]

Given the compositional history that underlies the Greek text, there are two possibilities to understanding the function of the resurrection here. First, it might at some point been intended to counteract the idea of the finality of death sometimes expressed in the book. Second, since the concept is not denied throughout the Greek text, the narrator says that the concept "is written." The narrator's audience appears to take it for granted that there will be a general resurrection, and the pressing question for the audience (and therefore for the narrator) appears to be whether Job will be part of it. The emphasis, then, is not just on the fact that Job will rise[120] but also that he will rise *with* those whom the Lord raises. With the legendary character of Job emerging in works such as the *Testament of Job*, it may have become easy to focus on those areas in the Greek text where his faith and life resonated with the audience's beliefs. But because Job was not immediately and clearly portrayed as an Israelite in the text, it was necessary to show how he was related to Israel and Israel's beliefs. To accomplish this, the narrator forged a theological argument about Job's resurrection in which he probably not only focused on texts that express the concept of a future life, but also associated Job with those whom God will raise. This theological rationale is later justified by the name change from Jobab to Job, signaling conversion. In addition to the theological argument, the narrator also forged a genealogical link between Job and the patriarch *par excellence*, Abraham.[121]

---

117 Literary evidence of the Hellenistic context includes the use of Amalthea's Horn as the name of Job's third daughter (42:14); Bosorra is interpreted as Job's mother rather than as the pre-exilic capital of Edom and Jobab's geographical origin (Gen 36:33); the name Uz is rendered Ausitis. Elsewhere in the book, there is the use of Hades in 33:22 and mention of sacrifices to Graecism (4:2; 31:31; 38:12). See Fernández Marcos, "Septuagint Reading," 257–258; Dhorme, *The Book of Job*, cxcvi.
118 See, Henry B. Swete, *An Introduction to the Old Testament in Greek* (Cambridge: Cambridge University Press, 1914), 256, 337. Swete ascribes the concept of the resurrection to the Pharisees and the Church. Tremblay, *Job 19, 25–27 dans la Septante*, 214–215, ties the concept to the Maccabean period and sees the resurrection as the ultimate divine reversal of injustice in the world.
119 See, Reed, "Job as Jobab," 48; Judith R. Baskin, *Pharaoh's Counsellors: Job, Jethro, and Balaam in Rabbinic and Patristic Tradition* (ed. Jacob Neusner et al.; BJS 47; Chico, Calif.: Scholars, 1983), 9.
120 As we shall see later, the *Testament of Job* has it that Job will rise.
121 See Reed, "Job as Jobab," 50–53.

2.2.3 Summary

In my study of the 11QtgJob and LXX-Job, I have identified two broad trajectories. First of all, the translators operated within an exegetical tradition. That is, prior to and following the canonization of the Hebrew text, a number of literary and theological features were increasingly emphasized to the extent that they easily became part of the collective psyche of the community. Secondly and related to this, however, the different contextual and historical moments in which the translators were immersed led to a certain amount of exegetical freedom or innovation. That is, the ability of the translators, while in the process of translation and transmission of the account, to build on the exegetical tradition within which they worked while also including, for diverse reasons some of which are lost to the modern reader, particular emphases on particular issues, expansions, omissions, and additions. It is a combination of the authors/editors interactions with specific exegetical traditions and their respective interpretive and historical contexts that shape the character of Job throughout history.

In the process, Job emerges as an individual who is restored partly because he is righteous and, in the Qumran text, partly because of divine mercy. It was this character that was easily appropriated especially within religious contexts. Yet, underlying this character, there is the tension between the divine rebuke and approval of Job,[122] thereby underscoring the impossibility of describing the experience of loss and restoration exclusively in simple linear retributive terms. In LXX-Job appendix, the focus appears to be on creating a theological and genealogical association between Job and Israel through association with Abraham. In order to accomplish this purpose, the narrator reintroduces Job to the Hellenistic audience and associates Job with Israel through the resurrection. Although there is no unambiguous literary evidence in the book of Job itself for the narrator's claim that Job will be raised "as it is written," the Hellenistic context with its assumed general resurrection allows the narrator to make such associations. The pressing issue for the audience and therefore for the narrator appears not to be whether Job will rise, but whether he will be raised *with* those whom God raises. Through a genealogical connection with Abraham and a religious conversion signaled by the name change, Job is guaranteed a place with those whom God raises.

---

122 Jürgen Ebach, »Hiob/Hiobbuch,« *Theologische Realenzyklopädie* 15 (1986): 370, describes Job as both »Recht« and »unRecht«; "Righteous" because he endured the contradictions of the world, and "Unrighteous" because he questioned God from his limited strength and limited insight.

2.3 Early Jewish and Christian Interpretation

2.3.1 Rabbinic Interpretation

In her work on rabbinic interpretation of Job, Judith Baskin underscores the diversity of opinions and interpretive moves that characterized the work of the rabbis. Two reasons are given for this diversity. One reason is theological, and deals with the merit of Gentiles in general and Job in particular. This gestures back to the tension about the nature of the relationship between Job as an outsider and the community of God's people in the LXX appendix. The other reason is literary, and deals with the composite nature of the book itself and the complexity of its ideas. Baskin concludes that the issue of Job's origin was paramount among the rabbis and played a significant role in the process of interpretation.[123] Drawing upon Baskin's remarks, I will examine the Epilogue as a text (in relation to the rest of the book) and as a paradigm for Israel and the church.

2.3.1.1 The Epilogue as a Text

Concerning the traditional Joban image in rabbinic circles, Robert Gordis argues that the ready acceptance of the Book of Job into the canon of Scripture is to be explained by the fact that only the Job of the prose tale likely impinged on the consciousness of the ancient readers. Furthermore, Gordis continues, "traditional views could be read into the text homiletically, thus softening the impact of heterodox ideas."[124] Three aspects of the Epilogue played a significant role in the interpretive process that resulted in the dominant image of a pious character: (a) the divine approval of Job in 42:7 and the rebuke of the friends; (b) Job's intercession for his friends; and (c) the restoration of Job's possession and status. Concerning the divine rebuke of the friends and approval of Job, there is at least one instance where some of the rabbis tried to understand the reason for the approval, given the nature of Job's words in the Dialogues. In Baba Bathra 16a, we are told that "a person may not be held responsible for what he does in his anguish," and Job's anguish is known to have been very great. Hermeneutically, this softens the sting in Job's words without really denying their rebellious character. Accordingly, the audience is led to focus not so much on what Job said in the

---

123 Baskin, *Pharaoh's Counselors*, 9–10; J. Weinberg, "Job Versus Abraham: The Quest for the Perfect God-Fearer in Rabbinic Tradition," in *The Book of Job* (ed. W. A. M. Beuken; BETL 114; Leuven: Leuven University Press, 1994), 281.
124 Robert Gordis, *The Book of God and Man: A Study of Job* (Chicago: University of Chicago Press, 1965), 222.

Dialogues but on the fact that he made such utterances because he suffered overwhelmingly.[125]

Job's virtue in the midst of suffering is, however, much more readily evident when we turn to his intercession for his friends. About Job's intercession, Spiegel writes: "A particularly poignant example of self-abnegation probably served as the climax of the story, when Job, mindless of his own misery, invoked mercy upon someone else."[126] In Baba Kama 9:29, this intercession carried a significant component of the moral force of the entire story, portraying Job as a selfless individual who suffered in God's service, and through his intercession set an example of forgiveness.[127] As we shall later see, this virtuous character of Job's is developed to a high degree in the *Testament of Job* where Job not only intercedes for his friends but also leads them in acts of charity on behalf of the poor and needy.

Finally concerning the restoration, Spiegel describes it as an idea that reaches back "to the world of myth and tale," where "a loss can be retrieved, life recalled from the beyond, and the joys of a former day restored by the grace and goodness of a god who can make bygones come back."[128] This understanding of the divine ability to reverse situations of loss influenced the idea of rewards and restoration. A conversation between Rabbis Gamaliel, Joshua, Eleazar b. Azariah, and Akiba recounts that once when they approached Rome and heard the boisterous noise of the city traffic, all the rabbis with the exception of Akiba started to cry; Akiba laughed instead. When he was asked why he laughed when the temple of God was destroyed and Gentiles lived secure and prosperous, he answered: "That is precisely why I was laughing. If this is how he has rewarded those who anger him, all the more so [will he reward] those who do his will." This explanation about God's expected restoration of God's people turns out to be a source of comfort to the other rabbis.[129]

These three components of the Epilogue (the divine approval, the intercession, and restoration) fit into the larger theological view of rabbinic thought. As Ephraim Urbach has shown, a major part of rabbinic thinking about God revolved around the divine attributes of justice and mercy (Exod 24:5-6; Ps 103:7–13). This translated into the idea that God's merciful actions indicate that, "retribution should not be according to the full measure

---

125 This "justification" for the divine approval was not exactly popular in rabbinic literature. Apparently, rabbi Johanan used it only once. However, in the 15th century CE, Jews who were being expelled from Spain used it to justify certain actions undertaken by their persecuted friends. See, Delmaire, "Les Principaux Courants," 73.
126 Spiegel, "Noah, Danel, and Job," 328.
127 Jacob Neusner, *The Tosefta Translated from the Hebrew with a New Introduction* (Peabody, Mass.: Hendrickson, 2002), 1007.
128 Spiegel, "Noah, Danel and Job," 329.
129 Jacob Neusner, *The Presence of the Past, The Pastness of the Present: History, Time, and Paradigm in Rabbinic Judaism* (Bethseda, Md.: CDL, 1996), 117–118.

of the sin."[130] In fact, the merciful character of God was pervasive in rabbinic thinking and was even personified. Rabbi Akiba, for example, is known to have said, "All that the All-Merciful does is for good." This meant that suffering could be seen as something "precious," resulting not as a consequence of retributive justice, but as a token of God's love.[131] This teaching of Rabbi Akiba's was interpreted in two ways: (a) that God's mercy is superior to divine justice and is granted to those who are righteous in their time of trouble (so Rabbi Eliezer); and (b) that God's mercy comes in response to human mercy, and it is within humankind's power to change the attributes of justice to compassion and vice versa (so Rabbi Gamaliel).[132]

Applied to the Epilogue, the superiority of the divine mercy may explain the softening of Job's utterances in Baba Bathra 16a; better still, it may explain the divine approval as a gift of God's love. It also explains God's decision to forgive the friends who, according to some Jewish legends, were also rewarded for consoling Job.[133]

2.3.1.2 The Epilogue as a Paradigm

The perception of Job as a righteous individual was, however, not unanimous in rabbinic thought. This is particularly clear when Job was compared with Abraham. For example, in Genesis Rabbah 49:9, Rabbi Levi is quoted as saying that whereas Abraham wondered whether God would destroy the righteous and the wicked together (Gen 18:25), Job on the other hand simply stated it as a fact that God does destroy both (Job 9:22). Furthermore, Rabban Joḥanan b. Zakkai argued that Job served God out of fear that stemmed from dread of punishment and the possibility of losing one's reward rather than fear inspired by love as was the case with Abraham (Gen 22:2). Although Rabbi Me'ir challenged this view in his homilies, it persisted among some rabbis and, perhaps, contributed to Rabbi Gamaliel's instruction that the book of Job be withdrawn from circulation.[134]

Rabbinic thought developed an interpretive paradigm that covered Abraham, Israel, and the world to come. In this paradigm, Abraham was the model; Israel had to conform to that model; and the world to come was the mark of the fruition of that model.[135] This interpretive paradigm that portrays

---

130 Ephraim E. Urbach, *The Sages: Their Concepts and Beliefs* (trans. Israel Abrahams; Jerusalem: Magnes, 1987), 448.
131 Urbach, *The Sages*, 454. As we have already seen, the concept of divine mercy is expressed in 11QtgJob and plays a significant role in the restoration of Job and his friends.
132 For further analysis of the rabbinic understanding of the divine nature, especially concerning justice and mercy, see Urbach, *The Sages*, 448–461.
133 See, Louis Ginzberg, *The Legends of the Jews*, vol. 2, *From Joseph to the Exodus* (trans. Henrietta Szold; London: John Hopkins, 1948), 242.
134 Urbach, *The Sages*, 406–411. See also Syring, *Hiob und sein Anwalt*, 25–50, for a discussion on the critical evaluation of Job especially within rabbinic circles.
135 Neusner, *The Presence of the Past*, 116.

Abraham in a highly favorable light partly explains the distinction between Job's fear of God and Abraham's. The idea that Job feared God, however, was also used to locate Job within the context of Israel's emergence as a nation. Rabbi Ishmael identified Job with the God fearer mentioned among Pharaoh's counselors (Exod 9:20). According to this rabbinic interpretation, the argument goes that during the Exodus, Balaam convinced Pharaoh to execute the Jewish first-born males; Job sat silent and did not oppose the decision, while Jethro escaped and later on was converted to Judaism. Along this line of reasoning, Job's suffering was seen as just dessert for his failure to prevent Pharaoh's onslaught against Israel.[136]

In the presentation of Jewish understanding of biblical chronology, under its treatment of covenant and slavery, Job's lifespan was seen as a sign for Israel's national experience. For example, one such understanding of biblical chronology reads:

> "It is said to our forefather Abraham at the covenant between the pieces (Gen 15:13): 'You shall certainly know that your seed will be strangers in a foreign land for 400 years.' Who is this seed? That is Isaac of whom it is said (Gen 21:12): 'because Isaac will be called seed for you.' About Isaac it says (Gen 25:26): 'Isaac was 60 years of age when they were born.' Our forefather Jacob said to Pharao (Gen 47:9): "the days of the years of my wandering are 130 years.' This makes together 190 years, this leaves 210 years, a sign for the lifetime of Job who was born at that time as it is said (Job 42:16): 'Job lived thereafter 140 years' and it is said (Job 42:10): 'The Eternal added double to all that Job had.' It turns out that Job was born when Israel descended into Egypt and he died when they left."[137]

According to this computation and rationale, the Epilogue corresponds to the time of Israel's deliverance from slavery. In the Jerusalem Talmud (Sota 5:8), the discussion on Israel's stay in Egypt equally places Job at the center, though with slight but significant variation. R. Yose bar Halaphta maintains that when Israel went down to Egypt, Job was born and when Israel left, Job died. But he goes on to add that a simile for this situation is a shepherd (God) who offers a he-goat (Job) to a lion (Satan) in order to divert the lion's attention from the sheep (Israel). Accordingly, Job's suffering is possibly portrayed in a positive manner as having been on behalf of Israel.[138]

Perhaps the most striking portrayal of Job's life as a national paradigm is in Pesiqta deRab Kahana 16:6 which deals with the issue of comfort and restoration for those in trouble. Job is explicitly compared with Jerusalem, the point being to show the close parallels between Job's experience and Israel's. These parallels include Job's fate in the hands of the Chaldeans (Job 1:17 // Jer 32:24), fire from heaven (Job 1:16 // Lam 1:13), the use of the potsherd (Job 2:8 // Lam 4:2), silence in the face of destruction (Job 2:13 // Lam 2:10),

---

136 See, Baskin, *Pharaoh's Counselors*, 15.
137 *Seder Olam: The Rabbinic View of Biblical Chronology* (trans. and commentary by Heinrich W. Guggenheimer; Northvale, N. J.: Jason Aronson, 1998), 37.
138 See, Weinberg, "Job Versus Abraham," 286.

the act of putting on of sackcloth (Job 16:15 // Lam 2:10), the need for pity (Job 19:21 // Jer 16:13), and the experience of trouble from God's hand (Job 19:21 // Is 40:2). Concluding from these parallels, R. Joshua bar Nehemiah said: "Now if in the case of Job, who was smitten twofold, he [God] gave his compensation twofold, so Jerusalem will be comforted twofold: Comfort, comfort my people, says your God." (Is 40: 1–2).[139]

In summary, the divine approval of Job in the Epilogue continued to pose interpretive problems for rabbinic scribes in light of the poetic section. In attempt to resolve the tension, some of the scribes focused on the divine attribute of Mercy, which transcends retributive justice. Accordingly, and as we saw in the case of 11QtgJob, the restoration of Job in Epilogue becomes more of an act of divine favor. Within the context of the Epilogue as a paradigm for Israel as a nation, Job's suffering is interpreted either as just dessert for failing to oppose Pharaoh's onslaught against Israel or as "sacrificial" suffering in order to enhance Israel's liberation.

2.3.1.3 The Testament of Job

The *Testament of Job*[140] is perhaps the most elaborate attempt to portray Job as a righteous person who endured his troubles and eventually triumphed.[141] On a literary level, it takes the form of a farewell address from Job to his new children prior to his death. Also, Job's verbose protests in the MT are missing; instead, it is one of the friends, Eliphaz, who engages in laments on Job's behalf.[142] Theologically, Job suffers not just because God wants to find out his religious motives but also primarily because Job accepts a divine mission to destroy a pagan temple.[143] In spite of these differences, the

---

139 See, Jacob Neusner, *A Theological Commentary to the Midrash* (ed. Jacob Neusner, SAJ 1: Pesiqta deRab kahana (New York: University Press of America, 2001), 168–169.
140 Robert A. Kraft et al., eds., *The Testament of Job According to the SV Text: Greek Text and English Translation* (Missoula, Mont.: Scholars, 1974).
141 The *Testament of Job* is an embellished account of the biblical story of Job along the lines of such works as the *Testament of Abraham*. Probably written between 100BCE-200CE, it celebrates the virtue if patience or endurance, and deals with a wide variety of other issues such as opposition to idolatry, Jewish burial rites, inter-racial marriages, Jewish mysticism, care for the poor, and female prophetic utterances. There is no consensus among scholars as to its authorship. See Russell P. Spittler, "The Testament of Job," *ABD* 3: 869–871.
142 For an examination of the differences between the *Testament of Job* and the MT, see D. Rahnenführer, »Das Testament des Hiob und das Neue Testament,« *ZNW* 62 (1971): 68–93; John J. Collins, "Structure and Meaning in the Testament of Job," *SBL Seminar Papers*, 1974 (2 vols.; SBLSP 7; ed. George MacRae; Cambridge, Mass.: Society of Biblical Literature, 1974), 35–52.
143 See, Baskin, *Pharaoh's Counselors*, 31. Irving Jacobs, "Literary Motifs in the Testament of Job," *JJS* 21 (1970): 1–10 discerns a number of religious themes within the Testament, including conversion, a new name symbolizing the conversion, and suffering for one's new faith.

Testament does resonate to some degree with LXX-Job, particularly with the partly "recreated" Job of the LXX-Job appendix.[144]

The material constituting the Epilogue is significantly expanded, although many details in the MT are left out. The friends are rebuked for not speaking truthfully κατὰ τοῦ θεράποντός μου' Ἰώβ ("against/according to my servant Job.") Although God rebukes the friends from the whirlwind, the prepositional phrase "to/concerning me" in the MT is dropped. After Job intercedes on their behalf and they are forgiven, Eliphaz sings a song of praise to God in gratitude (T.Job 43:1–13). The human assembly that gathers to console Job, we are told, holds festivities to God's delight, and on Job's demand the friends give him "one lamb for clothing the poor and naked." Thus Job's work of charity, apparently interrupted by his suffering, is now resumed; he has demonstrated his faith not only by praying for his friends, but also practically by working for the poor and the naked. He then exhorts his children to do likewise (T.Job 45:1–5).

The section dealing with the inheritance of Job's daughters and his eventual death is transformed into a spiritual experience. God's challenge to Job to gird up his loins (MT, 40:7) is interpreted as part of the healing process for Job. In the Testament, the bands that God asked Job to wear for his healing now constitute the inheritance of his daughters. Although they originally protest, Job explains the spiritual value of the bands to them.[145] Once they put the bands on, they are given angelic voices with which they sing. As a result, they pay little attention to the things of this world, portraying thereby a significant aspect of the book.[146] At his death, Job's soul is taken to heaven by angels in a chariot, while his body is buried and he is mourned in the city.

Although far removed from the MT, the *Testament of Job* turned out to represent part of the tradition about Job that came to be dominant among later interpreters. One notes, for instance, the character of Job that is referenced in

---

144 The similarities include the genealogical note (T.Job 1:3–5), the name change (T.Job 2:1), Job's expected resurrection (T.Job 4:9), Job as king (T.Job 28:8; 31:3), and Job's friends as kings (T.Job 29:3; 30:1). For a detailed description of the parallels between the *Testament of Job* and LXX-Job, see Berndt Schaller, »Das Testament Hiobs und die Septuaginta-Übersetzung des Buches Hiob,« *Bib* 61 (1980): 377–406. For a more thematic study and character analysis of the similarities and differences between the *Testament of Job* and LXX-Job, see C. T. Begg, "Comparing Characters: The Book of Job and the Testament of Job," in *The Book of Job* (ed. W. A. M. Beuken; BETL 114; Leuven: Leuven University Press, 1994), 435–445. For a general treatment of the Testament, see R. P. Spittler, "Testament of Job: A New Translation and Introduction," *OTP* 1: 829–868.
145 See, Peter Machinist, "Job's Daughters and the Inheritance in the Testament of Job and its Biblical Congeners," in *The Echoes of Many Texts: Reflections on Jewish and Christian Traditions: Essays in Honor of Lou H. Silberman* (ed. William G. Dever and J. Edward Wright; Atlanta: Scholars, 1997), 67–80.
146 See, Pieter W. van der Horst, "The Role of Women in the Testament of Job," *NedTT* 40 (1986): 273–289; Collins, "Structure and Meaning," 42, writes: "The real issue between Job and his friends is awareness of heavenly reality. Job has insights into heavenly things while the friends have not." See T.Job 33:5–9; 38:2–4; 40:5–6.

Jas 5:11: "Indeed we call blessed those who showed endurance. You have heard of the endurance of Job, and you have seen the purpose of the Lord, how the Lord is compassionate and merciful." Two words are important for the discussion on endurance. These are μακροθυμία and ὑπομονή. The first essentially describes divine virtue associated with God's steadfast love (see LXX, Exod 34:6), while the second is largely a human virtue associated with hope and expectation (see LXX, Ps 25:3; 37:9). However, there are instances of overlap where ὑπομονή is perceived as a gift of God to humans (Rom 15:5, 13; Heb 13:20) and μακροθυμία is a human virtue of self-restraint (2 Sam 16:5–13). The author of the letter of James refers to Job's ὑπομονή, probably referring to its meaning as a basic attitude of the righteous who endure suffering and wait for God's deliverance.[147]

LXX uses ὑπομονή to translate a number of Hebrew words in Job, including קוה – "to wait" (3:9; 17:13), יחל – "to wait," "to await" (6:11; 14:14; 32:16 – restored by Origen), and שלם – "to be at peace" (9:4; 22:21). The idea of expectation or hope is, therefore, present in the use of ὑπομονή. However, there is a difference between the use of the verb in LXX-Job and its use elsewhere. Unlike in the Psalms and even in the letter of James, for example, where the individual or community waits for God's deliverance, we find that in LXX-Job such deliverance is absent and in some instances actually resisted. Thus, in 3:9 Job wishes that the hope for the light of deliverance should not materialize; equally in 17:13, Job's hope is for the world of the dead. In 7:3, LXX misreads the MT נחל for יחל and thus translates: "I have endured months of vanity." This misreading may underscore an aspect of the way in which ὑπομονή is used in Job: it does have the idea of endurance, but lacks any explicit positive end result that is associated with its use elsewhere.[148]

The LXX uses the word ὑπομονή more than the *Testament of Job*. And in all its occurrences in LXX-Job, ὑπομονή is used only within the poetic section of the book,[149] where Job is most impatient. If one assumes that the author of the *Testament of Job* knew the work of the LXX translator and used

---

147 In Jas 5:7–11, μακροθυμία is used together with ὑπομονή, both exhorting the community of believers to endure and persevere in expectation of the *parousia*, the coming of God as just Judge. For further study of the theological significance of these terms, see J. Horst, "μακροθυμία," *TDNT* 4: 374–387; Kossi A. Ayedze, "Tertullian, Cyprian and Augustine on Patience: A Comparative and Critical Study of Three Treatises on a Stoic-Christian Virtue in Early North African Christianity" (Ph.D. diss., Princeton Theological Seminary, 2000), 63–100.
148 In 22:21, we come closest to the idea of associating ὑπομονή with some expected reward. The text is, however, part of the traditional conception that Job is now challenging. Elsewhere in 8:15, ὑπομονή is used to describe the enduring capacity of a house, translating the MT קום that V renders *stabit*, and that O and Symm. render with the verb ἴστημι – "to raise up," "to remain fast," "to be fixed." Therefore, it seems that in LXX-Job, ὑπομονή expresses the idea of enduring some form of adversity without any explicit association of endurance with imminent reward.
149 The word occurs in LXX-Job 3:9; 6:11; 7:3; 8:15; 9:4; 14:14; 15:31; 17:13; 20:26; 22:21; 32:4, 16; 33:5; 41:3.

mostly the prose section of the work to compose his own,[150] or perhaps that both works belong to a common tradition, then the author of the Testament has adopted the concept of endurance from the poetic section of LXX-Job and re-used it in his own work. Whereas in LXX-Job the idea of divine intervention is either minimal or even resisted, the author of the *Testament of Job* appears to make his most significant move on that very point. As a result, one finds that not only is Job born with the virtue of patience and endurance (T.Job 1:5), but he also asks his wife whether humans should not endure troubles even as they receive the good from God (T.Job 26:5) before urging his children to exercise that virtue (T.Job 27:7). But even more important is the fact that Job's endurance is closely associated with God's plan, as God urges Job to endure the sufferings from Satan in view of divine intervention (T.Job 4:6).[151] When God sends Job to destroy the pagan shrine and spells out the possible risks, the promise of a restoration is associated with Job's endurance. That is, because of his endurance, Job is promised not only double material reward but also future resurrection. But the restoration is also intended to show that God is impartial in retributive justice (T.Job 4:5–9). Perhaps, the very essence of Job's outbursts in the MT, where he often blames God for the injustices of the world, is being corrected and balanced with an emphasis on God's justice.

2.3.2 Early Christian Interpretation

Christian interpretation of Job was influenced by a number of factors. First, the text that many Christians used (LXX-Job) was in no small way different from the MT. Secondly, the Hellenistic world where early Christianity flourished provided an intellectual climate that helped to shape the understanding of Job. Finally, the fact that Job was immediately understood to be a non-Israelite allowed Christians to focus on him as a model for Jewish and especially non-Jewish audiences.

By the time of James' epistle, there appears to be an existing tradition about Job's endurance, a tradition that the audience has "heard" and probably accepts without questioning (Jas 5:11).[152] Moreover, the story that the audience has heard is that of Job's endurance and its association with God's

---

150 See, Spittler, "Testament of Job," 836.
151 The *Testament of Job* is, however, more complex than is represented here. Job suffers not only from the assault of Satan but also (like in the MT) from God who tests Job (see T.Job chs. 19–26), and in the course of his suffering, Job is ready to die as a martyr. I am interested here in examining the way in which his endurance is related to the idea of reward and divine intervention. For detailed discussion on the various aspects of Job's perseverance in the *Testament of Job*, see Cees Haas, "Job's Perseverance in the Testament of Job," in *Studies on The Testament of Job* (ed. Michael A. Knibb and Pieter W. van der Horst; Cambridge: Cambridge University Press, 1989), 117–154.
152 See, Bruce Zuckerman, *Job the Silent: A Study in Historical Counterpoint* (New York: Oxford University Press, 1991), 13–15.

gracious character. This perception of Job as one who endures in the hope of a restoration is prominent in the *Testament of Job*. Perhaps through a gradual process beginning with LXX-Job and proceeding to the *Testament of Job*, the character has been transformed and, in fact, recreated. This disparity between the Hebrew text and subsequent translations caused some of the early Christian interpreters such as Origen and Jerome to attempt to go back to what they considered to be the *Hebraica Veritas*. Whether the truth lies in any particular text may be debatable, but the feeling among these scholars of the need to return to the "truth" in the Hebrew text is indicative of the sense in which there is a difference between the Hebrew text and later writings. Christian understandings of Job were partly derived from a tradition that was sometimes significantly though not completely different from the Hebrew text.[153] Hermeneutically, this is indicative of the vital interaction that must constantly occur between tradition and text.

The second factor (which was not peculiar to Christians) was the influence of the Hellenistic world. Of particular importance was the Platonic idea of transcendental intelligible reality that could be approached and encountered. In Alexandria, for example, the Hebrew text was read using ideas from Greek philosophy. This meant in part that the spiritual world and its importance were favored over the physical. Texts that were difficult to interpret because of their moral connotations were, as a result, interpreted using methods that yielded different dimensions of meaning (other than the plain, literal sense). Accordingly, allegory and typology were developed as significant modes of interpretation.[154] Even in Antioch, where there was significant emphasis on the literal/historical meaning, the use of allegory was not abandoned. As a result, one finds in the patristic exegetes the reference to Job as a type of the church and even of Christ.

The third factor that influenced Christian interpretation was related to Job as a non-Israelite who antedated Moses and the Jewish law. Accordingly, he attained a high level of spirituality not with the help of the law but from

---

153 On the New Testament's interpretation of the Old, see Hans Hübner, "New Testament Interpretation of the Old Testament," in *Hebrew Bible, Old Testament: The History of Its Interpretation. Part 1, Antiquity. Vol. 1, From the Beginning to the Middle Ages in Co-operation with Chris Brekelmans and Menahem Haran* (ed. Magne Sæbø; Göttingen: Vandenhoeck & Ruprecht, 1996), 332–372.
154 See, J. F. Procopé's instructive essay, "Greek Philosophy, Hermeneutics and Alexandrian Understanding of the Old Testament," in *Hebrew Bible, Old Testament: The History of Its Interpretation. Part 1, Antiquity. Vol. 1, From the Beginning to the Middle Ages in Co-operation with Chris Brekelmans and Menahem Haran* (ed. Magne Sæbø; Göttingen: Vandenhoeck & Ruprecht, 1996), 451–477, especially pages 459–460; J. N. B. Carleton Paget, "Christian Exegesis of the Old Testament in the Alexandrian Tradition," in *Hebrew Bible, Old Testament: The History of Its Interpretation. Part 1, Antiquity. Vol. 1, From the Beginning to the Middle Ages in Co-operation with Chris Brekelmans and Menahem Haran* (ed. Magne Sæbø; Göttingen: Vandenhoeck & Ruprecht, 1996), 478–542; James McEvoy, "The Patristic Hermeneutic of Spiritual Freedom and its Biblical Origins," in *Scriptural Interpretation in the Fathers: Letter and Spirit* (ed. Thomas Finan and Vincent Twomey; Cambridge: Cambridge University Press, 1995), 1–25.

natural (internal) religion that God provides to all humankind. Also, Job was a prophet of sorts, announcing not only the incarnation of Christ, but also his suffering and redemptive work for both Jews and Gentiles. Thus, Job was an easy *point d'entrée* for Christian interpreters who saw him as an outsider.

These three factors influenced early Christian interpretation to varying degrees. Partly through the re-creation of the text, Job's character as a moral exemplar was reinforced; through the Hellenistic worldview that privileged the spiritual world, Job's restoration took on explicit spiritual and eternal dimensions; and through his Gentile origin, he was easily accessible to non-Jews.

In this section, I shall focus on three early Christian interpreters, Ambrose, Chrysostom, and Gregory the Great. Although these scholars were only part of the larger group of ancient interpreters, they produced considerable works on Job. Furthermore, they are fairly well representative of the Alexandrian (Ambrose and Gregory) and Antiochene (Chrysostom) schools of exegesis that helped in shaping Christian thought.[155]

2.3.2.1 Saint Ambrose of Milan (337/339–397)

One of the important themes in Ambrose's treatment of Job in *De Interpellatione Job et David*[156] is that of consolation, which comes in response to the troubles that humans undergo. These troubles pose a theological problem relating to innocent suffering and the prosperity of the wicked. According to Ambrose, the problem of innocent suffering is a perilous issue on which "even holy men have scarcely been able to keep track of sound belief."[157] In the introduction, Ambrose states that just as there are "many disturbances" that humans undergo, so too there are "many consolations that are at hand." These consolations, however, "indeed outweigh the discomforts, because they impart calm in present difficulties and the hope of things to come (cf. Rom 8:18)."[158] David prayed for such consolations (cf. Ps 41); but before David, Job had done the same, the only difference being that while David prayed from "the viewpoint of the moral lesson," Job acted "with greater vehemence."[159] Because the remedy for such troubles is consolation, Ambrose understands the mission of Job's friends as

---

155 For helpful introductions to the work of these scholars, see Christopher A. Hall, *Reading Scripture with the Church Fathers* (Downers Grove, Ill.: Inter Varsity, 1998), 56–200; G. R. Evans, *Fifty Key Medieval Thinkers* (London: Routledge, 2002), 11–15, 31–35; John Moorhead, *Ambrose: Church and Society in the Late Roman World* (ed. David Bates, The Medieval World; London: Longman, 1999), 71–101.
156 This work is published in the collection on the Church Fathers, Saint Ambrose, *Seven Exegetical Works* (trans. Michael P. McHugh; Washington: Catholic University of America Press, 1972).
157 Ambrose, *Seven Exegetical Works*, 352.
158 Ambrose, *Seven Exegetical Works*, 329.
159 Ambrose, *Seven Exegetical Works*, 330.

essentially consisting of trying to bring consolation to Job, even though they failed.

Ambrose's understanding of consolation is largely derived from his interpretation of the poetic section of the book and is closely related to two things: present piety and future resurrection. On Job's piety, Ambrose states:

> "One kind of consolation for those who find themselves in wretchedness and sorrow is to be free from guilt, so that they may not appear to be bearing their suffering and adversities as a punishment for sin. But his friends tried to take even this from the holy man Job, so that he might appear as an instigator of his own wretchedness, as one who had contracted the Lord's displeasure by grievous offences."[160]

Ambrose suggests that consolation comes from piety or innocence from guilt. Yet, in his comments on Job's response to the charges of the friends, Ambrose refers to Job 9:2–11 which portray the fact that humans cannot be righteous before God and the awesome power of God manifested in the universe. Ambrose then concludes that when such sovereign divine power is manifested, it brings about "help, not destruction" for those who are just. As Job's friends made their arguments against him, Job

> "withstood and carried the burden of the words next to that of the wounds. The President of the contest saw him; from out of the cloud and the storm, He gave His hand to him as he struggled, declared that Job's opponents had suffered a grievous fall, proclaimed him the victor, and gave him the crown."[161]

Ambrose here interprets the Epilogue from the context of the theophany, and largely sees the friends in a negative light. Although humans are not without sin, God's awesome power comes to provide help. Through his great ordeal, Job was purged of his sin and was then able to enter into a state of blessedness.[162] On the one hand, Job is portrayed as a righteous individual in line with the prose tale and especially the divine approval at the end. But on the other hand, Job is linked with the sinfulness of humankind, and his suffering is interpreted in the context of redemption. Job's righteousness is transformed into a state of blessedness through his suffering and purification. One senses in this reading the underlying theme of salvation through the sufferings and death of Christ. The issue is no longer mainly framed around the topic of retributive justice (although that is where Ambrose begins) and how it affects one's reading of Job and his friends, but around a redemptive process and how it transforms suffering into a purification tool.

The consolation that comes at the end of this process is not just a temporal or this-worldly experience; it ultimately involves the resurrection. Ambrose finds textual evidence for this in LXX-Job 14:13–17 where Job asks God to

---

160 Ambrose, *Seven Exegetical Works*, 334.
161 Ambrose, *Seven Exegetical Works*, 357.
162 See, Judith Baskin, "Job as Moral Exemplar in Ambrose," *VC* 35 (1981): 226; Pierre Cazier, "Lectures du Livre de Job Chez Ambrose, Augustin et Grégoire le Grand," in *Le Livre de Job* (Lectures de l'Écriture, Graphè 6; Paris: Presses de l'Université Charles-de-Gaulle, 1997), 83–84.

hide him in Sheol until God's anger is passed. Commenting on this text, Ambrose states:

> "What a fine passage, for it strengthens us in regard to the resurrection!...Holy Job rightly preferred to rise to the judgment rather than to the time of God's wrath, which is terrible even to the innocent. At the same time, in saying "You will set a time for me, when you would remember me," Job is understood to be prophesying that he was going to be raised up in the passion of the Lord, as is shown clearly in the conclusion of that book."[163]

Ambrose has clearly interpreted the text in light of the future resurrection. Furthermore, he has linked his interpretation of the text to the Epilogue of the book in LXX-Job where the concept of resurrection is for him clearly affirmed. With this concept of the resurrection and the allegorical interpretation that placed more emphasis on the spiritual sense of the text, Ambrose interprets Job's laments as a desire to flee from this present life in order to experience the far greater joys of the resurrected life.

2.3.2.2 John Chrysostom (347–407)

In his work on John Chrysostom, Laurence Brottier argues that Chrysostom made a significant effort to actualize Job. This actualization, Brottier argues, was done in two ways: (a) Chrysostom presented Job as a moral exemplar who, although a "pagan," lived a godly life inspired by the "inner law," different from Jewish law; and (b) Job's experience of suffering provided spiritual consolation to the audience, since Job is presented as someone who not only endured severe troubles but also ultimately won a prize.[164]

On Job's piety, Chrysostom saw Job not just as a wrestler (a concept that was quite common among early Christian interpreters and the *Testament of Job*) but also as a "wrestler of self denial."[165] Furthermore, unlike Adam who easily succumbed to the devil's tricks, Job resisted, thereby demonstrating piety that is worth imitating. In riches and poverty, Job was a model; his riches did not make him arrogant and his poverty did not overwhelm him. The reason for this is that Job was not lavish, his riches mostly being agricultural. Even more, he used his riches for the service of others.[166] Thus for Chrysostom, the saintly and submissive Job of the prose tale was more appealing than the rebellious character of the poetic section. It is this

---

163 Ambrose, *Seven Exegetical Works*, 346.
164 Laurence Brottier, "L'Actualisation de la Figure de Job chez Jean Chrysostome," in *Le Livre de Job Chez les Pères* (Cahiers de Biblia Patristica 5; Strasbourg: Centre d'Analyse et de Documentation Patristique, 1996), 64–68.
165 Saint John Chrysostom, *Homilies on the Gospel of Saint Matthew* 33.10 (NPNF 10: 224–226).
166 Chrysostom, *Commentaire sur Job* (trans. Henri Sorlin; Paris: Cerf, 1988) 1: 83, 91.

character of the prose tale who endured his troubles, an example that Chrysostom urged his audience to follow.[167]

Chrysostom was, however, not unaware of the nature and force of Job's words in the Dialogues. Thus, the fact that God continually refers to Job as "my servant" in 42:7 indicates to Chrysostom not that Job has been right all along but that "all that precedes has been wiped away," especially given Job's self-abnegation in 42:6.[168] Job spoke rightly by speaking of his good acts whereas the friends were wrong in condemning him.[169] The number of animals required for the sacrifice on behalf of the friends testifies to the severity of their guilt. However, acting like a priest, Job interceded for them. To Chrysostom, this suggests that God already honors Job and the material gifts that follow are only a sign of the respect that Job now enjoys.

Having lived prior to Moses (and therefore prior to the Jewish law) Job attained perfection without the aid of the law. He therefore prefigured the gospel. Chrysostom even goes as far as to argue that because Job lived such a noble life of patience and inner knowledge of God prior to the time of the law, Christ did not teach anything new or unusual.[170] Job set an example for all believers to follow, in the hope of receiving all the blessings that God has in store for all who love God and resist the devil. Job's patience in suffering is an example to imitate, and his restoration at the end is a sign that those who love God will also be rewarded.[171]

2.3.2.3 Gregory the Great (540–604)

Gregory's exposition of Job is a combination to varying degrees of three senses of scripture – historical, allegorical, and moral. This is immediately evident in the introduction to his work:

> "Be it known that there are some parts, which we go through in a historical exposition, some we trace out in allegory upon an investigation of the typical meaning, some we open in the lesson of the moral teaching alone, allegorically conveyed, while there are some few which, with more particular care, we search out in all three ways together, exploring them in a threefold method."[172]

---

167 Nahum N. Glatzer, *The Dimensions of Job: A Study and Selected Readings* (New York: Schocken, 1969), 25–26.
168 On 42:6 Chrysostom notes that the reason God acted in Job's life was to bring him to the point where he would make this confession. Once Job recognized his limitation, retracted and condemned himself, then God justified him.
169 Chrysotom, *Commentaire sur Job*, 2: 237.
170 Chrysostom, *Commentaire sur Job*, 1: 82. Chrysostom also sees Job as a model for the Israelites while they were in Egypt, deprived of the guidance of the law.
171 Chrysostom, *Commentaire sur Job*, 2: 241.
172 Saint Gregory the Great, *Morals on the Book of Job* (A Library of Fathers of the Holy Catholic Church Anterior to the Division of East and West 51, Parts 1 and 2; trans. Members of the English Church; Oxford: John Henry Parker, 1844), 7.

As will become evident, this is the procedure he employs in the Epilogue, although he is more interested in exploring the allegorical and moral senses of the text.

The divine approval of Job in 42:7 creates a moral problem for Gregory, one that puts humans at variance with God. Gregory finds it quite difficult to understand the reason for the divine approval, given the nature of Job's outbursts in the Dialogues. But he also holds firmly that God would not have allowed Job to be tested unless God was sure that Job will not sin. The approval reveals "how much our blindness is at variance with the light of divine uprightness." Consequently, "whoever considers that blessed Job sinned in his words after he had been scourged, plainly decides that the Lord had been the loser in His pledging."[173] Thus, although human perception would easily suggest that Job had sinned, God's perception is different. The hermeneutical clue for Gregory here is the prepositional phrase אלי which, following the LXX and Vulgate, he reads as "before me." He writes:

> "As far as concerns human judgments, his friends might be believed to have said in their words many things better than himself, yet Truth bringing forth another rule from the secret place, says; "Ye have not spoken before Me the thing that is right, as My servant Job." Before Me, He says, that is, within, where the conduct of many often displeases, even if outwardly it is pleasing to men."[174]

The "presence" of God where Job and his friends have spoken has been internalized and spiritualized, thus making a distinction between outward appearance and inward reality. This inward-outward distinction, which is part of the larger interpretive strategy associated with allegory and typology, allows Gregory to resolve the tension that readers perceive in the divine approval of Job and rebuke of the friends. Thus even though the friends might have spoken, in Gregory's own words "many better things than" Job, yet God's ability (in contrast to human inability) to perceive the inner reality of Job's words, allows God to approve of Job to humankind's dismay. Furthermore, Gregory argues that the fact that God refers to Job as "my servant" here is significant and indicates that all of what Job said in the Dialogues "he had said not with haughty pride, but with humble truth."[175]

Yet, the forcefulness of the divine rebuke of Job from the whirlwind could not be ignored. Commenting earlier on Job's approval in spite of the divine rebuke, Gregory argued that Job was reproved from the whirlwind in his own person, and yet was preferred to the friends because Job "surpassed all men by virtue of his merits, and yet, inasmuch as he was man, could not possibly be without blame before the eyes of God."[176] Ironically, the divine ability to

---

173 Saint Gregory the Great, *Morals on the Book of Job* in (trans. Members of the English Church; *A Library of Fathers of the Holy Catholic Church Anterior to the Division of East and West*, vol. 3 Part 2; Oxford: John Henry Parker, 1850), 668.
174 Gregory, *Book of Job*, 3:2, 668.
175 Gregory, *Book of Job*, 3:2, 669.
176 Gregory, *Book of Job*, 3:2, 667.

perceive what humans cannot that allows God to approve of Job is the same "divine eyes" before which Job as a human could not be without fault. Accordingly, there is tension between rebuke and approval in the text and Gregory finds the tension to be a result of human experience in the presence of God. Gregory partly resolves this tension by resorting to the difference between inward and outward appearances.

This tension is equally extended to the friends whom Gregory considers to be heretics. By asking them to go to Job for prayers, God graciously forgives and converts them. At this point, the allegorical/typological interpretation almost completely takes over. Job now represents the church and has to intercede for the friends (heretics); the bulls represent pride and the rams represent the leadership of heretics. Thus "to offer bulls and rams in sacrifice, is to sacrifice proud leadership with the humility of conversion, so that they, who before endeavored to take the lead in teaching, may tame the neck of pride and learn to follow by obedience."[177] Furthermore, the fact that God accepts Job's face rather than that of the friends indicates that the heretics can be accepted into the body of Christ only through the merits of the church. Job's "latter days" that are blessed refer to the end times when Jews are brought into the church. And the human assembly that gathers around Job to comfort him is a reference to the conversion of the Jews, while the sheep and earrings given to Job refer to innocence and obedience respectively, both of which are virtues of the church.[178]

Job's children remain ten "in order that those who had been destroyed may be shown to be alive." This expresses the idea of a resurrection. But Gregory goes even further to argue that since God is said to have restored everything twofold, one should understand that when God "restored him as many children as he had lost, he also added to him a double number of children, to whom he afterwards restored ten in the flesh, but reserved the ten that had been lost in the hidden abode of souls." The fact that Job's daughters inherit among their brothers signals the new era and rewards in the kingdom of God.[179]

In summary, all three scholars recognize the tension between the Epilogue and the preceding section of the book. Particularly, they see the tension in the divine approval of Job in the Epilogue after the rebuke from the whirlwind. On the one hand, all three see this tension as resulting from the human condition of imperfect beings in God's presence. And although all three recognize and speak about this human condition in God's presence, Gregory makes a distinction between inward and outward appearances and uses that distinction to resolve the tension; while God can see the inside, humans can see only the outside (which in this context is considered to be a less reliable basis for evaluation). Chrysostom on his part interprets the divine approval in

---

177 Gregory, *Book of Job*, 3:2, 671.
178 Gregory, *Book of Job*, 3:2, 669–687.
179 Gregory, *Book of Job*, 3:2, 668–700.

42:7 in close conjunction with the literary context of 42:6, which he see as a sign of Job's confession of helplessness. All three scholars view Job as a type of the church, and employ the concept of the resurrection to interpret the text.

2.4 Later Medieval Interpretation

Medieval interpretation demonstrated a high level of sensitivity on several fronts: 1) sensitivity towards the large corpus of extra-biblical material that resulted from the work of the Jewish Sages and Church Fathers, 2) sensitivity towards the contemporary cultural and intellectual climate, and 3) sensitivity towards the biblical text itself. For every interpreter, the second and third sensitivities are (and should be) obvious and expected. The first, however, requires comment. The complexity and diversity of interpretation during the rabbinic and patristic age had resulted in the development of different layers of meaning in the text. Furthermore, the fall of Athens in 86 BC had brought with it another factor that led Seneca to note that, "what was philosophy has become philology." That is, students in learning institutions had begun to focus not just on the formulation of new philosophical ideas, but also increasingly on the study of what the founders of these schools had propounded.[180] In its own way, this was a significant step in the field of the history of interpretation because, henceforth, the interpreter had to deal not only with the biblical text and the exigencies of the contemporary situation but also with the diverse material from previous authors. For the medieval interpreters, this was particularly important because the patristic and rabbinic formulations were quickly becoming authoritative. Traditional interpretation was becoming a significant component of interpretation, and interpreters had to react to this development in one way or in another: reject it, absorb it almost wholesale, or incorporate parts of it.

Accordingly, medieval interpreters had to develop methodologies for sorting through the emerging and even established traditional interpretations (represented by the work of the Sages and Fathers), contemporary culture (dominated by rational philosophy and science), and the biblical text itself. To varying degrees, interpreters operated between these three poles. The resulting overarching interpretive grid revolved around the interaction between the plain sense of the text (*peshat*), its wider midrashic/patristic interpretation, and the text's influence on the socio-cultural and religious life of the audience (*derash*).[181] In examining the medieval period, I shall focus

---

180 See, Procopé, "Greek Philosophy, Hermeneutics and Alexandrian Understanding," 459–460.
181 See, Barry D. Walfish, "An Introduction to Medieval Jewish Biblical Interpretation," in *With Reverence for the Word: Medieval Scriptural Exegesis in Judaism, Christianity, and Islam* (ed. Jane Dammen McAuliffe, Barry D. Walfish, and Joseph W. Goering; Oxford: Oxford University Press, 2003), 1–12. Other important essays in the same

2.4.1 Jewish Interpretation

2.4.1.1 Saadiah Gaon (882–942)

Medieval Jewish exegesis may be said to have begun with the work of the Geonim of Babylonia (9th-11th century) headed by Saadiah Gaon. A major concern of Saadiah's was that of exegetical freedom found in lots of allegorical interpretations (largely but not exclusively within the Christian community), and the largely literalist interpretation of the Karaites. Accordingly, Saadiah forged a hermeneutical methodology that principally favored the plain sense of the text over allegorical interpretation. But he also laid down a number of exceptions to the plain sense of the text. These include situations where (a) the plain sense contradicted sense perception, (b) the plain sense contradicted reason, (c) another clearer text could be used to obtain a different or better meaning, and (d) when some reliable tradition modified the plain sense of the text. When the plain sense of the text did not agree with reason and tradition, then exegesis was brought in to resolve the apparent contradiction.[182]

This interaction between exegetical freedom and tradition was employed in his treatment of the book of Job. In his introduction to the book, Saadiah lays down three reasons for the human experience of suffering. One reason is for the purpose of instruction (Prov 3:12). A second reason is for the purpose of purgation and punishment. Although it is punishment, its purpose is that of grace, intended to deter the transgressor from repeating the offenses and purifying such a person from offenses already committed. A third justification is for the purpose of trial and testing. This comes upon those that God knows will be able to endure burdens. Such persons are later rewarded with a blessed life.[183] Saadiah follows these three reasons with three aspects of God's providence or "bounties," as he calls them. These include (a) God's

---

volume dealing with the same issues include: Stephen D. Benin, "The Search for Truth in Sacred Scripture: Jews, Christians, and the Authority to Interpret," 13–32; Michael A. Signer, "Restoring the Narrative: Jewish and Christian Exegesis in the Twelfth Century," 70–82; Joseph W. Goering, "An Introduction to Medieval Christian Biblical Interpretation," 197–203.

182 Saadiah, *The Book of Theodicy*, 148 n. 68; Hans Lewy, Alexander Altmann, and Isaak Heinemann, eds., *Three Jewish Philosophers* (New York: Temple Book, 1974), 25–47. See also, Haggai Ben-Shammai, "The Tension Between Literal Interpretation and Exegetical Freedom: Comparative Observations on Saadia's Method," in *With Reverence for the Word: Medieval Scriptural Exegesis in Judaism, Christianity, and Islam* (ed. Jane Dammen McAuliffe, Barry D. Walfish, and Joseph W. Goering; Oxford: Oxford University Press, 2003), 33–50.

183 Saadiah, *Book of Theodicy*, 125–126.

goodness to all creation (Ps 145:9), (b) the requital of rational beings, this being remuneration for their work (Is. 40:10; 54:17), and (c) recompense for "tribulations with which He has afflicted us and which we have borne with fortitude. This can be called reward because the tribulations are not on account of some past sin on the servant's part."[184] Noticeably, Saadiah uses personal pronouns in describing the third aspect, suggesting that he interpreted the experience of suffering within the Jewish community from this perspective.

This description of the rational explanation for suffering is, however, placed within the larger rabbinic traditional interpretation. Saadiah writes:

> "we have the record of the history of one righteous person who was tested and bore the test with fortitude that was acknowledged. He was assured eternal bliss in the hereafter and granted far more than he had hoped for in this life. That was the prophet Job."[185]

This remark corresponds to the two major parts of the Epilogue and shall be treated in turn. First on the divine approval of Job, Saadiah's interpretation of 42:7–9 was guided by the understanding that although the friends are rebuked, there is much in their words that is true; in fact, he argued that, together with Job, they did not ascribe any injustice to God.[186] Accordingly, in his translation of 42:7 Saadiah argues that the friends' sin was not against God but against Job: God rebukes the friends for not speaking the truth "to me as to my servant Job."[187] Saadiah's translation of 42:7 suggests that for him the issue was not just about a theoretical theological formulation about the divine nature or character, but about the friends' depiction of Job's situation. The words of the friends have been "to" God but also "about" Job. Accordingly, their sin is essentially ethical and not theological, consisting of their attempt to interpret Job's experience as resulting from sin. It is because they sinned against Job that God asked the friends to go to Job for intercession. When they did, God "approved of all," granting "blessings in this world prior to the great reward of the hereafter."[188]

Secondly, and related to the restoration proper, the idea of resurrection suggests that although Saadiah understands Job's reward in material terms, he is also careful not to limit it to that. In fact, part of the very purpose of suffering is to enable humans to submit to God's wisdom and guidance. This in turn perfects the human character.[189] Thus, although Job was right in maintaining his innocence, he was ignorant of God's superior design, and

---

184 Saadiah, *Book of Theodicy*, 127.
185 Saadiah, *Book of Theodicy*, 127.
186 Job's words, the words of the friends, the arguments of each, and Elihu's rebuttal are recorded to show what is in people's hearts when they have reached the limit of endurance. But on one thing they all agree, namely, that there is no injustice in God. Saadiah, *Book of Theodicy*, 128.
187 Saadiah, *Book of Theodicy*, 412 n. 5.
188 Saadiah, *Book of Theodicy*, 411.
189 Saadiah, *Book of Theodicy*, 139 n. 36.

only through his suffering and encounter with God was he brought to an understanding of "the grace in the governance and decree of the All-wise (42:6).[190] Job had assumed that God's sovereignty meant that God does not make any distinctions between the fate of the just and the unjust. In that, Job had "walked doctrinally in the company of the wicked." But through his experience with God in the theophany, Job admits "that he has been enlightened: there is a moral difference between the lives of just and unjust men."[191]

Overall, Saadiah holds that a just deity cannot but compensate both humans and even animals for undeserved suffering; this is only the right thing to do in a world guided by divine grace. God blessed Job in this world prior to the great reward of the hereafter to teach all humans to submit to God's wisdom and guidance.[192] The Epilogue is, therefore, both a material restoration and a demonstration of moral enlightenment for Job.

2.4.1.2 Rashi (1040–1105)

In contrast to Saadiah (and later on Maimonides), Rashi did not employ philosophical concepts in interpreting biblical texts. In forging the relationship between the plain sense of the text, *peshat*, and its homiletical sense, *derash*, his work on Job was not an elaborate commentary close to what we have in Saadiah. Rather, it is made up of brief philological notes and comments on the text. In the process, he combines Jewish traditional interpretation and exegesis of the text. As Signer notes, it is the fusion rather than fission between text and tradition that occurs in Rashi's commentaries that constitute their great achievement.[193]

The interaction between text and tradition is evident in Rashi's interpretation of the divine approval of Job and rebuke of the friends. On the one hand, he holds that Job rebelled against God in some of his remarks (9:22–23). In fact, Job did not speak correctly when he stated that the world is ruled by constellations.[194] But then Rashi draws upon traditional rabbinic interpretation to argue that if Job continued to speak, "he spoke because of the severity of the pains that burdened him and overwhelmed him" (cf. Baba Bathra 16a). That is why he is called God's "servant" in the Epilogue. The friends, on the other hand, sinned by condemning Job.[195] Thus, like Saadiah, Rashi interprets the sinfulness of the friends in terms of their condemnation of Job.

---

190 Saadiah, *Book of Theodicy*, 410.
191 Saadiah, *Book of Theodicy*, 412 n. 5.
192 Saadiah *Book of Theodicy*, 411.
193 Signer, "Restoring the Narrative," 72.
194 Rashi, *The Book of Job*, 237.
195 Rashi, *The Book of Job*, 237.

2.4.1.3 Maimonides (1186–1237)

In his *Guide for the Perplexed*, Maimonides understands the book of Job to be essentially about divine providence. He refers to the book as a "strange and wonderful" book; strange because it contains "great and profound mysteries," and wonderful because it "removes great doubts, and reveals most important truths."[196] Following Saadiah's lead, he understands the book as an attempt to explain the different opinions that people hold on divine providence. But more than Saadiah, he reorganizes the different perspectives in the book to correspond to various philosophical concepts. First, he describes four philosophical theories on divine providence: (a) that which argues that there is no providence in the world; (b) part of the world is under a ruler and another part is abandoned to chance; (c) nothing is left to chance; rather, everything is willed into being; and (d) humans have free will, though it is not absolute. God has ultimate will, and rewards present suffering. Secondly, in his application of these theories to the book of Job, he dismisses the first one as utterly false and attributes the other three to characters in Job as follows: Job corresponds to position (b), Zophar to (c), and Bildad to (d). Eliphaz, on the other hand, expounds the biblical teaching that suffering is a result of sin, and Elihu introduces a new interpretation by making reference to the intercession of angels (Job 33:29).[197]

Crucial to Maimonides' understanding of Job's suffering and restoration is the idea of God's sovereign justice and providence. Maimonides refers to Aristotle's idea that while a part of the universe owes its existence to Providence and is under the control of a ruler or governor, another part is abandoned and left to chance.[198] But whereas Aristotle argued that providence is extended to species only and not to individual beings, Maimonides argued that humans, by virtue of their intelligence, are under God's rule while the rest of nature is not. Maimonides writes:

> "Divine Providence is connected with Divine intellectual influence, and the same beings which are benefited by the latter so as to become intellectual, and to comprehend things comprehensible to rational beings, are also under the control of Divine Providence, which examines all their deeds in order to reward or punish them."[199]

Underlying this was Maimonides' firm conviction that divine justice transcends human notions of providence and is beyond moral categories of

---

[196] Moses ben Maimon, *The Guide for the Perplexed* (trans. M. Friedländer; 2nd ed. New York: George Routledge, 1919), 296.
[197] Moses ben Maimon, *The Guide for the Perplexed*, 299–302. See also, Arthur Hyman, "Demonstrative, Dialectical and Sophistic Arguments in the Philosophy of Moses Maimonides," in *Maimonides and His Time* (ed. Eric C. Ormsby; Washington: Catholic University of America Press, 1989), 35–51.
[198] Moses ben Maimon, *The Guide for the Perplexed*, 282. For further analysis of this point, see A. Reines, "Maimonides' Concepts of Providence and Theodicy," *HUCA* 42 (1972): 169–206.
[199] Moses ben Maimon, *The Guide for the Perplexed*, 287.

good and evil. Accordingly, "all evils and afflictions as well as all kinds of happiness of man, whether they concern one individual person or a community, are distributed according to justice."[200]

In developing his argument, Maimonides draws upon Elihu's description of God's sovereignty and providence in nature to argue that humans should not fall into the error of imagining that God's knowledge is similar to ours or that God's intentions, providence, and rule are similar to those of humans.[201] With this, Maimonides critically engages the traditional interpretation of the Epilogue. He particularly refers to the rabbinic interpretation of Job in Baba Bathra 16a where Job is both rebuked for denying the resurrection and pronouncing words considered to be blasphemous, and then later justified on the basis that a person is not responsible for what they say in their affliction. According to Maimonides,

> "This explanation does not agree with the object of the whole allegory. The words of God [in 42:7] are justified...by the fact that Job abandoned his first very erroneous opinion, and himself proved that it was an error.... He is represented to hold this view only so long as he was without wisdom, and knew God only by tradition, in the same manner as religious people generally know Him. As soon as he had acquired a true knowledge of God, he confessed that there is undoubtedly true felicity in the knowledge of God; it is attained by all who acquire that knowledge, and no earthly trouble can disturb it. As long as Job's knowledge of God was based on tradition and communication, and not on research, he believed that such imaginary good as is possessed in health, riches, and children, was the utmost that men can attain; this was the reason why he was in perplexity.... On account of this last utterance [42:5–6], which implies true perception, it is said afterwards in reference to him, "for you have not spoken of me the thing that is right, as my servant Job hath."[202]

Maimonides interprets the Epilogue from the understanding that neither is divine justice to be understood within the limited scope of good and evil nor is the human response to God's actions dependent on whether God provides for humans or abandons them. In fact, suffering may actually enable one to develop a greater love for God.[203] To arrive at this goal, Maimonides first perceives of the story as an allegory for the learning process. And second, within this allegorical interpretation, renunciation of erroneous beliefs leads to divine approval. Thus he links Job's approval in 42:7 to Job's words in 42:5– 6, in a manner similar to what Chrysostom does within the Antiochene tradition. But also, like the Alexandrians and Saadiah, he speaks of "true felicity" that no earthly trouble can disturb. In all, Maimonides emphasized the role of reason and knowledge, and perceived Job as an ignorant person who, through his suffering, came to understand that his wealth, children, and

---

200 Moses ben Maimon, *The Guide for the Perplexed*, 285.
201 Moses ben Maimon, *The Guide for the Perplexed*, 303.
202 Moses ben Maimon, *The Guide for the Perplexed*, 300–301.
203 Moses ben Maimon, *The Guide for the Perplexed*, 303.

body were not of utmost importance in his relationship with God. Only then was he in the process of uniting with the active intellect, the divine being.[204]

2.4.2 Christian Interpretation

2.4.2.1 Thomas Aquinas (1224/5–1274)

Medieval Christian exegesis inherited the multiple senses of scripture developed during the patristic period.[205] Aquinas, however, proposed to carry out a "literal" exposition of Job.[206] He defined the "literal" sense as "that which is primarily intended by the words, whether they are used properly or figuratively."[207] It was through this literal interpretation that he explored the problem of suffering in Job and how it is related to divine providence. Like Maimonides, he was influenced by Aristotelian philosophy and made the distinction between rational beings (including humans) and the rest of creation, which he considered to be irrational.[208]

Top on his list of noble rational beings are the saints for whom everything, including evil, is ordered for good (Rom 8:28). Thus, divine providence ensures that human experience of pain should result in some form of good. This good need not be perceived exclusively in material or this-worldly terms.[209] Aquinas espoused the view widely held during the medieval period by Jews and Christians that divine justice extended to the next world.[210] For

---

204 Oliver Leaman, *Evil and Suffering in Jewish Philosophy* (Cambridge: Cambridge University Press, 1995), 81.
205 See, Edward Synan, "The Four 'Senses' and Four Exegetes," in *With Reverence for the Word: Medieval Scriptural Exegesis in Judaism, Christianity, and Islam* (ed. Jane Dammen McAuliffe, Barry D. Walfish, and Joseph W. Goering; Oxford: Oxford University Press, 2003), 225–236.
206 Aquinas refers to Gregory's mystical treatment of Job before indicating that he plans to carry out a literal interpretation. See, Thomas Aquinas, *The Literal Exposition on Job: A Scriptural Commentary Concerning Providence* (trans. Anthony Damico with Interpretive Essay and Notes by Martin D. Yaffe; Atlanta: Scholars, 1989), 69.
207 Aquinas, *Literal Exposition*, 76.
208 See, Aquinas, *Summa Contra Gentiles* (trans. The English Dominican Fathers from the Latest Leonine Edition; London: Burns Oates & Washbourne, 1928) 3:1,112; In *Literal Exposition*, 101, Aquinas makes a distinction between rational and sensual perceptions, and applies this distinction to Job's soul; the sensual part cursed the day of his birth because of his suffering while the rational part believed in some ultimate good in the midst of the pain.
209 See, Aquinas, *Literal Exposition*, 89; see also, Eleonore Stump, "Aquinas on the Suffering of Job," in *Human and Divine Agency: Anglican, Catholic, and Lutheran Perspectives* (ed. F. Michael McLain and W. Mark Richardson; New York: University Press of America, 1999), 195–196.
210 Aquinas, *Literal Exposition*, 225: "the time for man's retribution, however, is not in this life, as Job's friends opined, but in that life to which man is restored by resurrection." For an elaboration and critique of this view, see Timothy P. Jackson, "Must Job Live Forever? A Reply to Aquinas on Providence and Freedom, Evil and Immortality," in *Human and Divine Agency: Anglican, Catholic, and Lutheran Perspectives* (ed. F.

him, the ultimate source of happiness and justice was not to be associated with this world but with the resurrection. Therefore, the painful experiences of the present life may indeed be overshadowed by the goal in view, the blessedness of the next life.[211]

Thus, Aquinas' task of demonstrating how suffering is related to divine providence is worked out within a philosophical and theological framework. Philosophically, God belongs to the higher level of intelligence and knowledge. For human beings interacting with God, this calls for a continuous search for greater knowledge and understanding. Theologically, God's justice spans both this life and the next, and the experiences of this earthly life have to be interpreted in conjunction with the next. He thus combined philosophical rationale and religious conviction in his writing in general and in Job in particular.[212]

In his interpretation of the Epilogue, Aquinas situates the divine anger against the friends within the context of the theophany, and sees it as chronologically following the rebuke of Job and Elihu. While Elihu sinned from inexperience and Job from levity, the friends are said to have asserted "perverse dogmas" (cf.13:4).[213] Unlike Job, who did not "withdraw from the truth of faith," the friends did not profess "faithful dogmas" before God. Furthermore, the friends who now represent the "faithless" can be reconciled with God only through the mediation of the "faithful." God will listen to Job's prayer because of his "faith" and not impute the foolishness of the friends, that is, their "unfaithful dogmas" to them.[214] Yet, Job's intercession benefits not only the friends but also Job himself since (the Vulgate that Aquinas used mentions that) God turned to Job in response to Job's penitence. It is in response to Job's prayers that God restores him.

For Aquinas, happiness does not depend on wealth, health, or honor, but rather on the contemplation of God. But he also sought to distinguish himself from the Stoics who thought that material goods were of no effect to one's spirituality.[215] To reconcile this tension, he used Aristotelian science (which categorized the world into inferior and superior spheres) and his religious conviction of the better life to come. Therefore, in his interpretation of the restoration, he writes:

Michael McLain and W. Mark Richardson; New York: University Press of America, 1999), 220–223.

211 See, for example, his comments on Job 1:20–21; 2:7–11.
212 Joseph P. Wawrykow, "New Directions in Research on Thomas Aquinas," *RelSRev* 27, no. 1 (2001): 32–38; Norman Kretzmann, "The Metaphysics of Providence: Aquinas's Natural Theology in Summa Gentiles III," *Medieval Philosophy and Theology* 9, no. 2 (2000): 191–213; Martin D. Yaffe, "Providence in Medieval Aristotelianism: Moses Maimonides and Thomas Aquinas on the Book of Job," in *The Voice From the Whirlwind: Interpreting the Book of Job* (ed. Leo G. Perdue and W. Clark Gilpin; Nashville: Abingdon, 1992), 111–128.
213 Aquinas, *Literal Exposition*, 471.
214 Aquinas, *Literal Exposition*, 471.
215 Aquinas, *Literal Exposition*, 87.

> "Although Job did not base his hope on recovering temporal prosperity but on achieving future happiness, nevertheless the Lord also restored to him abundantly his temporal prosperity."[216]

Material prosperity is not denied, but is a temporary part of a larger goal or reward that stretches into the eternal realm (cf. Matt 6:33). As a result, Job's restoration played a double significance, one symbolic and the other practical. Symbolically, Job's restoration is analogous to what happened in the Old Testament where "temporal goods were promised so that in this way, through the prosperity which Job had recovered, an example might be given to the others so that they might turn back to God." Practically, the restoration was consistent with Job's character and was intended to "restore his reputation to him" since that reputation had been damaged among some people because of Job's adversity.[217]

As for the number of Job's children, Aquinas proposed two alternative interpretations. First, regarding the future life, the children had not totally perished but were reserved to live with Job in the future life; and second, regarding the present life, the children are not doubled because then the prosperity would have been divided among them and would not have increased per person. Rather, it was more proper that Job's offspring be increased not in numbers but in value as is insinuated by the exceptional beauty of the daughters.[218] This increased prosperity of Job's lasted until his death since he is said to have seen his children and grand children to the fourth generation. Furthermore, the "abundance" of life that he enjoyed refers not only to his material prosperity but also to the grace that led him to future glory.[219]

2.4.2.2 John Calvin (1509–1564)

Like Maimonides and Aquinas before him, Calvin was interested in the literal interpretation of Job, and his *Sermons on Job*[220] contribute to that endeavor. His interest in the plain sense of the text was fueled in part by his interest in the humanities as well as his conviction about the inspiration of the biblical text. This meant that the biblical text had a human and a divine component.[221]

---

216 Aquinas, *Literal Exposition*, 472.
217 Aquinas, *Literal Exposition*, 472. This corresponds to the consolation that Job receives from his former acquaintances and the gifts of sheep (which represent the animals lost) and earrings (which represent the household goods lost). It is these gifts that God doubled.
218 Aquinas, *Literal Exposition*, 473.
219 Aquinas, *Literal Exposition*, 474.
220 John Calvin, *Sermons on Job* (trans. Arthur Golding; London: Banner of Truth, 1574).
221 On Calvin's understanding of the ultimate divine authority of scripture, see John Calvin, *Institutes of the Christian Religion* (ed. John T. McNell; trans. Ford Lewis Battles; 2 vols.; The Library of Christian Classics 20–21; Philadelphia: Westminster, 1960), 1.8.1. For an examination of Calvin's interpretive and exegetical method, see David L. Puckett, *John Calvin's Exegesis of the Old Testament* (Louisville: Westminster, 1995).

In his interpretation of Job, these two sides meet and indeed stand in tension with one another because of the nature of the problem posed by the book, namely, the problem of innocent suffering. Calvin's interpretation is largely situated within the context of divine providence. He focuses not only on the divine attributes of mercy, justice, and sovereignty that are crucial for him, but also on the human ability or lack thereof to understand the workings of God in the world as a whole and in each person.

In articulating his view, Calvin first argues that "in administering human society," God "so tempers his providence that, although kindly and beneficent toward all in numberless ways he still by open and daily indications declares his clemency to the godly and his severity to the wicked and criminal." Furthermore, the "unfailing rule" of God's righteousness "ought not to be obscured" by the fact that God "frequently allows the wicked to exult unpunished for some time, while the upright are tossed about by many adversities."[222] This "unfailing rule of God's righteousness" stretches into the next world, so that ultimately, "iniquity is to have its punishment and righteousness is to be given its reward."[223] Next, under a more developed theory of providence and its practical application, Calvin notes that although God's providence is often clearly displayed in the world, "nevertheless sometimes the causes of the events are hidden. So the thought creeps in that human affairs turn and whirl at the blind urge of fortune; or the flesh incites us to contradiction, as if God were making sport of men by throwing them about like balls." Instead of this, Calvin states that if humans would have "quiet and composed minds ready to learn," then we would see that God always has some best reason for God's plan. This purpose or plan may include creating a virtue (e.g., patience, humility, repentance), or casting down the proud and arrogant, or simply displaying the glory of God (Ps 40:5; Jn 9:3).[224]

In his understanding of providence, therefore, Calvin combines a number of issues including divine justice, mercy, and mystery, as well as human inability to understand some of God's actions.[225] Experientially, this translates into a hope that even if the troubles of this world are not immediately righted, they will be righted in some future time. Knowing that God has a purpose that is sometimes beyond human comprehension may prevent the experience of adversity from being one of complete *anomie*.[226]

This description of the experience of divine providence is further developed in the *Sermons on Job*. In his first sermon where Calvin tries to

---

222 Calvin, *Institutes*, 1.5.7.
223 Calvin, *Institutes*, 1.5.10.
224 Calvin, *Institutes*, 1.17.1.
225 See, Susan E. Schreiner, "Exegesis and Double Justice in Calvin's Sermons on Job," *CH* 58 (1989): 322-338; idem, "'Through a Mirror Dimly': Calvin's Sermons on Job," *CTJ* 21, no. 2 (1986): 175–192.
226 David J. A. Clines, "Job and the Spirituality of the Reformation," in *The Bible, The Reformation and the Church: Essays in Honour of James Atkinson* (ed. W. P. Stephens; Sheffield: Sheffield Academic Press, 1995), 66.

bring his audience to "understand the sum" of the book, he lays down four guiding principles: (a) that humans are in God's hands; (b) that it is up to God to determine the course of life, and dispose of its fame at God's pleasure; (c) that it is humankind's duty to submit to God in humble obedience; and (d) that when it pleases God to lay God's hand on humans, although we do not perceive for what cause, yet we should glorify God and acknowledge God's justice.[227] Thus, Calvin creates an interpretive framework that incorporates divine sovereignty, allowing God to do as God pleases, but also one that refuses to give up the attribute of divine justice. He drew upon Eliphaz's words in 4:18 that not even the angels can stand divine judgment, as well as the divine approval of Job at the end to probe into the nature of divine justice and the relationship between divine justice and divine power. He posited a concept of double justice with a higher, hidden justice in God that transcends the law and could condemn even the angels. Interpreting Job's experience as a test, Calvin concluded that though God can "act" according to the higher, hidden divine justice, God can only "judge" according to the justice that is known.[228]

This interpretive framework is immediately discernible in his treatment of the Epilogue. For Calvin, God can chastise God's people with a "fatherly gentleness," but at the same time extend God's justice upon them. Calvin begins interpreting the Epilogue by noting that the words, "after the Lord spoke these words to Job," refer to the divine rebuke of Job from the whirlwind. Drawing upon Jer 25:29a and 1 Pet 4:17 which speak of divine judgment beginning with God's own people, Calvin argued that the rebuke is a process that begins with Job.[229] According to Calvin, Job was rebuked because although he pursued a good cause when he brought his case before God, he mishandled the case. Although Job rightly believed that God does not treat people according to strict retribution, Job uttered "excessive and outrageous" words, and in many cases seemed like "a desperate person" who even appeared to "resist God." Accordingly, we see "a good case mishandled."[230] The friends, on the other hand, sinned because they made an assumption, "which was quite besides the case, which was that Job was punished for his misdeeds." This, according to Calvin, was a "false doctrine" that essentially took away the hope of everlasting life and shut God's favors out of this frail and temporary life.[231]

The divine approval that Job spoke "rightly" prompts Calvin to ask, "how was that?" seeing that God had "condemned him as an ignorant,

---

227 Calvin, *Sermons on Job*, 1.
228 See, Susan E. Schreiner, *Where Shall Wisdom be Found?: Calvin's Exegesis of Job from Medieval and Modern Perspectives* (Chicago: University of Chicago Press, 1994), 105-115.
229 Calvin, *Sermons on Job*, 742.
230 Calvin, *Sermons on Job*, 1.
231 Calvin, *Sermons on Job*, 743. Apart from this assumption, Calvin argues that the Holy Spirit inspired the friends' words. See Calvin, *Sermons on Job*, 1.

overweening, and impatient person."[232] Calvin resolved this by arguing that Job was a person who feared God; although he sinned, he was a God fearer. Furthermore, Calvin makes a distinction between two forms of divine judgments, one that comes upon the righteous, and the other that comes upon people outside the church and intended to bring them into the church. This distinction is then applied to Job and his friends, and the second form of divine judgment is applied to the friends to justify God's decision to have them make offerings while Job intercedes for them. This, to Calvin, once more showed that God "handles men in diverse fashions" but also that God does procure welfare for those whom God has not forsaken completely.[233]

Calvin's focus on the mysterious aspect of God's sovereignty and the salvific aspect of God's actions continues to be significant in his second sermon on the Epilogue. The fact that God threatens to do an outrageous thing to the friends suggests to Calvin that there is "a strangeness in God," but he also adds that God can be "a rough rider to a rough horse," that is, act retributively.[234] But the focus immediately returns to God's mercy as the friends obey and bring the sacrifice. In response to Job's prayer, God turned Job's captivity and restored him.[235] However, the restoration was not included in the text for Job's sake, but rather for the sake of the audience in order to teach three lessons: (a) that adversity lasts only for a while; (b) that adversity serves God's people as medicine; and (c) that it results in happiness, because it leads to a time of deliverance by God.[236] Like Ambrose, Calvin partly interprets suffering in a redemptive manner, and the material restoration is not overly emphasized. In fact, the doubling of Job's property is not always the case in life. The more sure fact is that God brings afflictions to an end, and although temporal blessings are good, Calvin (like Maimonides) argues that there is something more that is gained in suffering. For Calvin, suffering leads to the assurance of God's goodness and the exercise of faith in times of affliction. Isn't this "very much?," asks Calvin.[237]

The beauty of Job's daughters and Job's long life are all interpreted as a demonstration of God's goodness in Old Testament times before the final revelation in Christ. However, Calvin argues that because of the revelation of a better life in Christ, we do not need to live that long; we ought to be satisfied with life no matter how short it is, seeing that we look forward to a better life even as Abraham did.[238] The Epilogue is thus interpreted with a focus on the future.

---

232 Calvin, *Sermons on Job*, 743.
233 Calvin, *Sermons on Job*, 745.
234 Calvin, *Sermons on Job*, 743.
235 Calvin noted that there are two possible readings of the text: "God turned at Job's repentance," (following the Vulgate) and "God turned the captivity of Job." But he maintained that the second reading is the "plain sense of the text."
236 Calvin, *Sermons on Job*, 749.
237 Calvin, *Sermons on Job*, 749.
238 Calvin, *Sermons on Job*, 750.

In summary, the foregoing analysis of some Jewish and Christian interpreters indicates that there are three things to note about the interpretation of the Epilogue from the early rabbinic and patristic period to the medieval period. First, there is tension between the nature of Job's words in the Dialogues leading up to divine rebuke and the divine approval at the end, and this tension is resolved in various ways: (a) the rebuke of Job was interpreted on the basis of the general sinfulness of humankind in God's presence. Although both Jewish and Christian interpreters employed this understanding of Job, they differed on how Job's sinfulness practically plays out as well as its role in the interpretation of the text. Within a "redemptive" framework, the rebuke of Job becomes part of God's strategy of bringing Job to a better realization of who God is. Once that lesson is learnt, Job is then approved; (b) Job's approval in 42:7 was related to his confession in 42: 1–6. Job's approval is thus closely associated not with the divine theophany, but with Job's words immediately preceding the Epilogue. This was particularly true of Maimonides; and (c) the approval was interpreted in line with divine providence and mercy. This interpretive strategy emerges in the work of early rabbinic scribes as well as in Calvin. On the rebuke of the friends, a number of Jewish and Christian interpreters (Saadiah, Gregory, Calvin) recognized the credibility of the friends' arguments in the poetic section of the book. For Saadiah, their rebuke was caused by their description of Job's suffering as a result of sin; their fault was not theological but ethical. For Gregory the Great and Calvin, the friends' fault was theological; they propounded "false dogmas" that, in Calvin's view, deprived Job of the hope of a resurrection in the life to come. For both Jewish and Christian interpreters, reconciliation between Job and his friends is created by the divine demand that the friends go to Job for prayers and sacrifices.

The second point to note from the foregoing survey is the use of allegorical interpretation, which resulted in the text being read as symbolic of Israel's experiences as a nation or the experiences of the church. For early rabbinic scribes, Job's experience of suffering was linked to the emergence of Israel in Egypt and particularly with the Babylonian exile. Accordingly, the Epilogue was associated with the message of restoration proclaimed by Second Isaiah. For Maimonides, the allegory of Job was applied to the individual person and related to the process of learning wisdom and becoming united with the transcendental Intelligence. For Christian interpreters, the Epilogue represented the experience of the Church, where Job was the Church and the friends represented the pagan world in need of conversion.

The third point to note is that the restoration was perceived as a blessed life in this world, but especially of life in the next world. That is, a fully developed concept of the resurrection is applied to the reading of the text. In the process of these various interpretations, a number of divine attributes emerge as major factors. These include divine sovereignty, providence, justice, and mercy. Depending on the interpreters and their contexts, these attributes are emphasized to varying degrees.

2.5 Historical-Critical and Literary-Critical Work on the Epilogue

In his book, *The Eclipse of Biblical Narrative*, Hans Frei succinctly describes the character and force of the historical-critical method of interpretation. It represented the engrossment of scholars in the Bible as a written document, so that the written source, in the particular shape in which it has come down to us, was part of the evidence to be examined. Criticisms of the writings went along with, indeed became part of, the criticism of facts. And what counted as evidence for or against the biblical reports was not only the extent to which they could be corroborated externally, but also the origin, development, and internal consistency of the writings.[239] Although some form of critical work had been done by preceding scholars such as Origen, Jerome, Rashi, Maimonides, Calvin and the like, it was not until the late 18th century that the historical-critical method was self consciously used as an interpretive tradition. The human component, which had always been recognized as part of the process of the production of the biblical text, now became the primary object of critical investigation. This included issues related to the historicity, date, place, and compositional history of the account. For the Epilogue of Job, this also meant, among other things, examining the dissonances between the prose and the poetic sections of the book. These dissonances are both literary and theological.

2.5.1 Critical Analysis

Historical-critical and analytical work on Job has been diverse and complex. The book has been examined not only in the light of other biblical material, but also in the light of ancient Near Eastern material (e.g., *Ludlul bêl nêmeqi* and the so-called "Babylonian Job").[240] An important conclusion from this comparative study of Job with other ancient Near Eastern material is that

---

239 Hans W. Frei, *The Eclipse of Biblical Narrative: A Study in Eighteenth and Nineteenth Century Hermeneutics* (New Haven: Yale University Press, 1974), 157.
240 These works deal with issues of innocent suffering and, in the case of the *Ludlul bêl nêmeqi*, of deliverance. See, John Gray, "The Book of Job in the Context of Near Eastern Literature," *ZAW* 82 (1950): 251–269; Carol A. Newsom, "The Book of Job: Introduction, Commentary, and Reflections," in *1 & 2 Maccabees, Introduction to Hebrew Poetry, Job, Psalms* (ed. Leander E. Keck; vol. 4 of *The New Interpreter's Bible: General Articles and Introduction, Commentary, and Reflections for each Book of the Bible Including the apocrypha/Deuterocanonical Books in Twelve Volumes*; Nashville: Abingdon, 1996), 330–334; Pope, *The Book of Job*, lvi–lxxi; Yair Hoffmann, "Ancient Near Eastern Literary Conventions and the Restoration of the Book of Job," *ZAW* 103, no. 3 (1991): 399–411.

older works dealing with issues of innocent suffering and theodicy may have influenced the book of Job. This conclusion then raises the issue of the possible compositional history of the book of Job.[241]

Critical examination of the book of Job itself leads to the recognition that there are not only different literary techniques (prose and poetry) employed in the book, but also that underlying these various literary techniques are more substantive and divergent perceptions of reality. A number of such differences are worth noting. First, the moral view of the prose Prologue and Epilogue, which portrays a situation of stability and order, appears to be at odds with that of the poetry. In the prose section, God permits God's servant to be afflicted without cause, and this does not seem to be particularly problematic, since Job appears to be quite patient in enduring his trouble because as he himself states, God gives and takes. The poetic section, however, portrays a different character that is ready to argue with God and resist the idea of his suffering. Second, the Adversary who plays a significant role in the Prologue is not mentioned at all in the poetic section or in the Epilogue. Third, in the prose section, sacrifices are used to approach the deity, while in the poetry no mention is made of sacrifices. And fourth, the divine names also differ. In the poetic section (with the exception of the divine speeches), God is referred to as El, or Elohim, or Shadday, or Eloah, while in the prose section, the names YHWH and Elohim are used.[242]

Because of these features within the book, scholars have reflected on the possible sources that were used for the composition of the book, and on its possible history of composition.[243] For the present purpose, however, I shall focus on the prose section of the book. Arguments relating to the prose section are generally formulated in three ways: 1) that the Prologue and Epilogue are the work of the author of the poem, because without the framework of the Prologue and Epilogue the poetic section does not stand; 2) that the author took the prose framework from some existing source, written or oral, and used it for his purpose. In this case, the author probably used it to replace or modify an "original" framework; and 3) that some later editor added the prose framework. Of these three hypotheses, the first and second have attracted the most attention from scholars, although the second appears to be the most credible.[244] Therefore, even though Richard Simon argued that

---

241 For a summary presentation on the various ancient Near Eastern works relating to the problem of innocent suffering and the various interpretive concepts that have been used to understand this problem, see James L. Crenshaw, *Urgent Advice and Probing Questions: Collected Writings on Old Testament Wisdom* (Macon; GA: Mercer University Press, 1995), 438–442.
242 See, Driver and Gray, *The Book of Job*, xxxiv–xxxvii; Pope, *The Book of Job*, xxi–xxvii.
243 See, Norman H. Snaith, *The Book of Job: Its Origin and Purpose* (SBT² 11; London: SCM, 1968), 19–33
244 For arguments in support of the first hypothesis, see Harold H. Rowley, *From Moses to Qumran: Studies in the Old Testament* (New York: Association, 1963), 151–162. For arguments in favor of the second hypothesis, see Duncan B. MacDonald, "The Original Form of the Legend of Job," *JBL* 14 (1895): 63–71; idem, "Some External Evidence on the Original Form of the Legend of Job," *AJSL* 14, no. 3 (1898): 137–164; Emil G.

the Prologue and Epilogue were later additions,[245] most scholars argue that the issue appears not to be one of determining whether the final editor was influenced by older material, but rather the extent to which such existing material was used. Along this line, some scholars argue that the Prologue and Epilogue were excerpted from a *Volksbuch*, but this has been challenged in favor of the argument that the author reworked existing legendary material on Job.[246]

The possibility of an existing tradition, written or oral, that depicted Job as a righteous individual, is partly preserved in the mention of Job, Noah, and Daniel as examples of righteous individuals in Ezek 14. In the Hebrew text of Sir 49:9, Job is equally mentioned as a person of steadfast righteousness. Moreover, a number of literary features in the Epilogue point to the possibility of an older corpus that was reworked. For example, a) the absence of the Adversary from the Epilogue means that YHWH assumes the responsibility for Job's trouble;[247] and b) the use of the expression פלל בעד in 42:10 together with the late form פלל על in 42:8 suggests that there may have been an older framework that was reused by the final editor.[248] Developing the idea of a reworked legend, some scholars proposed that only parts of the Epilogue belong to the original story,[249] and portions of the Epilogue were used to link the Epilogue to the poetic section.[250]

Kraeling, *The Book of the Ways of God* (New York: Charles Scribner's Sons, 1938), 197–217; Martin Noth, "Noah, Daniel und Hiob in Ezechiel xiv," *VT* 1 (1951): 251–260; Spiegel, "Noah, Danel, and Job," 305–355; Sarna, "Epic Substratum in the Prose of Job," 13–25; Cyrus H. Gordon, "Homer and Bible: The Origin and Character of East Mediterranean Literature," *HUCA* 26 (1955): 43–108, but especially pages 67, 75, and 95.

245 Richard Simon, *Histoire Critique du Vieux Testament* (Rotterdam: Leers, 1685), 30. See also Friedrich Delitzsch, *Das Buch Hiob: Neu Übersetz und Kurz Eklärt Ausgabe mit Sparchlichen Kommentar* (Leipzig: Hinrichs, 1902), 13; Kember Fullerton, "The Original Conclusion to the Book of Job," *ZAW* 42 (1924): 135, thinks that the book could have ended at 40:3–5. The framework of the book, however, unfortunately allowed subsequent revisers to append 40:6–42:7 "in the interest of a crass and obvious orthodoxy." Kautzsch, *Das sogenannte Volksbuch von Hiob*, 18–22. Kautzsch argues that the present text probably did not appropriate much from the existing legend except perhaps the name of the protagonist and his righteousness.

246 See, Driver and Gray, *The Book of Job*, xxvi; Pope, *The Book of Job*, xxii–xxiii.

247 Bruce Zuckerman, *Job the Silent: A Study in Historical Counterpoint* (New York: Oxford University Press, 1991), 27, writes: "the Epilogue probably presents the story as though the Satan never played a role in the action because in the more ancient tradition – in the story of Job that plays beneath the authorized prose version – the Satan did not exist. In the ancient story of Job, it was God *alone* who tested Job."

248 See, Hurvitz, "Date of the Prose Tale," 19; MacDonald, "The Original Form of the Legend of Job," 65–67; Pope, *The Book of Job*, xxvi; Snaith, *The Book of Job*, 1–18.

249 Moses Buttenwieser, *The Book of Job* (New York: McMillan, 1922), 67–68, argues that only 42:11 belonged to the original story; Albrecht Alt, »Zur Vorgeschichte des Buches Hiob,« *ZAW* 55 (1937): 265–268 argued that the story had two frames, chapter 1 and 42:11–17 constituting the outer frame, and chapter 2 together with 42:7–10 constituting an inner frame.

250 Robert Gordis, *The Book of Job: Commentary, New Translation, and Special Studies* (New York: Jewish Theological Seminary of America, 1978), 575, argues that 42:7–10 was written by the poet who wanted to link the prose frame to the dialogues. Elsewhere,

Other scholars have argued that without the Prologue and Epilogue, the Dialogues are without any plot and consequently would not make much sense. The Epilogue, in its entirety, is thus required by the form and plot of the story.[251] Thus beyond issues of sources and compositional history, studies in Job have employed literary critical methods as opposed to historical-critical methods. Prominent among such literary works are those of David Clines and Norman Habel, among others. Using the literary methods of New Critics such as Robert Alter, Habel and Clines have analyzed the text in terms of plot structure and narrative development, breaking down the book into three portions: narrative Exposition (chapters 1 and 2), Complication (chapters 3–31) and Resolution (chapters 32–42).[252] For Habel, the opening verses of the book (Job 1: 1–5) provide a background not just for the first movement in the story but also for the total narrative. Furthermore, Habel argues that in the presentation of the story, the narrator "employs the technique of repeating an earlier scene with significant variations and additions. These variations force a reinterpretation of the earlier scene."[253] On the basis of an analysis of a number of linguistic/literary and thematic echoes in the Prologue, Habel argues that the rest of the Prologue is presented in a way that its themes anticipate some of the major themes that are developed in the latter part of the text, including the Dialogue with the friends and the divine theophany. Habel then concludes that

> "the so-called prologue is not an independent story (even if some such story once circulated orally), but the first movement of a complex plot which foreshadows and requires subsequent movements for its appropriate development and resolution."[254]

Similarly, although David Clines identifies different modes of viewing the shape of the book of Job, his argument favors the tripartite structure of

---

The Book of God and Man: A Study of Job (Chicago: University of Chicago Press, 1965), 73, Gordis writes: "Having decided to utilize the traditional folk tale for his purposes, the poet then found it necessary to effect a transition from the prose prologue to the dialogue and from the dialogue to the prose epilogue. This he achieved by adding two brief jointures, one at the end of the original prologue (2:11–13), the other (42:7–10) before the epilogue." Carol Newsom "Narrative Ethics, Character, and the Prose Tale of Job," in *Character and Scripture: Moral Formation, Community, and Biblical Interpretation* (ed. William P. Brown; Grand Rapids, Mich.: Eerdmans, 2002), 124, also argues that 42:7–10 was a later addition intended to link the dialogues to the more original frame story.

251 See, Harry Ranston, *The Old Testament Wisdom Books and their Teachings* (London: Epworth, 1930), 114, 172; Dhorme, *The Book of Job*, xxxv; Rowley, *From Moses to Qumran*, 160, writes: "The epilogue was not demanded by the message of the book; but it was demanded by its form. The trial was over and the case against Job proved to be empty. The epilogue is merely the author's way of indicating this and rounding off his book."

252 See, Norman C. Habel, *The Book of Job: A Commentary* (Old Testament Library; Philadelphia: Westminster, 1985) 25–35; David J. A. Clines, *Job 1-20* (WBC 17; Texas: Wordbooks, 1989), xxxv–xxxvi.

253 Habel, *The Book of Job*, 28.

254 Habel, *The Book of Job*, 29.

Exposition, Complication, and Resolution. Clines argues that the credibility of this method is that it allows one

> "to speak of the narrative of the book as a whole, that is, of a narrative that does not only *frame* the book, but which runs *through* it. And we can now speak of argument not just of the *speeches* in which the characters are obviously arguing with one another, but of *the book as a whole*, narrative and speeches included."[255]

Overall, critical analysis of the book of Job in general and the Epilogue in particular largely begin with the recognition of some form of tension (literary, thematic, theological etc) within the text. The resulting effort of historical and literary critics is to provide interpretive contexts that do justice to the history of composition of the text (and thereby take seriously the historical contexts of the writers/interpreters) and to the final form of the text (and therefore take seriously the historical contexts of the final editors and the final readers). Both historical critics and literary critics thus begin with the final form of the text, but seek to resolve the issues within the text in different ways. A basic factor, perhaps dictated by the final form of the book, is that in spite of its significant differences the characters of Job in the prose and poetic sections really belong to the same person; that is, the story is about one Job, not two.

2.5.2 Theological Analysis

Scholars have highlighted a number of theological issues related to the form and content of the Epilogue. The following are worth noting. The character of Job that we find in the Dialogue is appropriately described as "anti-Job"[256] of the Prologue-Epilogue. So uncharacteristic are Job's comments and mannerisms in the Dialogues that, instead of divine approval as is the case in the Prologue, he is rebuked by God in the theophany.[257] In spite of this rebuke, in 42:7 we are told that God is angry with the friends, "for you have not spoken rightly to/about me as my servant Job." How is it that Job who has just been rebuked for speaking without knowledge is now said to have spoken rightly? Furthermore, how is it that the friends who have defended God all along are now said not to have spoken rightly like Job? The friends may have falsely accused Job of being a sinner, or as Elihu put it, they may

---

255 Clines, *Job 1-20*, xxxvii-xxxviii.
256 This expression is credited to Zuckerman, *Job the Silent*, who understands the dialogues as having been created as a parody of the traditional pious Job. See also H. L. Ginsberg, "Job the Patient and Job the Impatient," *Conservative Judaism* 21, no. 3 (1967): 12–28.
257 The divine rebuke, beginning in chapter 38, has several allusions to some of Job's most powerful utterances in protest in chapter 3. For instance, the allusions to creation mythology including ideas such as the shutting of the sea (38:8 // 3:23, the shutting of humans); images of light and darkness, day and night and the power to control them (38: 12, 15, 19 // 3:3, 4); images of the sea, its creatures and the netherworld (38: 8, 16, 17 // 3:8); reference to Job as גבר (38:3 // 3:1). All these allusions together as a cluster suggest that God is responding in part to Job's speech in chapter 3.

have made Job look like a bad person (32:3), but what is it that they said about God that is not true?[258] This is a question that we have seen in the survey of the history of interpretation. For a number of ancient interpreters, the friends articulate cogent theological points that do resonate with much of ancient Israelite religious worldview. How then does one interpret the divine rebuke of the friends?

Furthermore, the restoration with its 'happy ending' seems to undermine the integrity and force of Job's penetrating arguments presented in the Dialogues in which Job argues that God does not always guarantee 'happy endings.'[259] But if the restoration of Job in the Epilogue creates theological tensions with the preceding section, it provides an opportunity for the redemption of the divine character. As Leo Perdue argues regarding the image of God in the Prologue, the theological portrait of a divine tyrant who is willing to destroy even those who are rumored to be disloyal cannot stand in the face of overwhelming crisis. Accordingly, God must act to set things right, and Job's restoration leads to the redemption of God as God appears to be the true Judge.[260]

2.5.3 Interpretive Issues

The foregoing analysis indicates that there are a number of interpretive issues that relate to the form and function of the Epilogue in the story.[261] There are two distinct but related issues involved in the interpretation of the first section of the Epilogue (42:7–9). On the one hand, the tension between the divine approval of Job in the Epilogue and the rebuke in the theophany that calls for serious thought. It has been argued that the approval of Job is of such a magnitude and nature that it throws the entire discussion into narrative confusion. According to David Penchansky, the approval actually reverses the notions of traditional piety:

> "The traditional view of piety is bifurcated. The piety demanded by the God of the Prologue and the Speeches of Yahweh conforms to the traditional theological framework of Israel, but the painful exclamations in the center gain the approval

---

258 For a summary of the dissonances between the Epilogue and the rest of the book, see Pope, *Job*, xxiii-xxvi; Gordis, *The Book of God and Man*, 70–72.
259 See, Crenshaw, *Urgent Advice*, 431.
260 Leo G. Perdue, *Wisdom and Creation: The Theology of Wisdom Literature* (Nashville: Abingdon, 1994), 182.
261 Sandmel Samuel, *The Hebrew Scriptures: An Introduction to their Literature and Religious Ideas* (New York: Knopt, 1963), 299, refers to the Epilogue as a "lame" and "pathetic conclusion" given the nature of the dialogues. Carl G. Jung, *Answer to Job* (trans. R. F. Hull; Princeton: Princeton University Press, 1973), ignores the Epilogue completely, preferring to end with Job's repentance in 42:6. He argues that God had a shadow side that led God to pound Job into submission in 42:1–6. Reacting to this view, Suzanne Boorer, "The Dark Side of God? A Dialogue with Jung's Interpretation of Job," in *Pacifica* 10 (1997), 297, argues that God does appear to have a shadow side, but this is balanced by God's life giving character as portrayed in chapter 42.

of Yahweh in the epilogue. Notions of piety are reversed: the Job of the center becomes the pious figure of whom God approves; the Job of the prologue, a hopeless sycophant."[262]

On the other hand, it is not just the approval of Job that calls for reflection but also the divine rebuke of the friends. Accordingly, other scholars have argued that in the rebuke of the friends, God

> "acts like the kind of person he praises Job for denying him to be. Concerning Job's friends, at the same time as he says they are wrong in their naïve insistence that he always punishes evil, he threatens to punish them for being evil. He will avert disaster from them if they repent and admit that he does not always avert disaster from the repentant."[263]

Furthermore, the rebuke of Eliphaz and his friends for not speaking rightly is "shocking" since Eliphaz had cited a heavenly voice to reinforce his admonition to Job (4: 12–19), but now he hears God's voice without qualification declaring him and his friends wrong.[264] Since Eliphaz's argument is that humans are *de facto* sinful by their being human, the narrator's portrayal of the divine character in the Epilogue refuses to place the entire cause of suffering at the feet of humans, creating thereby significant tension with the law of retribution: if humans are not to blame for everything evil that occurs, or more precisely, if God now takes part of the blame, where does that leave the divine credibility as just Judge?[265]

Therefore, the second section of the Epilogue (42:10–17) that deals with the restoration proper also has dissonances both with the Prologue and the Dialogues. The exceptional material restoration has a naivety about it that warrants explanation, coming as it does after the heated debate in the Dialogues.[266] Is the restoration an act of divine freedom enacting itself in felicity?[267] Or should one see a close connection between the restoration and the law of retribution, signaled by the twofold restoration which elsewhere is

---

262 David Penchansky, *The Betrayal of God: Ideological Conflict in Job* (Louisville: John Knox, 1990), 54.
263 Robert Polzin, "The Framework of the Book of Job," *Int* 28 (1974): 186.
264 So, J. H. Eaton, *Job* (Sheffield: JSOT Press, 1985), 47. Although in his vision Eliphaz is unsure of the form and nature of the "spirit" that made the revelation, he is sure about the message, namely, that humans are not righteous before God (the MT can also be read to mean that humans are not more righteous than God). Ironically, what this implies is that "the distinction between the righteous and the impious is not a black-and-white one." See Clines, *Job 1-20*, 128.
265 The reader is left to ponder over and echo Abraham's question to God, "Shall the Judge of all the earth not do what is just?" (Gen 18:25).
266 Gutiérrez, *On Job: God-Talk and the Suffering of the Innocent*, 12, states that although the ending of the book is naïve, "the poet wants to give human and material expression to the deep spiritual joy that Job has experienced in his final encounter with God."
267 Janzen, *Job*, 267, writes: "In the light of the Dialogues we may no longer interpret any specific aspect of experience – positive or negative – in terms of a strict law of rewards and punishments .... When we see Job blessed, in the end, we are invited to interpret this as arising out of God's freedom enacted toward Job."

enacted within the context of the law of rewards and punishment.[268] Furthermore, within the context of the restoration, how is one to understand the number of children? As Newsom notes, it is shocking that the narrator seems to overlook the fact that beloved children cannot be replaced by new ones, as wealth can be replaced.[269] Also, it is unclear why it is that every numbered possession or component of what Job lost in the Prologue is doubled in the Epilogue with the exception of the children.

Carol Newsom articulates the whole dissonance between the Epilogue and the rest of the book as follows:

> "Through its ironic dissonance with what has gone before, the prose conclusion makes it less clear which voice, if any, holds the key to the troubling issues raised by the book of Job. Just when one expects resolution, the book offers frustration instead. One could easily be angry at the book for having asked its readers to work hard at difficult moral and religious questions and then ended with a tease instead of an answer."[270]

The foregoing analyses that highlight different interpretive issues regarding the Epilogue result in different perceptions of the role of the Epilogue in the book. For some scholars, the Epilogue is anticlimactic. David Clines, for example, argues that by returning to retribution in the end the Epilogue actually deconstructs the book as a whole. Consequently, Clines argues that any attempt to "house the anti-retributionist philosophy within the dogma of retribution, as a kind of modification or tampering of it" will "denature the drama of the book."[271] Therefore, and in conjunction with much of historical critical analysis, God's rebuke of the three friends and praise of Job in 42:7 is more often seen in light of the Prologue, as part of a didactic tale structure wherein the hero is shown to be one of unconditional piety.[272] For some scholars who take the entire narrative into consideration, it is argued that the humbling of Job's friends comes about without any real motivation, and the restoration of Job's fortunes appears as capricious as the sufferings imposed upon him at the start of the narrative.[273] The problem then that besets the

---

268 Francis I. Anderson, *Job: An Introduction and Commentary* (Downers: Intervarsity, 1977), 293, writes: "It is a wry touch that the Lord, like a thief who has been found out (Exod 21:4), repays Job double what he took away."
269 Newsom, "The Book of Job," 635, writes: "without knowing more about the conventions of storytelling in ancient Israel, it is difficult to say whether such 'outrageous' features are supposed to be accepted simply as part of the way one tells a story like this, or whether the author is subtly using this detail to make readers uncomfortable with a story that they would otherwise accept without question."
270 Newsom, "The Book of Job," 636.
271 David J. A. Clines, "Deconstructing the Book of Job," in *The Bible as Rhetoric: Studies in Biblical Persuasion and Credibility* (ed. Martin Warner; London: Routledge 1990), 70, 72.
272 So, Newsom, "The Book of Job," 634. Peter P. Zerafa, *The Wisdom of God in the Book of Job* (Rome: Herder, 1978), 40, posits a lost dialogue in which the friends might have tried to pose as God's friends but were disavowed by God. He concludes that the friends had probably urged Job to curse God, which explains why they are rebuked in 42:7.
273 So, Michael P. Gillespie, *The Aesthetics of Chaos: Nonlinear Thinking and Contemporary Literary Criticism* (Florida: University of Florida Press, 2003), 85.

interpreter of the Epilogue is one of both form and content; that is, how do the prosaic form and the content of the Epilogue meaningfully respond to the diverse and conflicting voices expressed in the Prologue and Dialogues? Does the Epilogue contradict and ignore the challenge to the doctrine of retribution expounded in the Dialogues and finally turn out to be anticlimactic,[274] or does the Epilogue attempt to redeem the impatient Job of the Dialogues,[275] or does the Epilogue incorporate and transcend both the Dialogues and the Prologue?

In the next chapter, I will propose a hermeneutic for interpreting the Epilogue that attempts to do justice to the literary and theological resonance and dissonance between the Epilogue and the preceding sections of the book. I will suggest that such a hermeneutic ought not just to highlight the resonance or dissonance between the Epilogue and the preceding sections, but also the way in which these differences and similarities are brought together to constitute the form and content of the Epilogue.

2.6 Summary Conclusion

The foregoing analysis has highlighted a number of issues related to the interpretation of the Epilogue. First, there are a number of substantive dissonances between the Epilogue and the preceding sections of the book. For example, Job is approved in the Epilogue and this stands in tension with his rebuke in the divine speeches. Also, the human experience of the transcendent God of the poetic section stands in tension with the "accessible" God of the prose section. Furthermore, the moral view of retributive justice in the prose section of the book is challenged by the discussion in the poetic section. Second, some of these dissonances within the overall structure of the book can partly be explained as a result of the compositional history of the text. That is, the final form of the text is probably a result of a history of composition in which new perceptions and expressions of reality were placed alongside older ones. This combination is perhaps best illustrated in the fact that the narrator brings together sacrifice and prayer in the formulation about the cultic activity in the Epilogue. We have seen that part of the dissonance between the prose and the poetic section is demonstrated in the portrayal of

---

[274] Athalya Brenner, "Job the Pious? The Characterization of Job in the Narrative Framework of the Book," *JSOT* 43 (1989): 45–46, argues that the way in which the epilogue unfolds sabotages its own credibility in much the same way that the prologue negates itself. Brenner writes: "How can the sacrificial activity and prayer offered by Job on behalf of his friends (42:8–9) be religiously more effective than Job's own sacrifice in the prologue?... The seeming 'happy' ending, perhaps appropriate to the source tale, is ironic when it follows the poem." Similarly, K. Fullerton, "The Original Conclusion," 126, argues that the Epilogue actually "ruins the book artistically," and is "out of spiritual harmony with the Dialogue."

[275] Zuckermann, *Job the Silent*, 57, writes: "if Job superficially seems to be impatient and questioning, then perhaps, encapsulated within the framework of the traditional Joban legend, Anti-Job could once more be converted into Job the Silent."

human access to the deity; sacrifice in the prose Prologue and prayer in the poetic section. While sacrifices function to prevent the deity from acting in a particular, presumably punitive manner, prayer, on the other hand, functions within the poetic section as part of the process of restoration. In the Epilogue, both sacrifice and prayer are brought together, as the friends offer sacrifices and Job prays for them.

Beyond the recognition of such issues of compositional history, the interpretation of the final form of the text is what has been of particular concern to me. The interpretive question, then, has been whether one can read the text in its final form in a way that draws upon the insights of historical criticism but also attempts to do justice to the final form of the text? A survey of the history of interpretation of the Epilogue lays the groundwork for embarking on such an endeavor. In the next chapter, I will propose that the reader can, in the case of the Epilogue of Job, be attentive to the interpretive implications of historical-critical analysis while reading the text in its final form.

Chapter 3: Revisiting the Epilogue

Critical analysis of the Epilogue indicates that there are substantive dissonances between the Epilogue and the preceding poetic section. Given the credibility of these arguments raised in the previous chapter, one wonders whether the final editor placed the Epilogue where it is for nothing. If the character of Job in the Dialogues has progressively and successfully dismantled the theological rationale associated with the nature of retribution in the Prologue, what does the Epilogue again serve by seeming to return to this naïve state of rewards for the righteous and (threat of) punishment for the wicked? Hermeneutically, one may ask: does Job again worship God for naught? Is Job again approved for naught? On the other hand, do the friends defend God in the Dialogues for naught? Is Job's challenge of the traditional understanding of retributive justice in the Dialogues for naught? Here it seems to me that the answer to all these questions is a definite "no." The divine approval of Job and the rebuke of the friends serve to respond not only to issues raised in the Prologue (where retribution works until it is bypassed because of the decision by God and the Adversary to subject Job to trial), but also in the Dialogues (where the efficacy of the doctrine is seriously challenged and its limitations exposed).

In the development of the account, Job's story has also become the story of the friends.[276] That is, although the initial purpose of the attack on Job was to provoke Job to speak "to/about" God, the divine rebuke of the friends for not speaking rightly "to/about" God as Job has suggests that the friends (perhaps in a sub-plot of the book) are involved in the story's development and outcome. In the dynamic of the exchange between Job and his friends, they have represented the counter-testimony[277] to Job's expression of frustration with the system of retribution, as they have maintained that God is after all responsible and just. Carol Newsom thus rightly argues for the need to "rehabilitate" the friends in order to appreciate the strength of their arguments[278] – arguments that are deeply entrenched in Israelite religious

---

276 See, Roland E. Murphy, *The Tree of Life: An Exploration of Biblical Wisdom Literature* (2nd ed.; Grand Rapids, Mich.: William B. Eerdmans, 1996), 44–45.
277 The idea of testimony and counter-testimony is credited to Walter Brueggemann, *Theology of the Old Testament: Testimony, Dispute, Advocacy* (Minneapolis: Fortress, 1997).
278 Carol A. Newsom, "Job and His Friends: A Conflict of Moral Imaginations," *Int* 53 (1999): 241–242, writes about Eliphaz's opening discourse: "His narratives strategically privilege endings over beginnings. They are thus not stories of explanation but stories for the projection of a future. They serve to configure situations as open rather than closed. By opening up the space of a possible future, they are narratives of hope."

traditions. Through the friends' arguments, the retributive aspect of the divine-human relationship has persisted through the Dialogues into the Epilogue, where the narrator now uses it both in the divine rebuke and the restoration itself.[279] Consequently, what we have in the Epilogue is a situation where both Job and his friends move beyond their respective positions in the Prologue-Dialogues to some amount of conclusion and stability.[280] As such, there is some positive value that the Epilogue (as reconciliation and restoration) brings to the interpretation of the book, without which a significant aspect of its meaning is lost.[281]

3.1 Proposed Hermeneutic

As has been shown above, critical analysis of the text begins with the recognition of the differences between the prose and poetic sections of the book, and how the character of Job in the prose section is starkly different from that in the poetic section. Part of the basic question that underlies the focus on these differences is whether one is dealing with the same Job. In other words, what is it that allows the interpreter to assume or determine that one is dealing with the same character, rather than two Jobs? The larger hermeneutical issue here is that for historical-critical and literary-critical analyses, the final form of the text, which presents the story as that of a single individual, requires that the interpreter be able to establish some basic literary and thematic features that demonstrate that one is dealing with a single character in the prose and poetic sections of the book. In an ironic way, the credibility of critical work in identifying and even isolating different portions

---

Newsom presents a more developed argument in *The Book of Job: A Contest of Moral Imaginations*, 90–129. God's great acts (נפלאות) about which Eliphaz speaks (Job 5:9) are not new to Israelite theology (cf. Pss 71:19; 136:4; 145:3; Deut 10:21; Is 40:28). It is about these very acts that Job will later admit having spoken without knowledge (42:3), just before his restoration.

279 Clines, *Job 1-20*, 145, 147 writes: "The reversal of outward fortune or estate is a motif greatly beloved by biblical doxologists. The note of hope on which this doxology concludes evidences again Eliphaz's general attitude toward Job. As a righteous, though necessarily imperfect, human creature, Job can look to God as the reverser of fortunes to release him from his unhappy situation."

280 As I have argued above under my exegesis of 42:9, Job and his friends are closely related here; it is not a matter of either-or, either Job or his friends, but rather a matter of both-and. Although the Adversary had posed the issue of retributive religion in exclusive terms of either-or, and the friends and Job had largely continued along those lines, the narrator now combines the two aspects of the divine-human relationship, namely, retribution and its limitation.

281 William R. Thickstun, *Visionary Closure in the Modern Novel* (London: MacMillan, 1988), 39, notes that when one reaches the conclusion of a novel, "the problem of hinting at a centre of meaning which remains inaccessible to language becomes particularly acute," because much of a novel's strength lies "in its continual series of detours around an unseen centre, as narrative strategies and intellectual themes are repeatedly tried out and then rejected." Yet, "the process of deferral cannot continue indefinitely."

of the book and treating them as such partly lies on an antecedent credibility of the final form of the text. For there is a sense in which, without credible literary and thematic features that hold the Job of the prose and poetic sections together in the final form of the text, one may not really speak of dissonances between the characters of Job in the prose and poetic section, but rather of different Jobs altogether.

Accordingly, my analysis of the Epilogue will seek to argue that the hermeneutical value of the Epilogue lies in its demonstration that no single perception of the relationship between the deity and humankind is sufficient. Neither the moral and theological value of retributive justice nor that of its limitation (both expressed in the prose and poetic sections of the book) is enough; both are needed in dynamic tension.[282] Accordingly, the confrontational model of interpretation that has sometimes been used to pit Job against his friends explores only part of the problem. A different approach is proposed here – one that transcends the confrontational model and builds on the respective positions held by Job and his friends. Thus the Epilogue, to use Dennis Olson's description of the value of Deuteronomy, "holds together law and human responsibility with promise and divine mercy," and "ought to accommodate plurality while also finding a common center."[283] To demonstrate this hermeneutical strategy, I will examine how the Epilogue is related to the Prologue and to the Dialogues; then I will show how the Epilogue is at dissonance with both the Prologue and the Dialogues; finally, I will argue that the Epilogue, in its form and content, draws significantly from both the Prologue and Dialogues, but also transcends both. It is this ability of the Epilogue to rise above the preceding sections that illustrates the uniqueness of the Epilogue and contributes to its significance for reading and interpreting the book.

3.1.1 The Literary and Thematic Function of the Epilogue

Although scholars differ in opinion with regard to the nature and extent to which the Epilogue adequately responds to the various moral and theological problems raised in the preceding sections of the book, there appears to be no doubt that the narrator attempts to do just that – that is, bring the book to an end.[284] To anticipate what I shall develop in greater detail later, one notes that unlike the prose Prologue and the poetic Dialogues, the Epilogue is a series of speeches expressed in turns by the narrator and YHWH. This artistic

---

[282] See, John C. L. Gibson, *Job* (Philadelphia: Westminster, 1985), 264–266.
[283] Dennis T. Olson, *Deuteronomy and the Death of Moses: A Theological Reading* (Minneapolis: Fortress, 1994), 3, 4.
[284] Frank Kermode, *The Sense of an Ending* (Oxford: Oxford University Press, 1966), 12, remarks that it is "one of the great charms of books that they have to end." What the Epilogue does is that it brings the literary work to an end, but not necessarily to an interpretive end.

feature of the text is significant because of the diverse voices expressed in the Prologue and Dialogues. At the end of the book, the "polyphonic" character of the text is being reframed, as God's voice from the whirlwind continues.[285]

In bringing the work to a literary end, the narrator has the entire scope of Job's experience in view. After presenting the protagonist with the fourfold characterization in 1:1, followed by a concrete representation of that special status of his (1:2), the narrator takes the reader to the heavenly council where God and the Adversary agree that Job's piety will be tested only after God touches "all that belongs to him," (1:11) and "all that belongs to a person" (2:4). This refers to the attacks on Job's possessions and health respectively. That is, Job is touched with respect to the material and the immaterial aspects of his life. In the Epilogue, the narrator has this scope of the problem in view, for God is said to restore "all that Job had" (42:10), which again refers to his material and immaterial status.[286] Thus, with respect to the scope of Job's experience, the Epilogue seeks to address it in full.

But what about the details of Job's experience? How does the Epilogue respond to them? In interpreting the Epilogue, attention has to be given to as much detail as possible. This means looking at the differences and similarities between the Epilogue and the preceding sections. Only by identifying such differences and similarities, and showing how important they are will the literary and thematic function of the Epilogue be further determined and illustrated.

3.1.1.1 The Epilogue and the Prologue

After several chapters of complex poetry in the Dialogues, inter-spaced with brief prose (27:1; 29:1; 32:1–6), the reader comes to the Epilogue, which, like the Prologue, is written, in simple clear prose.[287] Because the historical-critical method isolates the poetry and prose, it is often easy to see the Epilogue as having little, if any difference vis-à-vis the Prologue. Of course,

---

285 Mattitiahu Tsevat, "The Meaning of the Book of Job," in *Sitting with Job: Selected Studies on the Book of Job* (ed. Roy B. Zuck; Grand Rapids, Mich.: Baker, 1992), 196, argues that if the last chapter does not provide an answer, then the book will constitute "a literary torso, an anthology of verbalized doubts; it would betray an utter lack of appreciation of the controlling conceptions which are everywhere in evidence in the work." Since the monophonic character of the Epilogue engages the polyphony of the Dialogues, one is to expect that such "answers" will necessarily be provisional and multidimensional.
286 I use "immaterial" here to refer to the attack on Job's body in the second round of attack, leading up to the soliloquy in chapter three and the debate in the Dialogue.
287 In his description of Hebrew narrative, Robert Alter speaks of a "rhythm" that alternates between dialogue and narration. He writes: "beginning with narration, they [the Hebrew writers] move into dialogue, drawing back momentarily or at length to narrate again, but always centering on the sharply salient verbal intercourse of the characters, who act upon one another, discover themselves, affirm or expose their relation to God, through the force of language." Robert Alter, *The Art of Biblical Narrative* (New York: Basic Books, 1981), 75.

there are good reasons to associate the Epilogue with the Prologue, for the literary similarities between these two parts are quite obvious. For instance, (a) God refers to Job as "my servant" (42:7, 8), a characterization that is closely related with God's approval of Job's religious life (cf.1:8; 2:3); (b) the setting is that of the patriarchal period where wealth is measured in terms of livestock and sacrifices are offered to God by family heads (42:12, 9 // 1:3, 5); (c) as God's servant, Job can effectively intercede on behalf of those who (may) have wronged God (42:8–9 // 1:5); and (d) people come around him to show their grief and comfort him (42:11 // 2:11).[288]

Precisely because of this close affinity with the Prologue, it is important to be attentive to the differences between the Epilogue and the Prologue. The reader or interpreter of the text progressively processes information about the characters, and, in the course of doing that, constructs a "situation model," that is, a mental representation of the situation described by the text.[289] In the process of reading, van Oostendorp argues, a number of things may happen. First, there is the "skipping hypothesis" – that is, readers may skip new information because they erroneously think they already possess the relevant information; and second, there is the "rejection hypothesis" – that is, new information may be rejected because the information the readers have relating to their situation model is hard to change even if the text requires this change. Such readers actively hold onto the first perspective once it is established. Van Oostendorp concludes: "a situation model is not something static, but a mental representation that is in constant flow, adapting itself dynamically to new, incoming information."[290] Consequently, any new information or different portrayal of a previous situation, any modification or expansion or retraction of a previous idea become crucial because it is these new nuances that constitute the content of the new situation model and characterize the unique dimension of the current experience of reading.

With this in mind, and having examined the resonances between the Epilogue and the Prologue, one must also examine how the Epilogue both attempts to bring the story to an end as well as carry it further beyond the Prologue. That is, it is important to show the dissonances between the Prologue and Epilogue, those features in the text that reveal how the Epilogue modifies, transforms, or transcends the Prologue. A number of points are worth noting: (a) there is the absence of the divine council and with it the Adversary. Although the image of the Adversary is historically late,[291] his

---

288 For further analysis of the literary links between the Prologue, Dialogues, and Epilogue, see Susan F. Mathew, "All for Nought: My Servant Job," in *The Bible on Suffering: Social and Political Implications* (ed. Anthony J. Tambasco; New York: Paulist, 2001), 51–57.
289 See, Herre van Oostendorp, "Holding onto Established Viewpoints during Processing News Reports," in *New Perspectives on Narrative Perspective* (ed. Willie van Peer and Seymour Chatman; New York: State University of New York Press, 2001), 173.
290 Van Oostendorp, "Holding onto Established Viewpoints," 175.
291 See, Hurvitz, "The Date of the Prose-Tale of Job," 19–20; Syring, *Hiob und sein Anwalt*, 91–95.

presence within the text as a narrative character is significant.[292] Accordingly, his absence from the Epilogue necessitates comment;[293] (b) among the human assembly, one finds the introduction of new family members (Job's brothers and sisters) coming to console him, perhaps alluding to the importance of family members in post disaster consolation (cf. Ezek 14:22); (c) Job's wife is silent, and this silence creates an interpretive "gap." On the one hand, her silence "eliminates" her ambiguous words (2:9) that reflect God's approval of Job in 2:3, the uncertainty that Job had about his children, and the Adversary's idea of 'blessing' God while under pressure.[294] On the other hand, her silence may also mean that her words in 2:9 are left unmodified with all their ambiguity, and stand in tension with Job's response in 2:10; and (d) Job does not speak; in fact, the reader is completely deprived of any information about the protagonist's words or even thoughts (contrast 1:5).[295] This creates another interpretive "gap," inviting the reader into the final moments of the narrative in a significant way.[296]

What all these literary features together as a cluster indicate is that although the Epilogue draws significantly from the Prologue (thereby creating the necessary context and sense of literary familiarity and stability), the Epilogue also modifies that material, thereby moving the narrative

---

292 Carol Newsom, "The Book of Job," 348, describes the Adversary as "the externalizing of divine doubt about the human heart." In this light, see the Chronicler's use of the Adversary to describe what is elsewhere a manifestation of divine anger (1 Chron. 21:1 // 2 Sam 24:1). Elsewhere in "Narrative Ethics, Character, and the Prose Tale of Job," 129, Newsom draws upon the work of Emmanuel Levinas and Zachary Newton to argue that ha-satan represents interrupted speech. That is, the Adversary's words are "interpreted as 'Saying' which interrupt God's 'Said.'"

293 Zuckerman, *Job The Silent*, 27, argues: "since it was the Satan's challenge to God that set in motion all the action of the Job story, one expects him to play at least some role in the story's conclusion. The story almost demands that God direct some comment towards the Satan, and the fact that no such comment is forthcoming constitutes a rather glaring loose end." However, if the Adversary is simply the hypostasis of divine doubt, then his absence suggests the suppression or elimination of that doubt. From the point of view of plot structure, this would be fitting for the conclusion.

294 Although her words in 2:9 (עדך מחזיק בתמתך) have traditionally been construed as an unmarked interrogative ("are you still holding onto your integrity?"), it is worth noting that she echoes God's word in 2:3 rather significantly: ועדנו מחזיק בתמתו ("he still holds onto his integrity.") Like God's, her words are unmarked as an interrogation. Though the explicit marker of interrogation is not always used in Hebrew, one may note that the narrator has used it before (1:8; 2:3). Thus, its omission in 2:9 may be deliberate and leaves the text open. Her use of ברך (with Job as the subject) and immediate association of the word with death, however, also echoes the Adversary's idea (1:11; 2:5) as well as Job's uncertainty about his children's possible sin (1:5).

295 In the entire narrative, the reader's perception of Job's character is fostered in two ways: through the narrator, a process that Dan Shen calls "external focalization" and through direct interaction with the protagonist, when Job speaks, what Shen calls "internal focalization." See Dan Shen, "Breaking Conventional Barriers," in *New Perspectives on Narrative Perspective* (ed. Willie van Peer and Seymour Chatman; New York: State University of New York Press, 2001), 167–169.

296 Perhaps at the end of the book, it is less about what Job and his wife think and feel, and more about what every reader thinks and feels, as has been shown from the history of interpretation.

forward. The character of Job that emerges even within the limited context of the prose section is dynamic and complex; it is a character that interacts with and is shaped by the different literary and thematic contexts in which he is found. But it is character that also contributes in shaping the themes and other characters in the text. As such, the Epilogue is both closure and openness.[297]

3.1.1.2 The Epilogue and the Human Discussion

There has been less interest among scholars in determining the affinities between the Epilogue and the Dialogue for the obvious reason that the dissonances between these two sections of the book are more glaring.[298] Nevertheless, it is crucial to examine the resonances between the Epilogue and Dialogue (some of which are simply linguistic or thematic echoes), for only by doing that will the strength of the dissonances be further highlighted and their significance more fruitful. These similarities include the following: (a) the rebuke of the friends for not speaking rightly (נכונה – 42:7) places the Epilogue in conversation with the Dialogues given that it is in the Dialogues that the friends articulate their ideas. Moreover, the root כון is used elsewhere only in the dialogues;[299] (b) the use of the idiom "to lift the face" (42:8, 9) also resonates with the Dialogues because it occurs elsewhere only in the Dialogues, where it is raised and discussed (11:15; 13:8, 10; 22:8; 34:19); (c) the idiomatic expression depicting the divine reaction to the friends, "my anger is kindled against you," (42:7) is found elsewhere in the book only in the exchange between Job and his human counterparts, specifically in Elihu's speech (32: 2, 3, 5); (d) the reference to Job's former life in comparison to the latter (42:12) exactly recalls Bildad's words in 8:7; (e) mention of Job's brothers, sisters, and former acquaintances gathering around him to comfort and console him (42:11) recalls and contrasts 19:13 where Job's family and acquaintances desert him; and (f) the fact that Job's daughters inherit property recalls the Dialogues where the concept of inheritance (נחלה) is discussed (20:29; 27:13; 31:2). Associated with the idea of inheritance is Job's acquisition of riches, particularly gold, which recalls the discussion about gold and silver in 27:16 and chapter 28. Taken together, all these echoes and resonances provide linguistic and, to some extent,

---

297 On the "openness" and "closure" of a text, see Mark C. Taylor, *Erring: A Postmodern A/Theology* (Chicago: University of Chicago Press, 1984), 74–93.
298 One should, however, note the recent work of Yohan Pyeong, *You Have Not Spoken What is Right About Me: Intertextuality and the Book of Job* (ed. Hemchand Gossai; Studies in Biblical Literature 45; New York: Peter Lang, 2003), who has argued that the divine approval of Job in 42:7–8 should be understood in light of the Dialogues. Pyeong focuses particularly on the first cycle of Dialogues and the possible religious traditions that underlie the Dialogues.
299 See 8:8; 11:13; 12:5; 15:23, 35; 18:12; 21:8; 27:16, 17; 31:15; 38:41. Particularly noteworthy is the use of the form נכון by Job (12:5 and 21:8), Bildad (18:12), and Eliphaz (15:23) to articulate their various perspectives on retributive justice, all within the context of the Dialogues.

thematic bases for creating a conversation between the Epilogue and the Dialogues as part of the interpretive process.

In spite of these echoes and similarities, there are differences too: (a) as is widely recognized, the divine approval of Job in 42:7 stands in tension with the rebuke in the theophany; (b) God's character in the Epilogue as one who brings trouble upon Job stands in tension with God's self-portrayed image in the divine speeches where God (very much like the friends) rebukes Job for trying to misconstrue the divine character in order to appear righteous (40:8); and (c) although the idiom "to lift the face" is used in the Dialogues, it is never used with God as subject; in fact, God does not lift the face of humans, specifically princes (34:19). The sense in which the expression is used in the Epilogue is thus a reversal of its use in the Dialogues. As we shall see, the concept of inheritance in the Epilogue is also used in a manner that is different from the Dialogues. All these similarities and differences suggest that the narrator uses language and concepts that echo the human discussion, but in doing so the narrator sometimes reverses the sense in which that language and those concepts are employed in the human discussion.

While the differences between the Epilogue and the Prologue may be broadly viewed within the framework of a linear progression (the differences are mostly additions, subtractions, and some modifications), the differences between the Epilogue and the Dialogues are in the form of contrasts or reversals (the Epilogue reverses the sense in which the concepts taken from the Dialogues are used), although this characterization should not be overdrawn.

3.1.1.3 Beyond the Prologue and the Dialogue

In interpreting the Epilogue, there are generally two trends that can largely be characterized as synchronic and diachronic. The first attempts to harmonize the Epilogue with the Prologue and, from that interpretive frame, hammer the discordant voices in the poetic section and the modifications of the prose section into a uniform whole. The result is that the dissonances between the Epilogue and the preceding sections are downplayed. Meir Sternberg, for instance, describes the tension between the prose Prologue and the Dialogues as an "apparent contradiction" that is resolved in the divine approval in the Epilogue. Sternberg writes:

> "Job acts counter to expectation not despite but because of the qualities specified on his first appearance; and his character gains in complexity not by appeal to new factors but to the new and newly assessed manifestations of the old.... The dissonance here is more illusory than real, laudatory rather than ironic, intended not

just to modify our view of a certain righteous man but to redefine the concept of righteousness itself."[300]

Worth noting here is the fact that Sternberg recognizes the dissonance between the character of Job in the poetic and prose sections. But this dissonance is described as more "illusory" than "real" and more "laudatory" than "ironic." The element of continuity in the presentation of the character is enhanced, so that even though Job gains in complexity, what one finds at the end are not new factors, but a "newly assessed manifestation of the old."

The second trend that highlights the dissonances tends to argue for the polyphonic character of the text and its open-endedness. Carol Newsom articulates this strategy as follows:

> "God's speech from the whirlwind offers yet another, strikingly different moral imagination, one that simultaneously challenges the friends' narratives and practices as well as Job's moral answerability. Far from resolving all questions, the divine speeches invite the reader to construct a further dialogue in which all three ways of apprehending the world might be set in conversation.[301]

According to this strategy, not only do Job and his friends offer different moral imaginations for dealing with the problem of innocent suffering, but also God's speech adds to the different perceptions of reality. Furthermore, the interpretive issues are not fully resolved; rather they are placed in conversation, with the possibility of creating significantly different conclusions about the definition and nature of righteousness and the appropriate human response to the problem of suffering at the hand of the deity. My proposal here is that an interpretation of the Epilogue should endeavor to combine aspects of the synchronic and diachronic approaches. As has been shown above, the Epilogue is both at some resonance and dissonance with each of the preceding sections of the book. It is, however, not enough simply to speak of resonances and dissonances within the book and how they may represent a "newly assessed manifestation of the old" or different traditions or perceptions of reality. One must further inquire into the possible *raison d'être* of putting these resonances and dissonances together in the Epilogue, with the understanding that the whole is greater than the sum of its parts.[302] This interpretive strategy is suggested by the fact that even though

---

300 Meir Sternberg, *The Poetics of Biblical Narrative: Ideological Literature and the Drama of Reading* (ed. Herbert Marks and Robert Polzin; Indiana Studies in Biblical Literature; Bloomington, Ind.: Indiana University Press, 1985), 346. See also M. Greenberg, "Job," in *The Literary Guide to the Bible* (ed. Robert Alter and Frank Kermode; Cambridge, Mass.: Harvard University Press, 1987), 285–286.
301 See Carol Newsom, "Job and his Friends," 253; idem, "Cultural Politics in the Book of Job," *BibInt* 1 (1993): 119–134. See also Rick D. Moore, "The Integrity of Job," *CBQ* 45 (1983): 31: "The poet has denied integrity to his character, and we should deny thematic integrity to the book."
302 As Habel notes about the author of the book, "It is a mark of creative genius that this author rarely appropriates literary forms or genres in their ideal traditional form. Rather, they are adapted, modified, and transformed to meet particular artistic and theological ends." Norman C. Habel, "Literary Features and the Message of the Book of Job," in

the Epilogue is a series of alternating monologues, its formulations about the divine approval of Job, rebuke of the friends and restoration of Job all echo the preceding sections of the book where dialogue is prominent. My interpretive dynamic emerges as three-dimensional: inwards towards the center in search of unity; outwards towards other experiences in search of diversity; and finally, forward towards the transcendent in search of meaning.

This interpretive strategy will be further illustrated by reference to Michael Gillespie's description of folktales. In his study of folktales, Michael Gillespie finds that they consistently represent some form of struggle. Gillespie argues that folklore "represents the rudimentary values and fundamental conflicts of the culture. It stands as the oldest example of a literary tradition, and it acts as the foundation of all that supersedes it."[303] This feature of folklore is created by what Gillespie calls "the deft juxtaposition of the quotidian and the bizarre."[304] Three things are significant for my purposes here: (a) the element of conflict that appears in folklore, often created by the unfamiliar or bizarre features of the text; (b) the element of familiarity or the quotidian in folklore that provides the sense of security and continuity; and (c) the idea that in the interaction between the quotidian and the bizarre, folklore becomes the foundation for that which supercedes it. The combination of these three factors indicates that while representing the "chaotic" or conflicting character of the culture, folklore is paradoxically the foundation for the development of culture. Whereas the quotidian is familiar, the bizarre is unfamiliar and sometimes even uncanny; whereas the familiar provides a sense of stability in the midst of the fluctuations and chaos of life, the bizarre represents the untamable and mysterious component of the story that captures the readers' imagination and brings them into new experiences. Only through continuous combination of both the familiar and the bizarre is folklore developed in a meaningful way.[305] The result of this interpretive process is increasing stability (as new situations and experiences are interpreted and appropriated into the domain of the familiar) and increasing open-endedness (as more of the familiar is continually taken up into interaction with the mysterious). For the Epilogue, this triple aspect of folklore is preserved through the narrator's ability to describe Job's current situation in terms that incorporate, confirm, modify, contrast, and finally transcend the Prologue and Dialogues.

Sitting with Job: Selected Studies on the Book of Job (ed. Roy B. Zuck; Grand Rapids, Mich.: Baker, 1992), 98.
303 Gillespie, *Aesthetics of Chaos*, 44.
304 Gillespie, *Aesthetics of Chaos*, 49.
305 Gillespie, *Aesthetics of Chaos*, 56, focuses on the bizarre and argues that it points to unconventionality in traditional interpretation, and ultimately frees the reader from the burden of constructing arguments that offer moral justification for behavior. I would argue that folklore by its very nature is traditionally expected to have some "moral lesson." The danger for the reader, however, is with any attempt to transform a circumstantial characterization into a permanent or static evaluation.

Such a conceptual frame of interpretation is not unique to the Epilogue of Job. Probably at the climax of his several "better than" sayings in chapter seven, Qoheleth states: טוֹב אַחֲרִית דָּבָר מֵרֵאשִׁיתוֹ – "The end/latter part of a thing/matter is better than its beginning/former part." (Eccl 7:8) These words, especially the juxtaposition of "former" and "latter," immediately resonate with two texts in Job: Bildad's words in 8:7 and even more so the narrator's in 42:12a where we read that וַיהוָה בֵּרַךְ אֶת אַחֲרִית אִיּוֹב מֵרֵאשִׁתוֹ ("the Lord blessed the latter part of Job more than his former").[306] This evaluation, which not only compares Job's former life with his latter but also depicts the latter in qualitatively superior terms over the former, appears to be a theological cliché employed to describe the "happy" ending, and is made exactly midway into the Epilogue.[307] This immediately raises the question: what is it that separates the two poles of Job's life and thereby makes a comparison possible? The doubling of his property listed immediately after 42:12 suggests that the issue revolves around Job's loss of his possessions in the Prologue.[308] But another distinction is also signaled in 42:9, where Job is performing the task of intercessor for his friends. Accordingly, the better latter part of Job's life is already signaled in the first part of the Epilogue. In fact, Job intercedes not only to reconcile his friends with God, but also to prevent God from dealing outrageously with the friends.[309] His prayers are both reconciliatory (benefiting the friends) and preventive (stopping God from acting in a particular manner). Unlike in the Prologue where Job's

---

306 Qoheleth makes his declaration within a literary and theological context that deals with human limitation and divine sovereignty, stating that God does both good and bad (an idea that Rashi linked to Job 1:22 and 2:10), and no one can find fault with God (lit. "after him" – Eccl 6:12; 7:14). Similarly, Bildad talks about the former and latter times within a literary and theological context that emphasizes human limitations (Job 8:9), and divine sovereignty (8:5– 6) and freedom from moral fault (8:3, 20).
307 John McIntyre, *Theology After the Storm: The Humanity of Christ, Theology of Prayer, The Cliché as a Theological Medium* (Cambridge: Eerdmans, 1997), 264, argues that, "it would be wrong to abandon the cliché, for it would not have passed into theological folklore had it not originally contained a fair degree of commonsense as well as theological truth." Thus the task of "assessing the cliché as a medium of theological expression takes on a more involved complexion ... as it becomes necessary to judge, on the one hand, what credibility is to be assigned to the initial cliché, and, on the other, when a perfectly acceptable concept has begun to wear thin, or is discovered to contain elements which require closer consideration than was at first thought necessary."
308 In his article, "Theodicy in a Social Dimension," *JSOT* 33 (1985): 14, Walter Brueggemann argues that the book of Job is framed around the idea of loss and restoration, and that in this instance the focus is precisely on land, signaled by the mention in v.15 of Job's daughters having inheritance. Inheritance here in the Epilogue thus parallels possessions in 1:10.
309 Moore, "Raw Prayer and Refined Theology," 43, has proposed that the book is framed by prayer (1:5; 42:8). Similarly, Balentine, "My Servant Job Shall Pray for You," 502–518, has discussed Job's two intercessions in 1:5 and 42:8 under the categories of "conventional" (where Job prays for other humans) and "unconventional" (where he prays to stop God from acting against the friends) views of intercession, and concluded that both models are important for the community of faith: "There is something not only important but perhaps imperative – for the world and for God – in having someone like Job who risks praying like a מוֹכִיחַ for a restoration of the afflicted that transforms heaven and earth."

prayers for his children essentially deal with the human potential to sin against God, the narrator here suggests that God is facing the possibility of doing an "outrageous" act, and Job's intercessions will go to prevent that. Bildad was right; Job's latter life is turning out to be very great.

Between Job's former and latter lives stands his traumatic experience of loss and pain, depicted vividly in the Prologue and Dialogues. This loss and pain is part of the reason why Job's life is now depicted in terms of "former" and "latter." It cannot be ignored without losing a significant thrust of the book. The governing word or theme that the narrator uses to link the two parts of Job's life is exactly the word that has been crucial all along – ברך.[310] Thus, just as Job's former life was blessed by God (1:10), so too his latter life is anchored in divine blessing (42:12). The Epilogue thus looks back on Job's former life, not so much to imitate or reenact it but to surpass or transcend it. There is, on the one hand, an element of constancy in the entire account, namely, the role of the word ברך in the divine-human relationship. While this word provides spiritual and economic security for Job, it also contains the ingredient for potential debate (1:10) and ultimately for progress (42:12). In the Epilogue, the reality of progress is indicated by the use of the comparative preposition מן in the word מראשתו. In his former life, Job was greater than all the sons of the east (1:3); now his latter life is even greater.

This "more than" perspective from which the Epilogue looks back allows the narrator to do two things: (a) it allows the narrator to introduce God's qualitative and moral verdict on the preceding sections (42:7, 8), which paradoxically creates dissonance with the Dialogues, especially with the divine rebuke of Job in the theophany; and (b) it also allows the narrator to quantitatively describe Job's exceptional riches/possessions as well as his extended lifespan (42:12b–17). Therefore, there is both continuity and discontinuity between the Epilogue and the preceding sections, or to use Bildad's and the narrator's language, between Job's former and latter life. But this resonance-dissonance dynamic has been placed within a literary and theological context that is described as "more than," thus allowing one to preserve and develop that resonance-dissonance tension. A proper interpretation of the Epilogue should bear this new reality in mind. Precisely at this point in the narrative, the hermeneutical divide that the Epilogue presents for interpreting the book is twofold: (a) it revolves not only around noting the similarities and differences between the Epilogue and the

---

310 Meir Weiss, *The Story of Job's Beginning: Job 1-2: A Literary Analysis* (Jerusalem: Magnes, 1983), 61, notes that there are six occurrences of ברך in the Prologue, and the seventh occurrence is in the Epilogue, thus contributing to the integrity of the book. The verb occurs once in the Dialogues (29:13), but that is within a context of Job's nostalgia for the former times. As Carol Newsom, "The Book of Job: Introduction, Commentary, and Reflections," 346, rightly notes, each of the seven times that the word occurs in the prose tale (1:5, 10, 11, 21; 2:5, 9; 42:12), the reader must negotiate its meaning. In the present context of 42:12, the verb is used with God as the subject – this being only the second time that it is used with God as subject (the other time being 1:10). Since it is used positively in 1:10, the same likely applies here.

preceding sections, and highlighting them but also (b) around combining the similarities *and* differences between the Epilogue and the preceding sections and showing how they now transcend the preceding sections. The Epilogue has drawn and (re)used significant material from the Prologue and Dialogues and, in so doing, has preserved the major voices from the preceding sections and created new interpretive avenues. The resonances create narrative stability and the dissonances create narrative complexity. Together, within the literary and theological framework described as "more than," the new hermeneutical grid is the interaction between Job's former and his better latter life, predicted by Bildad (retribution), ensured by the divine blessing (pro and beyond retribution), challenged by Job in his protest and laments (counter strict retribution), and finally presented by the narrator at the end of the book (interaction between retribution and its suspension).[311]

The apparent naïveté of the Epilogue, especially the divine approval of Job, becomes a significant factor. The credibility of the divergent voices in the Prologue and Job's discordant utterances in the Dialogues is ultimately anchored in the fact that they are approved and refined through the divine response and verdict at the end; that is, they can no longer be perceived simply as human thoughts or as counter God, for now they receive divine approval, though limited they may be. It is, therefore, possible to apply Qoheleth's rationale about "the end of a matter" to the book of Job. Only through such a model or hermeneutic can one do justice to the elements of constancy, diversity, and change within the narrative. In the same way that the Prologue is not naïve or simplistic[312] and the poetic section is diverse and complex but also significantly consistent, so too the Epilogue is far from naïve and far from being a tease. It is an appropriate endeavor by the narrator to bring about some amount of positive resolution or closure, albeit partial, to the book. This provisional conclusion is recognized as a necessary tool in reading and writing.[313] On careful examination, the Epilogue demonstrates

---

311 Robert P. Carroll, "Postscript to Job," *MC* 19 (1976): 161, notes that if the divine approval of Job in the Epilogue is allowed to carry maximal content, "then it would open up a wide range of reference."
312 This point has been adequately made by David J. A. Clines, "False Naivety in the Prologue of Job," *HAR* 9 (1985): 127–136. See also Alan Cooper, "Reading and Misreading the Prologue to Job," *JSOT* 46 (1990): 69–79; idem, "Narrative Theory and the Book of Job," *SR* 11 (1982): 35–44.
313 Olson, "Biblical Theology as Provisional Monologization," 171–172, draws upon the work of Bakhtin to argue that provisional truths are an unavoidable part of reading and writing, and indeed of any dialogue. Olson writes: "In a sea of conflicting dialogues and voices which is constitutive of every localized and particularized context, rhetors can make provisional, temporary but adequate arguments about truth and value to a given audience or interpretive community that is persuaded by the character and competency of the speaker, the cogency of the arguments, and the artfulness by which the argument or appeal is made." So, too, Newsom, "Book of Job," 637: "What the book of Job models is a community of voices struggling to articulate a range of perspectives, each one of which contains valid insights as well as blindness to other dimensions of the problem. At different times and in different circumstances, one or another of the voices

the author's ability to raise the level of his narrative frame and weave in thematic issues that are both continuous and discontinuous with the preceding sections in order to describe Job's new experience and reality – a reality that is both a conclusion and a new beginning. This resonance and dissonance or continuity-discontinuity dynamic in the text has been appropriately recognized.[314]

3.1.2 Continuity and Discontinuity Between the Epilogue and the Preceding Sections

There are two major parts in the Epilogue: vv. 7–9 and vv. 11–17, with v.10 serving as the link between the two parts.[315] The first section is vertical, largely depicting the relationship between heaven and earth, and is framed by the word of God spoken in 42:7 and responded to in 42:9. This corresponds with the narrative movement between heaven and earth in the Prologue. The second section is horizontal, largely focusing on the human-human dimension. This distinction between the two sections should not be overdrawn, however, for there are overlaps (in the first section, the friends go to Job; in the second, God blesses the latter part of Job's life). I have already demonstrated that the Epilogue is both at resonance and dissonance with the Prologue and the Dialogues. I have also shown why it is important to adopt a new hermeneutic in order to properly interpret the Epilogue. Now I will examine how this resonance-dissonance dynamic is combined in the Epilogue. To do this, I will focus on vv. 7–8 in the first section and vv. 10–12 in the second.

42:7 God's word about human words

ויהי אחר דבר יהוה את־הדברים האלה אל־איוב
ויאמר יהוה אל־אליפז התימני חרה אפי בך ובשני רעיך
כי לא דברתם אלי נכונה כעבדי איוב

---

may seem more powerful, may be the word we need to hear in order to work our way through a particular experience."
314 Thomas F. Dailey, *The Repentant Job: A Ricoeurian Icon for Biblical Theology* (New York: University Press of America, 1994), 59, argues that, "the disparity engendered by the prose/poetry junctures is actually constitutive of the intrigue of the tale. What results is a structured movement that can be described in terms of orientation, disorientation, and reorientation." Similarly, Yair Hoffman, *A Blemished Perfection: The Book of Job in Context* (ed. David J. A. Clines and Philip R. Davies, JSOTSup 213; Sheffield: Sheffield Academic Press, 1996) argues that the story is structured around the anti-mimetic (unreal) and mimetic (real) depictions of Job's life. Hoffmann concludes on pages 275–276 that, "the counterpoint within the story bridges between the mimetic and anti-mimetic dimensions of the book. The introductory story contains within itself the code to the constant tension that characterizes the book as a whole."
315 The reference to prayer in v. 10a echoes the first part of the Epilogue (vv. 7–9), while reference to Job's restoration in 10b anticipates vv. 11–17.

(After the Lord spoke these words to Job, the Lord said to Eliphaz the Temanite, "My anger is kindled against you and your two friends, for you have not spoken rightly to/concerning me as my servant Job.")

- The expression ויאמר יהוה אל־אליפז (The Lord said to Eliphaz) echoes God's words to the Adversary, ויאמר יהוה אל השטן (The Lord said to the Adversary – 1: 8, 12; 2:2, 3, 6) in the Prologue. This particular resonance is worth noting because God's word to Eliphaz consists of two components, approval of Job and rebuke of the friends, which corresponds to God's approval of Job and rebuke of the Adversary in the Prologue.
- חרה אפי בך ובשני רעיך ("My anger is kindled against you and your two friends") echoes the linguistic parallel expression in which Elihu's anger was kindled against Job and his three friends in the Dialogues (32:2, 3): ויחר אף אליהוא...באיוב...ובשלשת רעיו. Only in these two instances in the book do we find the use of the idiom about anger to rebuke others about the content of their words.[316]
- נכונה is derived from the verb כון, which occurs only in the Dialogues. More important is the use of נכון in 12:5; 15:23; 18:12; and 21:8 to express the idea of the inevitability (or lack) of divine rewards and punishment.
- כעבדי איוב ("like my servant Job") echoes עבדי איוב in the Prologue, especially in conjunction with the qualifying phrase, כמהו אין ("there is none like him" –1:8; 2:3). Apparently, Job continues to distinguish himself from others.

In this verse, one can discern resonances/echoes in which the narrator combines elements of approval and disapproval from the Prologue and Dialogues.

42:8 Human action in response to divine command/promise

ועתה קחו־לכם שבעה־פרים ושבעה אילים
ולכו אל־עבדי איוב והעליתם עולה בעדכם
ואיוב עבדי יתפלל עליכם כי אם־פניו אשא
לבלתי עשות עמכם נבלה
כי לא דברתם אלי נכונה כעבדי איוב

("But now, take for yourselves seven bulls and seven rams and go to my servant Job and offer a sacrifice for yourselves. My servant Job will pray for you that, if I lift his face, I will not do to you an outrage, for you have not spoken rightly to/concerning me as my servant Job.")

- The expression ולכו אל־עבדי איוב והעליתם עולה ("And go to my servant Job and offer a sacrifice") echoes the association

---

316 See, Syring, *Hiob und sein Anwalt*, 109.

between עבדי איוב ("my servant Job" –1:8; 2:3) and his religious piety of offering sacrifices (1:5) in the Prologue.
- The idea of praying in the expression יתפלל עליכם resonates with other expressions of prayer (calling קרא – 5:1; seeking God דרש – 5:8; שחר – 8:5; spreading one's hands פרש יד – 11:13; interceding עתר – 22:27; 33:26), all in the Dialogues.
- The idiomatic expression, פניו אשא ("I will lift his face") echoes other occurrences in the Dialogues where the primary idea behind the idiom is that of showing favor to others, or even being partial (11:15; 13:7–8; 22:8; 34:19).
- The idiomatic expression, עשות עמכם נבלה ("do to you an outrage"), echoes a parallel idiomatic expression in the Prologue כדבר אחת הנבלות תדברי ("You speak as one of the outrageous" 2:10).

Once again, one can discern a number of literary and thematic features that resonate with the Prologue and Dialogues, and which, when considered as a cluster, do create the necessary framework for holding these portions of the book together in conversation.

The first part of the Epilogue thus shows a number of resonances with the preceding sections of the book. Yet, within this framework of resonance/echo, there is significant dissonance that contributes in creating the complete sense of the text. The following dissonances should be noted: (a) the divine approval of Job echoes that of the Prologue (1:8; 2:3), but instead of locating the approval in the divine council and directing it to the Adversary, the divine approval is done on earth and directed at humans. The test motif no longer appears to be an issue; (b) although sacrifices are offered to ward off potential divine action caused by human offenses (resonance with Prologue –1:5), it is Job's friends who offer the sacrifices while under divine threat (dissonance with Prologue). As we saw in the last chapter, LXX and Syr. tried to harmonize this text with the Prologue by stating that it is Job who offers the sacrifice; (c) the divine charge against the friends for not speaking נכונה resonates with the debate among Job and his friends in the Dialogues about the certainty of divine rewards and/or punishment (12:5; 15:23; 18:12; 21:8), but its complementary part "like my servant Job" creates tension with the theophany where Job is rebuked; and (d) the two idioms ("to lift the face" and "to do an outrage") resonate with the Dialogues and Prologue respectively, but the sense in which they are used here is at dissonance with the Dialogues and Prologue. For example, God's threat to do an outrage is used as intended punishment for the friends' wrongful speaking; in the Prologue, the parallel idiom (2:10) is the presumed offense itself. Also, within the context of the discussion on retributive justice in the Dialogue, the idea of partiality or favoritism conveyed by the idiom (to lift the face) is resisted, but in the Epilogue the idiom is used positively.

After the transition in v. 10 where linguistic features draw upon the Prologue and Dialogues, the second section is equally framed around the dynamic between the resonances and dissonances.

42:11 The enlarged human assembly

ויבאו אליו כל־אחיו וכל־אחיתיו וכל־ידעיו לפנים
ויאכלו עמו לחם בביתו
וינדו לו וינחמו אתו על כל־הרעה אשר־הביא יהוה עליו
ויתנו־לו איש קשיטה אחת ואיש נזם זהב אחד

(Then all his brothers, sisters, and former acquaintances came to him and ate bread with him in his house. They consoled and comforted him concerning all the trouble that the Lord had brought on him, and each gave him a *Qesitah* and a gold ring.")

- The phrase, ויבאו אליו ("Then ... came to him"), echoes the gathering of the divine assembly ויבאו בני האלהים...על יהוה ("the sons of God came to...the Lord"
  – 1:6; 2:1) in the Prologue. The enlarged human assembly now recalls the divine assembly and the gathering of Job's friends in chapter two. It is to part of this human assembly that the divine approval of Job in the Epilogue is made.
- The coming of כל־אחיו וכל־אחיתיו וכל־ידעיו לפנים ("all his brothers, sisters, and former acquaintances"), however, also echoes and contrasts the expression אחי מעלי הרחיק וידעי אך זרו ממני ("He distances my kin from me, and my acquaintances are wholly scattered from me" – 19:13) in the Dialogues.
- ויאכלו עמו לחם בביתו וינדו לו וינחמו אתו על כל־הרעה אשר־הביא יהוה עליו ("They ate bread with him in his house, and consoled and comforted him for all the trouble that the Lord brought on him") echoes the banquet scenario in the Prologue where Job's children were אכלים ושתים יין בבית אחיהם ("eating and drinking wine the house of their brother" – cf. 1:13, 18), and the mission of the friends who, after hearing about "all the trouble that came on him" (כל הרעה הזאת הבאה עליו), came "to console and comfort him" (לנוד לו ולנחמו – 2:11).

42:12–13 The divine blessing of Job

ויהוה ברך את־אחרית איוב מראשתו ויהי־לו ארבעה עשר
אלף צאן וששת אלפים גמלים ואלף־צמד בקר ואלף אתונות
ויהי־לו שבענה בנים ושלוש בנות

("The Lord blessed the latter part of Job more than his former; he had fourteen thousand sheep, six thousand camels, one thousand yoke of oxen, and one thousand donkeys. He had seven sons and three daughters.")

- The expression ויהוה ברך ("The Lord blessed") here echoes the Adversary's words to YHWH, saying מעשה ידיו ברכת ("You have

blessed the work of his hand") in the Prologue (1:10), this being the only other time that the verb ברך is used with God as subject.
- אחרית איוב מראשתו resonates with the juxtaposition of ראשיתך (your beginning) and אחריתך (your end) in the Dialogues (8:7).
- The rest of the text recalls the numbering of Job's children and possessions in the Prologue (1:2–3).

Again, there are resonances/echoes with the preceding section, but also significant dissonances: (a) the festive mood in the Epilogue echoes the Prologue, but it is also different since there is no mention of wine (a feature that LXX-Job added); and (b) although Job's numbered possessions in the Prologue are doubled in the Epilogue, the children remain ten.

The point here is not that there is perfect symmetry in the way the narrator uses the Prologue and Dialogues, but that there is a significant cluster of expressions that create resonance and dissonance. That is, the narrator draws from both the stable and unstable dimensions of Job's life in order to depict a new situation in the Epilogue.[317] The result is that the Epilogue makes its claim on the preceding section in a manner that enhances the dynamism of resonance and dissonance between the Epilogue and the preceding sections but, through the monologues of the Epilogue, also seeks to bring about positive control and stability. As Bruce Zuckerman writes,

> "The writer/editor of the prose supplements of Job can play things both ways in the conclusion. By showing his audience patient Job, he can reinforce the legendary image of the folk hero whose actions speak louder than words; but since the poem has just shown how vocal (and even impatient) this Job can be, the Epilogue can also be seen as the conventional response to the pleadings of an innocent man in distress. Hence Job can be silent folk hero and vocal Righteous Sufferer at one and the same time: the images superimpose on one another – or to put this in terms of counterpoint, they form a contrapunctal duet."[318]

In creating the "situation model" of the reading experience here, the narrator appears to be using the resonance-dissonance dynamic. These resonances and dissonances are consequently no longer just the end products of the reading or interpretive process, but its very foundation. It is this resonance-dissonance dynamic that constitutes part of the narrative strategy (form) and narrative substance (content) of the Epilogue.

---

317 Dhorme, *Book of Job*, lxxxv, notes a number of terms that occur in the Prologue, Dialogues, and Epilogue. Of importance for our purposes is the use of בעד in the sense of "on behalf of" in 42:8 and 6:22; נבל is used in 42:8; 2:10 and 30:8. On their own, such linguistic echoes may not be sufficient to sustain the argument about single authorship. However, and especially as a cluster, they create significant interpretive links between the different sections of the text.

318 Zuckerman, *Job the Silent*, 161. For more on the intricate nature of narrative connections and how they may combine to create different levels of meaning in a text, see Noël Carroll, "On The Narrative Connection," in *New Perspectives on Narrative Perspective* (ed. Willie van Peer and Seymour Chatman; New York: State University of New York Press, 2001), 21–41.

3.1.3 The Comic Aspect of the Epilogue

Attempts have been made to read Job as drama, with some scholars suggesting that Job is a modification of Greek tragedy. Central to this view is the argument that the book clearly depicts the problem of human suffering in the hands of divine beings that appear to be insensitive to human plight and pain.[319] With respect to the Epilogue, scholars like Hugh Pyper have argued that it is not so much a happy ending as it is one that continues the theme of suffering rather than restoration. Basing his argument on Job 2:6, where God permits the Adversary to torment Job without taking his life, Pyper interprets Job as a survivor with an ambivalent status: "both blessed and cursed, preserved from death to live a life of pain, outliving the beloved only to have to endure the knowledge of their absence."[320] In this light, "Job was left to live out 140 years brooding on the injustice he had suffered. The epilogue neither suggests this nor rules it out."[321]

Others have, however, argued for a comic reading of the book of Job.[322] Worth noting is the fact that those who argue for the comic character of the book do not ignore or undermine the tragic elements in the book. Theoretically, comedy does not so much ignore or downplay the tragic element as it transcends it.[323] As I have argued above, this perception of a possible transcending of Job's former life is perhaps the hermeneutical clue to interpreting and understanding the Epilogue and particularly its "happy" ending.

The comic aspect of the book is portrayed in the Epilogue through a number of literary clues that can be construed in two broad ways. First, there is the absence of the Adversary and the silence of Job's wife, both of which

---

319 As early as the 5th century CE Theodore of Mopsuestia argued that the book of Job is a drama created in a manner similar to Greek drama, and in the process the author distorted the original legend. Among modern scholars, one notes the work of Horrace Kallen, *The Book of Job as a Greek Tragedy* (New York: Hill & Wang, 1959). For an overview of some of the arguments in favor of reading Job as tragedy or comedy, see William J. Urbrock, "Job As Drama: Tragedy or Comedy?" *CurTM* 8 (1981): 35–40.
320 Hugh Pyper, "The Reader in Pain: Job as Text and Pretext," in *Text as Pretext: Essays in Honor of Robert Davidson* (ed. Robert P. Carroll; JSOTSup 138; ed. David J. A. Clines and Philip R. Davies; Sheffield: Sheffield Academic Press, 1992), 249.
321 Carroll, "Postscript to Job," 165.
322 See, William Whedbee, *The Bible and the Comic Vision* (Cambridge: Cambridge University Press, 1998); idem, "The Comedy of Job," *Semeia* 7 (1977): 1–39; John Morreal, *Comedy, Tragedy, and Religion* (New York: State University of New York, 1999); Conrad Hyers, *Comic Vision of the Christian Faith: A Celebration of Life and Laughter* (New York: Pilgrim Press, 1981).
323 In *The Symbolism of Evil* (trans. Emerson Buchanan; Boston: Beacon Press, 1967), 324, Paul Ricoeur writes: "On the one hand, the evil that is *committed* leads to a just exile; that is what the figure of Adam represents. On the other hand, the evil that is *suffered* leads to an unjust deprivation; that is what the figure of Job represents. The first figure calls for the second; the second corrects the first. Only a third could announce the transcending of the contradiction, and that would be the figure of the 'Suffering Servant,' who would make of suffering, of the evil that is undergone, an *action* capable of redeeming evil that is committed." See also William Whedbee, "The Comedy of Job," *Semeia* 7 (1977), 30–31.

are conspicuous because of the Prologue-like language employed in the Epilogue, and the role that they play in the overall plot. The absence of the Adversary eliminates the whole plot structure built around God's dispute with the Adversary in the Prologue. The silence of Job's wife limits the ambiguity around her words, and especially her inclusion of the idea of death into the entire debate. In contrast to Job 'blessing' God as the Adversary had argued and his wife had suggested, it is God who blesses Job. And in contrast to Job dying, the narrator speaks of him living on and on, as though in defiance of the retributive effects of moral corruption which is death at seventy or eighty years (Ps 90: 7–10).

The second way by which the narrator attempts to create a positive end for the book is through God's word. As is clear from the text, the Epilogue consists of speeches by God and the narrator; dialogue as expressed in the prose Prologue and in the poetic section is eliminated. The suppression of open debate in the Epilogue may suggest that the "polyphonic" character of the text is being restricted. Accordingly, God's approval of Job in 42:7, which linguistically parallels God's approval of Job to the Adversary in the Prologue, not only has the potential of becoming the ultimate verdict but more importantly now goes unchallenged. In fact, unlike the Adversary, who continues to be suspicious in 2:3, the friends participate in the process of Job's characterization (and restoration) as God's servant by offering sacrifices and having Job pray for them. Furthermore, as I shall argue later, the restoration not only surpasses the Prologue in that whatever Job lost is now doubled, but also through the fact that words and expressions that receive a largely negative portrayal in the poetic section (e.g., inheritance and "lifting the face") are now portrayed in a largely positive manner.

All these factors, woven into eleven verses of simple clear prose, allow the narrator to move towards a positive conclusion. As Robert Polzin accurately argues,

> "The framework of the story, then, is the work of a genius. By means of its remarkable resources it takes the reader on a journey, the beginning of which may be described as equilibrium without insight and whose conclusion is appropriately equilibrium with insight. The genius of this journey is that insight is conferred not by the avoidance of contradiction and inconsistency but precisely by the courageous integration of contradiction and resolution.... What is on the surface a diachronic linear treatment of a problem reveals itself as containing an underlying or latent synchronic structure.[324]

The Epilogue is not just a return to the old days; it is a partial transformation of Job's life and experience as recounted in the Prologue and poetic Dialogues. In an attempt to create this new image of Job, the narrator uses

---

324 Robert M. Polzin, *Biblical Structuralism: Method and Subjectivity in the Study of Ancient Texts* (Philadelphia: Fortress, 1977), 74. Similarly, Dailey, *Repentant Job*, 81, notes that the literary features in the text present the book "not as an ironic failure of wisdom, but as its optimistic summit."

language that is both Prologue-like and Dialogues-like, language that is exclusive to these two preceding sections, and thereby has the potential and reality of dissonance with one another. By this use of language and themes from the two preceding sections, the narrator not only brings the story to an end but also presents the reader with a new and profound interpretative lens that is both dialogic and synchronic. Of particular importance for my purposes is the fact that Job is now depicted in terms that are "more than" what he was in the Prologue and Dialogues. This allows the narrator to integrate the resonances and dissonances, the tragic and comic features of the text into the Epilogue.[325] The result is that the language and content of the Epilogue is complex and dynamic, drawing up enough from the Prologue and Dialogues to make them relevant to his conclusion, but also surpassing them in ways that give the Epilogue its own uniqueness and identity.

3.2 Interpreting the Epilogue

The Epilogue begins with a rather long introductory formula. The transition from 42:6 to 42:7 could very easily have been made with a simple *wayyiqtol* verb form that introduces YHWH's speech to Eliphaz. In fact, the literary formula, ויאמר X ויע/ויוסף ("Then X answered / added... and said") has been used twenty-eight times to introduce both human and divine words in the Dialogues and the theophany.[326] On account of this repetition, the reader may come to expect this almost stereotypical formula. Instead of this brief and rhythmic formula, the narrator gives a lengthy introduction that wraps up the divine words to Job before introducing the divine rebuke of Eliphaz and his friends. Although this lengthy formula is without parallel in the book of Job, one is fortunately not left in the dark as to its use in the Bible. Close parallels of this formula are repeatedly used to introduce or make transitions to a new phase in a plot or story line.[327]

Perhaps the narrator uses this lengthy introduction in order to enhance the continuity and discontinuity dynamic between the Epilogue and the preceding sections. Accordingly, one notes that the narrator makes double reference to

---

325 The integration of the comic and tragic aspects of the text in the Epilogue is demonstrated, for example, in v. 11: "Then all his brothers, sisters, and former acquaintances came to him and ate bread with him in his house. They consoled and comforted him for all the trouble (evil) that the Lord had brought on him. Each gave him a *Qesita* and a gold ring." The tragic feature in this verse is that the source of Job's troubles, elsewhere described in impersonal terms (2:11), is now explicitly described as the Lord's action. Nevertheless, there are some comic aspects in the verse too: (a) the mission of the friends in 2:11 which was to come and "to console and comfort him" is now fulfilled as they, together with Job's family, actually console and comfort him; and (b) they offer him gifts, which within the context of the restoration, become part of the "happy ending" as Job gets back everything he lost and even more.
326 3:2; 4:1; 6:1; 8:1; 9:1; 11:1; 12:1; 15:1; 16:1; 18:1; 19:1; 20:1; 21:1; 22:1; 23:1; 25:1; 26:1; 27:1; 29:1; 32:6; 34:1; 35:1; 36:1; 38:1; 40:1, 3, 6; 42:1.
327 See Gen 15:1; 22:1; 39:7; 40:1; 1Kg 17:17; 21:1; Ezr 7:1.

YHWH's speech: "after the Lord *spoke* these words to Job, the Lord *said* to Eliphaz...." In one full swoop, the narrator ends YHWH's words to Job from the whirlwind; the Epilogue is situated after these words have been spoken. But then the narrator immediately has the Lord speaking again, this time to Eliphaz. Thus, the narrator enhances both narrative continuity (as the Lord appears to have finished with Job and immediately turned to the friends) and narrative discontinuity (as the Lord bypasses Job's response in 42:1–6).[328] On the one hand, the continuity allows the narrator and reader to situate God's words to the friends within the context of the divine theophany. It also allows the narrator to introduce the divine verdict on the preceding section. On the other hand, the discontinuity allows the narrator to introduce a series of new events demanded by the Lord and carried out by Job and the friends in 42:7–9.[329] While the theophany is the context in which the narrator situates God's verdict on the narrative, God's demands on the friends introduce a new dimension to the story on the human plane. This new series of actions will lead up to the human gathering in 42:11 and, in conjunction with the divine words from the theophany, parallel the heaven-earth movement of the narrative in the Prologue. The Epilogue, then, is to be interpreted in close conjunction with the theophany; in fact, I suggest that the Epilogue is partly rooted in the experience of the theophany, and is part of its outworking.

3.2.1 Divine Rebuke and Approval (42:7–9)

Just as God opened up the theophanic manifestation with a rebuke of Job, so now God begins the address to the friends with a rebuke (42:7). This rebuke of the friends for not speaking rightly constitutes a major interpretive issue in the Epilogue. This interpretive problem is further compounded by the concurrent approval of Job's discourse to/about God. As Stanley Porter notes,

> "there are no anaphoric indicators in the words themselves to specify which specific words of Job are being referred to by God. So many things have been said by Job

---

328 See, in this connection, Budde's insightful remark that »der erste Satz übergeht die Erwiderung Hiobs ganz und gar, ähnlich wie Jahwe in 38:2 die Reden Elihu's.« Budde, *Das Buch Hiob*, 271. See also, Edwin Good, *In Turns of Tempest: A Reading of Job* (California: Stanford University Press, 1996), 380–382; Samuel Terrien, *Job* (CAT 13; Paris: Delachaux et Niestlé, 1963), 271–272. However, the Epilogue ultimately echoes Job's confession, and the whole picture that emerges from the literary and theological context created by this introduction that links the Epilogue to the theophany is one in which Job and his friends are both rebuked and approved. Obviously, Job's rebuke is more extended; but his approval is also more outstanding.

329 A similar method of continuity and discontinuity can be discerned in 3:1 where Job breaks with the silence and mannerisms of the Prologue but, in initiating the Dialogues, goes on to speak about issues related to his "day" – a recurring word in the Prologue, and brings up the death wish that he had earlier rejected from his wife. See Rick Moore, "The Integrity of Job," 25–26.

that it is difficult to believe that the words can refer undifferentiatedly to all that he has said in the dialogue with his friends."³³⁰

Still, attempts have been made to identify the context and, therefore, the words referred to in this rebuke. Some scholars have proposed that the appropriate context for this rebuke is the prose tale account of Job's piety.³³¹ The strength of this argument lies in the fact that in the rebuke of the friends, God refers to Job as "my servant," a characterization found elsewhere only in the Prologue. Furthermore, one may note that the idea of speaking falsely is often expressed in a different manner. Compare דבר שקר (Mic 6:12; Is 32:7); לשן שקר (Prov 6:17; 12:19; 21:6; 26:28). In the book of Job itself, one finds מלל שקר (Job 36:4) and דבר עול (Job 13:7; 27:4). Consequently, the expression לא דברתם אלי נכונה ("you have not spoken rightly to/concerning me") more readily echoes the attitude of the friends in the Prologue who, having seen the gravity of Job's pain, sat down in silence, ואין דבר אליו דבר – "and not speaking a word to him." In this sense, the rebuke calls attention to what the friends did *not* say; they have not articulated a theological response that adequately addresses Job's situation.

According to Albrecht Alt's theory about the prose framework, the three friends (in an original account) likely urged Job to curse God, thus provoking the divine rebuke.³³² The problem with this theory is, of course, that there is no such text in which the friends are said to have urged Job to curse God. Furthermore, the limitation of the argument that locates the context of the rebuke exclusively in the Prologue is that the root כון, which plays a significant role in this rebuke, does not occur in the Prologue. Moreover, when Elihu rebukes the friends in language that is closely similar to God's, he tries to distinguish himself from the friends precisely on the issue of false words (cf. 36:4). All these features suggest that one should also place the divine rebuke of the friends in conversation with the Dialogues.³³³ That is, the rebuke touches on Job's attitude of protest in his speeches in the Dialogues.³³⁴

---

330 Porter, "The Message of the book of Job," 292.
331 Carol Newsom, "Job: Introduction, Commentary," 634–635; Jean Lévêque, *Job et Son Dieu: Essai D'Exegese et de Theologie Biblique*, vol. 1 (Paris: Lecoffre, 1970), 125; Robert W. E. Forrest, "An Inquiry into Yahweh's Commendation of Job," *SR* 8, no. 2 (1979): 160.
332 Albrecht Alt, »Zur Vorgeschichte des Buches Hiob,« 265–268. This view is supported by C. Kuhl, »Neuere Literarkritik des Buches Hiob,« *TRu* 21, no. 4 (1953): 203; E. J. Kissane, *The Book of Job Translated from a Critically revised Hebrew Text with Commentary* (New York: Sheed & Ward, 1946), xxxv. Other historical-critical analyses that link 42:7–9 with the Prologue, particularly with 2:11–13 include: Friedrick Horst, *Hiob 1–19* (BKAT 16/1; Neukirchen-Vluyn: Neukirchener Verlag, 1968), 31; Ernst Kutsch, »Zu Problemen der Rahmenerzählung des Hiobbuches,« in *Zur Aktualität des Alten Testaments. Festschrift für Georg Sauer zum 65* ed. Siegfried Kreuzer and Kurt Lüthi (Frankfurt: Peter Lang, 1992), 78–83; Syring, *Hiob und sein Anwalt*, 111.
333 For arguments in favor of the Dialogues as the context for interpreting the rebuke, see G. Hölscher, *Das Buch Hiob* (HAT 17; Tübingen: Mohr, 1952), 101.
334 Marvin Pope, *Job*, 350, writes: "If this verse refers to the arguments of the Dialogue, it is as magnificent a vindication as Job could have hoped for, proving that God values the

As the survey of the history of interpretation indicates, some scholars have argued that the context for the divine approval is Job's utterance in 42:1–6. This argument is credible to the extent that the action demanded by God in 42:8 echoes Job's new experience in 42:5. However, it is important to note that prior to this time, the friends, unlike Job, have not had a theophanic encounter with God. It would be unfair to compare Job's post-theophanic understanding of God with the friends' pre-theophanic understanding. Finally, other scholars argue that the divine rebuke of the friends is a result of the fact that though they speak about God, they never speak to God. These scholars have insisted that the basic meaning of the preposition אל is not "about" but "to." Thus, Dale Patrick argues that an examination of chapters three through twenty-seven shows that Job's three companions never address God. "They speak a great deal about him, but he is never spoken to. Job on the other hand addresses 54 verses to God in the dialogue."[335]

I have already argued that the basic meaning of the prepositional phrase includes "to me" as well as "concerning me." Therefore, God's rebuke of Job in the theophany after Job's several addresses to God suggests that the issue here is not just about the attitude of speaking *to* God, though that is important, but also about what Job says. Prayer/lament (or direct speech to God) is part of the solution in this text. But the lack of it is not the cause of the problem. To focus on the direct address to God alone is to miss an important aspect of the book, namely, the human struggle to articulate a theology in the midst of one's own suffering or about the suffering of others.[336] Rick Moore goes further to argue that the friends represent modern interpretive attitudes that are driven by pure speculation and never get to reality. Most interpreters, he argues, may talk about God but they never talk to God; accordingly, theology is separated from prayer. He then proposes that theology and prayer ought to come together so that "talking about God and talking to God come together so intimately that a single term (like *'ēlay* in Hebrew) could refer to them both at the same time."[337]

It is likely that, in the interpretation of this rebuke, one has to take the context of both the Prologue and the human discussion in the poetic section into consideration. Although the root כון occurs only in the Dialogues, the

---

integrity of the impatient protester and abhors pious hypocrites who would heap accusations on a tormented soul to uphold their theological position."
335 Dale Patrick, "Job's Address to God," *ZAW* 91 (1979): 269.
336 See Gutiérrez, *God Talk*, 12.
337 Rick Moore, "Raw Prayer," 43–46. Similarly, Manfred Oeming, »Ihr habt nitch recht vom mir geredet wie mein Knecht Hiob: Gottes Schlusswort als Schlüssel zur Interpretation des Hiobbuchs und als kritische Anfrage an die moderne Theologie,« *EvT* 60, no. 2 (2000): 114, states: »Gott lobt nicht irgendeine einzelne Äußerung Hiobs, weder den geduldigen Leider des Anfangs, noch den wütend aufbegehrenden Rebellen des Mittelteils, noch den, der sich am Schluss besonnen hat und sich revoziert. Nicht eine bestimmte *Lehre von* Gott wird ins Recht gesetzt. Gott lobt vielmehr die Sprech*richtung* Hiobs, die innere Haltung, das Wissen darum, wohin und woher er zu denken hat: eine *Rede zu* Gott. Die Freunde warden umgekehrt nicht für das getadelt, *was* sie gesagt haben, sondern ihre Attitüde zu Gott, ihre distanzierte.«

comparative aspect of the charge "like my servant Job" broadens the context to include the Prologue. Both Job and his friends are temporally and sporadically silent in the Prologue (2:13), and again in the Dialogues (32:1 for the friends; 31:40 and 40:5 for Job). Furthermore, the idea of false words is hinted at and dealt with both in the Prologue (2:10 where Job does not sin with his lips) and Dialogues (13:7; 27:4; 36:4 where concern over false words is expressed). Therefore, the charge against the friends should be understood within the context of both the Prologue and Dialogue.[338]

What then is the possible meaning of the rebuke? I have argued that the idiomatic expression, דבר...כון is used to refer to something that is firmly established, either through divine sovereignty or human inquiry.[339] It is probable that this is the sense in which the expression is used in the rebuke. First, on the sovereignty of God, the friends repeatedly use traditional language and logic to argue that God is sovereign. In their articulation and defense of the concept of God's sovereignty, they argue from within the framework of opposing moral categories of good and evil. This is a necessary component of the argument, since it develops the moral aspect of the idiom and ultimately preserves the retributive component of the divine action.[340] However, the friends leave out another component of the idiom, that which deals with God's sovereignty in supra-moral categories, and consequently a vital component of Job's experience, namely, that God does bring trouble for no reason, or, better still, for reasons that exceed the limits of retributive justice.[341]

The sovereignty of God implies that God's freedom to act transcends the law of retribution as understood within such opposing moral categories. Therefore, when God rebukes the friends for not speaking firmly to/about God, it is unlikely that they are being indicted for something that they say that turns out to be inherently wrong, but for what they left unsaid in their diagnosis and description of Job's experience.[342] Unlike Job who repeatedly attributes everything (both good and bad) to God in a manner that assumes and then defies the proportionate retributive law of cause and effect, the

---

338 Daniel J. O'Connor, "The Cunning Hand: Repetitions in Job 42:7, 8," *ITQ* 57, no. 1 (1991): 24–25.
339 See above under textual analysis on 42:7.
340 Robert Forrest, "An Inquiry," 163–164, argues that the fact that Yahweh's sovereignty is 'established' implies the presence of divine righteousness and justice towards which humans are required in biblical thought to aspire. "It is this consciousness of this fact which Yahweh commends.... What distinguishes [Job] from his friends is his ability to speak with authority on the essential significance of creation, namely, the presence of the divine in it which makes human life religiously possible."
341 Jules-Marcel Nicole, *Le Livre de Job* (Cherbourg: EDIFAC, 1987), 2: 265: "En fait le dialogue ne visait pas à démontrer que la différence entre le sort du méchant et celui du juste était nulle. En règle générale, l'homme de bien est récompensé et le coupable est puni.... Mais si l'on prétend que la règle ne comporte pas d'exception, on se bouche les yeux sur la réalité."
342 See Melanie Köhlmoos, *Das Auge Gottes: Textstrategie im Hiobbuch* (FAT 25; Tübingen: Mohr, 1999), 353, who argues that the friends are rebuked because they misunderstand God's work of justice.

friends are guilty of half truths, sometimes emphasizing proportionate recompense (4:8–9; 8:11–13), or (in the heat of the debate), the graciousness of God in the face of human sinfulness in general and Job's sins in particular (5:8–11; 11:6). In the process, they ignore the fact that even within the context of retributive justice, God's actions are sometimes negatively disproportionate.[343] This appears to be the major point of the entire book, a point that Job repeatedly tries to make, and sometimes uses extreme language to make it to his friends. In the Prologue, the reader is informed that Job is attacked for nothing (2:3); then he is later on, with divine approval, struck with an evil disease (2:7), and the friends come precisely to comfort him because of the evil that has come on him (2:11); then in the Epilogue the narrator makes it clear that the source of this evil is God (42:11; Is 45:7). For Job, God sends both good and evil (2:10).

This double perception of God's character continues in the Dialogues. For example, in 9:14–20 and 10:19, Job argues that God's sovereignty overrides the categories of justice, and in 9:24 he argues that God even corrupts judges. But then he goes on to argue that God will be angry with the friends and will rebuke them for speaking deceitfully and showing partiality to God (13:9–10). In one instance, God appears to care less about moral categories and justice. Then in the next moment, God does. Although both images are contradictory, the character of Job that the narrator presents to the reader is one that experiences both, though painfully so. For the reader, such complexity, ambiguity, and uncertainty in the text suggest that closure of meaning is impossible and interpretive possibilities are varied.[344] On the other hand, though the ambiguity is unsettling and creates an interpretive dilemma, it is still possible that, "rather than suspend judgment, we grasp both horns of the dilemma, at least for now."[345]

When the friends come to console and comfort Job, they seem to have been overwhelmed by the severity of Job's pain; that is, the disproportionate nature of Job's pain renders the friends (and potentially their theological view) deficient. Job's experience is not a normal one; it is beyond the norm, and the friends recognize that fact. Therefore, the divine charge against the friends is not because of their mishandling of a normal case as far as retribution is concerned, but because of their failure to articulate a cogent theological response that befits and addresses what they themselves have recognized as "very great," as abnormal (2:12). This insufficient theological view of theirs finally becomes problematic when used as a limiting

---

343 Even within Israel's retributive justice system, God is theoretically portrayed as capable of punishing to the third and fourth generations and blessing to thousands of generations, thereby transcending the law of strict retribution (Exod 20:5–6). It was precisely about the negative imbalance in the law of retribution that the exiles complained, prompting God to promise an end to such disproportionate action (Ezek 18:1–3).
344 See, Terrence W. Tilley, "God and the Silencing of Job," *MTh* 5, no. 3 (1989): 268.
345 Stanley Porter, "The Message," 304.

framework for interpreting human experience, hence the rebuke for not speaking rightly about/to God.[346] Consequently, the rebuke places the friends in a situation where they come to experience the mysterious character of God who is not only angry with them, but who also reveals God's readiness to deal with them outrageously, that is disproportionately. The complexity of v. 7 continues in vv. 8–9, as the friends are asked to go to Job for prayers, but especially because of the reason why God requires such action: "so that I will not do an outrage to you." The command is introduced by a disjunctive phrase, "but now" (42:8). This disjunctive adverbial phrase echoes that of 42:5. In just the same way that Job's experience of God was partially changed and enriched towards the end of the theophany, so too the friends' relationship with God will experience a new dimension within the context of this encounter with God at the altar. A number of interpreters discern an ironic twist here, as the friends who had asked Job to pray for mercy are now themselves in need of Job's prayers.[347] The friends are asked to take animals, go to Job, and offer a sacrifice for themselves while Job prays for them. Job and his friends are held together in this cultic event.

The seven bulls and seven rams are reminiscent of the Balak/Balaam offering described in Num 23:1, 4, 14, 29. Although it is Balak who brings the animals and the offering is Balak's (Num 23:3, 6), it is Balaam who makes the offering (Num 23:4). Unlike Balak, however, the friends will encounter God at the altar; the offering that they are required to make is a step towards that encounter.

The tripartite command, "take! ... go! ... offer! ..." recalls God's command to Abraham in Gen 22:2, which is the only other text where one finds these three imperatives used together.[348] By analogy with Gen 22:1–19, then, the friends are put in a situation that, like Abraham's, will bring them into the presence of the mysterious God. This anticipated encounter explains the reason for their offering a sacrifice even though they have just been contrasted with Job the "servant," whose role in the Prologue consists exactly

---

346 Nam, *Talking About God*, 59, writes about the friends: "their theological argumentation remains the same in repeating the already established concepts of God, without responding adequately to the challenge of Job."
347 Moster, "The Punishment of Job's Friends," 214, writes: "Why did [God] have the friends punished? To introduce an 'exquisite' ironic twist: One of the friends had assured Job that if he repented God would then be able to intercede for other sinners (22: 26–30), and now Job has to intercede for the three friends." See also, Habel, *The Book of Job*, 584; Gordis, *Book of Job*, 493.
348 A number of literary features link the story of Job (mainly the prose section) with that of Gen 22:1–19. Among these features one should note the following: (a) the theme of the fear of God (Job 1:1, 8, 9; 2:3 // Gen 22:12); (b) the importance of sacrifices to God (Job 1:5; 42:8 // Gen 22:2, 13); (c) the reference to the protagonists' children as "son/daughter" (1:5, 13; 42: 13 // Gen 22:2, 3, 6, 7, 8, 10, 12) and "servant" (Job 1:19; 29:5 // Gen 22:5, 12); and (d) the conclusion of the story with divine approval and blessing (Job 42:7, 12 // Gen 22: 16–17). For a detailed study of the relationship between these two accounts, see Andreas Michel, »Ijob und Abraham,« in *Gott Mensch Sprache: Schülerfestschrift für Walter Groß zum 60* (ed. Andreas Michel and Hermann Josef Stipp; Ottilien: Verlag Erzabtei, 2001), 73–98.

of offering sacrifices on behalf of those who have wronged God. The irony is that although the friends have angered God and need Job's intercessions on their behalf, they still have enough moral authority to make sacrificial offerings to God on their own behalf; together with Job, they participate in the process of reconciliation with God and experience of God's sovereign mystery.

The entire divine command in 42:8 is expressed in a chiastic manner. In the first part of the verse, we have a twofold action from humans to the divine in the order of the friends (offering) and Job (praying); then in the second part, we have a description of action from the divine to humans in the order of God lifting Job's face and not punishing the friends. This creates the chiasm: Friends – Job – Job – Friends, with God at the center. Both Job and the friends are drawn into this new experience, one that is expressed in the irony that although Job's prayers are intended to prevent God from acting outside the norm, the response to those very prayers will be action that is hitherto largely unconventional in Israelite theology.

In the same way that the previous verse expressed a dynamic relationship between God, Job, and the friends, so too this verse continues with that dynamism. This dynamism is illustrated by the following: (a) there is no other biblical instance where God is said to lift the face of humans;[349] in fact, the very opposite appears to be the case: God does not lift the face of princes (Job 34:19). This presents a new challenge and experience to Job and the friends; (b) when the idiom "to lift the face" is used with respect to another person, that person receives the favor. Accordingly, one would expect that in this text, Job should be the beneficiary since it is Job's face that God lifts; and (c) the divine response to Job's intercession introduced by כִּי אִם can be read either as a sure outcome or as a conditional statement that becomes certain only in the next verse. In the latter sense, it creates narrative suspense and allows the friends to respond to the divine command.

Just as Job's prayer is accompanied by the sacrifice of the friends, so too the divine favor shown to Job in the lifting of his face paradoxically benefits the friends as well. The forgiveness of the friends is conventional, but the method by which such forgiveness is attained is unconventional. In order not to do a folly to the friends, God has to break with the traditional understanding of divine justice of perfect equity, by lifting Job's face; better still, God has to surpass it without contradicting it. The narrator combines the familiar with the unfamiliar or bizarre. This is reflected on the human plane by the fact that although Job is praised, he must now function together with his friends in this new experience; his story has become theirs too, and together they must transcend their limited perspectives as they encounter the transcendent and mysterious character of God at the altar.

---

349 The case of Gen 19:21 may be cited as an exception to this, although one should equally note that even there, the dialogue is between Lot and the angels who come to represent God.

Outside the folkloric framework of the book (1:5; 42:8), sacrifices are not the means of approach to the deity. In the poetic section, there is much more emphasis on praying. People can call (קרא– 5:1), seek God (דרש– 5:8; שחר– 8:5), spread one's hands towards God (פרש יד– 11:13), or intercede (עתר– 22:27; 33:26).[350] While sacrifice appears to be more of a defensive endeavor to ward off the possible vengeance of the deity, prayers appear to be more restorative in function. In the Epilogue, the divine threat is such that although the friends do not suffer physically, there is a combination of what would be the pre-disaster and post-disaster responses.[351]

Two other texts are particularly important for understanding this provisional conclusion. In 11:13–15a Zophar states:

אִם־אַתָּה הֲכִינוֹתָ לִבֶּךָ
וּפָרַשְׂתָּ אֵלָיו כַּפֶּךָ
אִם־אָוֶן בְּיָדְךָ הַרְחִיקֵהוּ
וְאַל־תַּשְׁכֵּן בְּאֹהָלֶיךָ עַוְלָה
כִּי־אָז תִּשָּׂא פָנֶיךָ מִמּוּם

("If you strengthen your heart and spread your hand towards him;
if you remove iniquity by your hand and injustice does not dwell in your tent,
Then you will *lift your face* high.")

Then in 22:26–27a Eliphaz states:

כִּי־אָז עַל־שַׁדַּי תִּתְעַנָּג
וְתִשָּׂא אֶל־אֱלוֹהַּ פָּנֶיךָ
תַּעְתִּיר אֵלָיו וְיִשְׁמָעֶךָּ

("Then you will delight in Shadday, and *lift your face* towards God;
You will pray to him and he will hear you.")

These two exhortations from the friends are important because they touch on the issue of prayer and the lifting of one's face. In both instances, prayer and the lifting of one's face go together and are related to one's moral uprightness. The friends do envision the possibility of Job lifting his face either as a result of his moral virtue or as part of his prayer for restoration. In the Epilogue, however, the narrator slightly but significantly changes the dynamic: it is God who lifts Job's face.

---

350 As Miller argues about the varied language of prayer in the biblical text, prayer designates "an occurrence in the midst of the affairs of life and without special accoutrements, simply as human communication with the divine; but it also speaks of the phenomenon of prayer with language that designates it as a particular speech-act and may at times point to prayer as an occurrence accompanied by varied acts of worship and ritual." See, Patrick D. Miller, *They Cried to the Lord: The Form and Theology of Biblical Prayer* (Minneapolis: Fortress, 1994), 32-48, especially page 47.
351 Similarly, in Abraham's test, we find that although Isaac is not killed, the divine verdict introduced by "and now" is presented in a manner that conveys the possibility that Isaac was sacrificed. God says to Abraham: "because you have done this thing and have not withheld your son from me..." (Gen 22:12, 15).

The narrator thus brings together the preventive and restorative aspects of religion (sacrifice and prayer, which correspond to the Prologue and Dialogues respectively), with the governing idea being the fact that God lifts Job's face. But in drawing upon these ideas from the preceding section, the narrator paradoxically creates a dissonance between the Epilogue and the preceding sections. God is not as one-dimensional as the friends had thought; God can act disproportionately and show favor to humans. But also, God is not as ambiguous as Job had sometimes argued; instead, God does respond favorably to human prayer as the friends had argued. Thus, what the friends come to realize in this encounter is that, although the component of retribution that underlies the divine-human relationship is present, God on whom the law of retribution ultimately depends is also superior to it.[352] On the one hand, the bizarre or unfamiliar element in this folkloric story is appropriated into the familiar, as God's favor to Job is incorporated into the forgiveness of the friends; on the other hand, the familiar element of retribution is taken up into the unfamiliar realm where God can act disproportionately.

In summary, the first section of the Epilogue ends on a positive note. The friends are obedient to God and Job's prayers are answered. The divine rebuke of the friends, the sacrifice at the altar, and Job's intercession all explore the retributive aspect of the relationship between the deity and humans. On the other hand, the divine threat against the friends and the lifting of Job's face explore the dimension of the relationship that goes beyond strict retribution. The friends make the sacrificial offering (in conjunction with the moral vision of the Prologue). Job prays for them (in conjunction with the vision of restoration discussed in the Dialogues). And God responds to Job and indirectly to the friends in a manner that affirms both visions (the friends are spared and Job is restored) but also surpasses both (Job and his friends together benefit from God's decision to lift Job's face). Within the overall setting of the theophany-epilogue, both Job and the friends have been rebuked and approved, although the approval of the friends is less obvious.

---

352 See Taylor, *Erring: A Postmodern A/Theology*, 82.

3.2.2 The Family and Social Restoration (42:10–17)

The narrator probably combines two ideas to express the nature of the divine response to Job. Read as fortunes, the expression שׁב שׁבית in 42:10 implies the reversal of Job's material loss in the Prologue. However, read in the sense of "captivity" the expression portrays the broader experience that Job goes through, beginning with the second round of attack and continuing in the Dialogues – an experience that is depicted in political, social, moral, and even cosmic terms. This (immaterial) experience is hinted at by the immediate association of the expression about the restoration with Job's prayer for his friends and God's promise to lift Job's face. Therefore, the expression can be perceived as responding to the context of the Prologue and Dialogues, to Job's material and immaterial loss.[353]

The first human assembly had come precisely to show grief and comfort Job (2:11). With the severity of his pain, Job ironically wished that God would crush him, perceiving his death as his only consolation (6:10). Eliphaz and the friends continued to portray themselves as messengers of God's consolation (15:11) but Job rejected their effort (16:2; 21:34), preferring to contrast the friends' endeavors with his own acts of consolation to other mourners (29:25). The second and enlarged human assembly described here probably fulfils the original mission of the three friends, with the clue being the inclusion of Job's brothers and sisters in the group.

The idea of family members serving as the source of consolation following troubles sent by God is equally expressed in Ezek 14:22. Incidentally, the text deals with Ezekiel's modification of a tradition according to which Noah, Daniel, and Job could effectively intercede on behalf of others to ward off divine anger. As Ezekiel modifies this tradition, repeatedly insisting that these three persons would not be able to save their children (Ezek14:15, 18, 20), he concludes with a scenario in which sons and daughters do survive the disaster (14:22). These surviving children become the source of comfort. When the people see these survivors, God says, "you will be consoled for all the disaster that I brought on Jerusalem" (אשׁר הבאתי על־ירושׁלם ונחמתם על־הרעה). The presence of Job's family members in the group and his children in 42:13 may, therefore, be suggestive of a tradition according to

---

353 The root שׁוב occurs several times in the book of Job (see 1:21; 6:29; 7:7, 10; 9:12, 13, 18; 10:9, 16, 21; 11:10; 13:22; 15:22; 17:10; 20:2, 10; 22:23; 23:13; 31:14; 32:14; 33:5, 25, 32; 34:15; 35:4; 39:4, 12; 40:4). Though its basic sense of "turn back" or "return" is maintained, its use has significant nuances that warrant further observation. Of importance is its use in the sense of stopping an ongoing action, particularly injustice (6:29) or restraining God from acting in a particular manner (9:12, 13; 11:10; 23:13). It is also used in the sense of restoring what has been lost (20:10), for example, human righteousness (33:26). The verb is thus used in a double manner to express the act of preventing or stopping something as well as restoring others. Both meanings can be understood in the present context. In its "preventive" sense, it depicts the end of Job's painful experience; in its restorative sense, it describes Job's material blessing and health.

which family survival was the "commensurate" or "acceptable" response to the gravity of disaster sent by God.

With the family reunion in view, the narrator reintroduces the issue of blessing in the relationship that Job has with God. In 42:12, the narrator not only expresses the fact that Job's life is blessed, but also compares it with his former life. The doubling of "all that Job had" mentioned in 42:10 is now laid out. With this doubling becoming a tangible reality, the fact that he has seven sons and three daughters, the same number as in the Prologue, comes as a bit of a surprise.

The interpretation of the number of sons as seven may further highlight the interaction between the tragic and comic aspects of the book in general and the Epilogue in particular. Although it would be logically coherent to double the number of children, the narrator seems to be aware of the ambiguous nature of the report about the children and their (supposed) death in the Prologue. As Habel notes, the most tragic disaster of all in the death of Job's family is not actually stated. It is left for the audience to deduce.[354] As the report about the disaster is made known, the narrator always concludes with mention of the death of the servants (נערים – Job 1:15, 16, 17). When we get to 1:18, we are told that Job's sons and daughters (בנים and בנות) were eating and drinking together. It is the perfect occasion for the Adversary to strike. After situating the sons and daughters together, the narrator states that the wind pushed down the house and it fell on the servants (נערים) and they died. One cannot but think about the narrator's choice of words here. Is the killing similar to the selective killing that was sometimes the case during the Exodus plagues (cf. Exod 9:3–6)?

David Clines explains that on looking back over the passage, we realize that it is for the sake of this text that the term נערים has been used throughout. These (namely, the children) are the נערים that really matter, though no doubt their attendant servants also died.[355] And yet, what comes more naturally is to assume that it is the servants who die; only on second thought can one bring in the children. This ambiguity allows the reader to raise the question about the children: what happened to them? This is further compounded by the fact that in the Epilogue, everything that Job lost in the Prologue is doubled with the exception of the children.[356] Therefore, the seven sons and three daughters in the Epilogue may be playing on the idea that the children did not die, that perhaps they underwent something similar to the binding of Isaac.

A similar ambiguity occurs in Gen 22:1–19, where Isaac is referred to as son and servant. Of particular importance is the reference to Isaac as נער in

---

354 Habel, *The Book of Job*, 93.
355 Clines, *Job 1-20*, 33.
356 See also 19:17 where Job still speaks of his children. Together with the ambiguity about the death of the children in the Prologue and the number of children in the Epilogue, this text further highlights the possible tension between death and survival in the narrative.

22:5 and 22:12. In 22:5, immediately after Abraham sees the place of sacrifice, he refers to Isaac as "lad": "The lad and I will go a little further; then we will worship and we will come back." Given the fact that the lives of the other servants are not in danger, one cannot but pause to think over Abraham's choice of words here when he refers to Isaac (hitherto called בן) as נער. In fact, he goes on to promise that Isaac will return from Moriah, a promise that stands in tension with what God has demanded. The second time that Isaac is referred to as "lad" is in 22:12 where the angel calls out urgently to prevent the death of Isaac. Thus, one sees that the times when Isaac is referred to as "lad" are significant because they present a different and positive agenda for him. Although נער and בן can be used interchangeably, I suggest that the choice of words here is more than just a result of such interchangeability. As far as Isaac the son (בן) is concerned, it is he who is demanded by God as sacrifice (22:2); it is he who carries the wood to Moriah and wonders where the animal for the sacrifice is (22:6–7); it is he who is bound and laid on the altar (22:9); and finally, it is he who is said not to have been withheld from God (22:12, 15). But as for Isaac the "servant/lad" (נער), it is he who is promised a return trip from Moriah (22:5) and timely saved by the angel from Abraham's knife (22:12). Within the story there are two components: with the exception of 22:8, every other time that Isaac is called "son" his life is in danger, but when he is called "lad" his life is spared. Both themes are developed together, and stand in tension with one another.[357]

If this analysis is accepted, it will shed further light on the book of Job. It is clear from Job 1:5 and especially 42:7–9 that divine threats are taken seriously enough to warrant sacrifices; intentions are as consequential as real actions. Thus, while the children are part of the restoration, thereby suggesting to the reader that they had been lost in the destruction, the fact that they remain the same number and the ambiguity about their death in the Prologue creates tension: their possible survival of the attack preserves the potential for a comic dimension, or at least reduces the tragic nature of the account, thereby creating the context for hope and continuity.[358] This survival

---

357 The religious objective the centers around the "test" motif warrants that Abraham should loose his son. But the practical concerns related to Abraham's need for children as well as the divine promise that the blessing would be through Isaac warrant that Isaac should live. The resulting paradox is presented in the reference to Isaac as "son" who is lost and "lad" who is retained or rescued. This paradox allows the narrator to portray Abraham as a hero of faith who underwent the toughest test but still retained his son.
358 Conrad Hyers writes: "The dismal and fated conclusion of the tragic flaw or circumstance is partially overcome in a comic flourish.... Comedy is [humankind's] stubborn refusal to give tragedy and fate the final say.... The fate that cannot be transcended, or the arbitrary will of the gods that cannot be overturned, is transformed and overturned in an heroic gesture of the human spirit. Incongruous though it may seem, man has the last laugh." See M. Conrad Hyers, "The Dialectic of the Sacred and the Comic," in *Holy Laughter: Essays on Religion in the Comic Perspective* (ed. M. Conrad Hyers; New York: Seabury, 1969), 232. It is important to note, however, that in the Epilogue of Job, the comic perspective does not develop in spite of the will of the divine, but rather in conjunction with it.

motif may be further suggested by the focus on the daughters, who are portrayed as receiving inheritance from their father alongside their brothers. Accordingly, it is important to examine the role that the daughters' inheritance may play within the overall context of restoration and family survival.

3.2.2.1 Daughters and Inheritance in the Ancient Near East

Inheritance in the ancient Near East was one of the social media by which family patrimony was preserved. Because of the dominant patrilineal structure of the society, it was sons who perpetuated the family line.[359] In the absence of a son, however, the daughter could inherit. At Nuzi, in the absence of a son, there were several options: (a) the daughter could be sole heir, (b) the daughter could become co-heir together with an adopted son (sometimes the son-in-law) or her brothers, and (c) the daughter could be granted the rank of "son" and would then become heir.[360] Daughters' ability to inherit, therefore, was not always dependent on the absence of sons. Sometimes they would inherit together with sons or even in spite of the presence of sons.[361] At Deir El-Medina, women are known to have owned property and handed it down to both sons and daughters. In one instance, a husband adopted his childless wife as a "daughter," and this adoption gave her the right to become heir. Jaana Toivari-Viitala notes that this practice underscored the role of the daughter (and implicitly that of the son) as one embodying the right to inherit the parent's property.[362]

---

359 See the detailed treatment of this issue by Hennie J. Marsman, *Women in Ugarit and Israel: Their Social and Religious Position in the Context of the Ancient Near East* (Leiden: Brill, 2003).
360 See, Jonathan Paradise, "A Daughter and Her Father's Property at Nuzi," *JCS* 32 (1980), 190–198. In Ugarit, one also finds that daughters could inherit in place of or in the absence of sons. In the legends of Kirtu and Dani'ilu, for instance, one finds that after the death of the kings' sons, their daughters took the responsibility of the sons. In the case of Kirtu, it was the last born of six daughters who received the birth-right (KTU 1.15:III.16). For a detailed treatment of this text, see Klaas Spronk, "The Legend of Kirtu (KTU 1.14–16): A Study of the Structure and Its Consequences for Interpretation," in *The Structural Analysis of Biblical and Canaanite Poetry* (ed. Willem van der Meer and Johannes C. der Moor; JSOTSup 74; ed. David J. A. Clines and Philip R. Davies; Sheffield: JSOT Press, 1988), 62–82.
361 A legal document at Elalah provides evidence for the fact that daughters could inherit alongside sons. Elsewhere at Elam, a text depicts a father giving property – a field, a house, and an orchard – to his daughter, which suggests that there were instances in which the daughter would be preferred over sons. See Zafrira Ben-Barak, "Inheritance by Daughters in the ANE," *JSS* 25 (1980), 28–31.
362 Jaana Toivari-Viitala, *Women at Deir El-Medina: A Study of the Status and Role of the Female Inhabitants in the Workmen's Community during the Ramesside Period* (ed. J. F. Borghouts et al.; Egyptologische Uitgaren 15; Leiden: Nederlands Instituut voor het Nabije Oosten, 2001), 107. In fact, by their very status as children, sons and daughters were entitled to inheritance from both parents. For further analysis on this right of succession, see P. W. Pestman, "The Law of Succession in Ancient Egypt," in *Essays on Oriental Laws of Succession* (ed. J. Brugman et al.; Leiden: Brill, 1969), 58–78.

While sons were generally expected to wait for their inheritance until the death of the father, daughters could receive their share when they got married, a practice that scholars refer to as "pre-mortem inheritance."[363] But such pre-mortem inheritance was not limited to daughters. In addition to the general possibility of inheriting from one's parents, both sons and daughters could receive property from their parents at their weddings.[364] The emerging conclusion is that, although sons were often preferred as heirs because of the patrilineal structure of the society, there is enough evidence to indicate that daughters too were heirs to family property.

3.2.2.2 Daughters and Inheritance in the Bible

The account of the daughters of Zelophehad inheriting family property after the death of their father (Num 27:1–11; 36:1–12) is the only other instance in biblical literature where daughters inherit. In that instance, as with the Epilogue of Job, the idiom X...ל נחלה נתן is used to describe the passage of family property from parent to child. Such inheritance was supposed to remain within the family or tribe (Ezek 46:16), hence Naboth's refusal to give his family property to Ahab (1Kg 21:3, 4). When the daughters of Zelophehad inherit their father's property (Num 27: 7, 10, 11), Moses promulgates a law that restricts daughters to inner-tribal marriages in order to protect the family inheritance (Num 36). As Katharine Sakenfeld notes, this marriage restriction meant that the woman who possessed the inheritance could not claim to have it "in her own right."[365] Rather, as the daughters themselves state the reason behind their request for inheritance, it was for the sake of their father's name, "so that our father's name" should not "be lost in the clan just because he had no son" (Num 27:4). As a result, they demand to be given inheritance "among the brothers of our father" (Num 27:4), thus placing their inheritance under the oversight of their father's brothers. Sakenfeld insightfully remarks that "the boundary between literary and cultural-context reading is not always easy to determine; but in this case attending to both sides of the boundary enables the reader to perceive both patriarchy and freeing from patriarchy in a single text."[366] Underlying this concern for family property expressed by the daughters of Zelophehad was a broader concern for social justice. As Dennis Olson argues, other rules could be broken and other precedents overridden in favor of justice in the economic

---

363 See, Katarzyna Grosz, "Bridewealth and Dowry in Nuzi," in *Images of Women in Antiquity* rev. ed. (ed. Averil Cameron and Amélie Kuhrt; Detroit: Wayne State University Press, 1993), 193–206; Martha T. Roth, "The Neo-Babylonian Widow," *JCS* 43–45 (1991–1993): 1–26.
364 Toivari-Viitala, *Women at Deir El-Medina*, 69.
365 Katharine Doob Sakenfeld, "Zelophehad's Daughters," *PRSt* 15 (1988): 42 n. 13.
366 Sakenfeld, "Zelophehad's Daughters," 41.

life of Israel. No one tribe was to benefit from situations that threatened to deprive other tribes of their land.[367]

Just as Zelophehad's daughters, Job's daughters inherit "among their brothers" (42:15). This suggests that although women were allowed to inherit, such rights of inheritance were restricted.[368] The significant issue in the interpretation of this text, however, is not so much the fact that Job's daughters inherit property together with their brothers (for that was fairly common in the ancient Near East as shown in the section above), but the way in which the concept of inheritance is used in the Epilogue with respect to the Dialogues. Apart from this text in the Epilogue, the word "inheritance" (נחלה // חלק) is used within the context of the discussion on retributive justice in the Dialogues. Zophar argues that the wicked person disappears from his place (20:7, 9), his children become poor (20:10), he returns (שוב) the wealth he has gotten (20:10, 18), and has no survivors (vv. 20–21). Then in emphatic fashion, Zophar concludes: "This is the wicked man's portion (חלק) from God; the inheritance (נחלה) ordained for him from God," 20:29). Thus for Zophar, God ensures that the wicked person is rightly punished, and inheritance is used as a reward for what one does.[369] In chapter 27, "inheritance" consists of a number of experiences such as the death of children (27:14), hunger (27:14), no survivors (27:15), and loss of wealth (27:16–17).[370] Job later confirms this use of the concept of inheritance within the context of another oath of innocence in 31:2. He asks, "What is God's portion from above and the inheritance of Shadday from the heights?" and then answers that it is calamity that comes on the iniquitous (31:3). Thus, the concept of inheritance is used in a moral sense within the context of retribution and the debate is whether or not the reward system is as functional as it should be. What is more, the concept is largely used in a negative sense to refer to the punishment that God dishes. In the Epilogue, however, the narrator presents inheritance as a positive experience for Job's daughters.

---

367 Dennis T. Olson, *Numbers* (ed. James L. Mays, Patrick D. Miller, and Paul J. Achtemeier; IBC 4; Louisville: John Knox Press) 1996, 165. See also Baruch A. Levine, *Numbers 21-26: A New Translation with Introduction and Commentary* (ed. William F. Albright and David N. Freedman, AB; New York: Doubleday, 2000), 355–361.

368 Marsman, *Women in Ugarit*, 288. However, during the fifth century BCE, there is evidence from Elephantine showing that daughters had the same status as sons, and could own and inherit property on their own right. See A. Cowley, *Jewish Documents of the Time of Ezra* (New York: MacMillan, 1919), 42–48.

369 Job, however, repeatedly uses the concept of inheritance in his argument about the failed retributive justice system (17:5; 21:17; 24:1–2, 18). See Habel, *The Book of Job*, 328; Pope, *The Book of Job*, 159. For a discussion of the theological concept of inheritance and its relevance to the whole land of Israel as a gift from God, see S. Joy Osgood, "Women and Inheritance of Land in Early Israel," in *Women in the Biblical Tradition* (ed. George J. Brooke; Lewiston: Edwin Mellen, 1992), 29–52.

370 Because of the linguistic and theological similarity between these words here and those of Zophar in chapter 20, some consider these words to be those of Zophar. However, the use of the masculine plural pronoun "you" in 27:11 and 12 shows that it is Job speaking. Furthermore, the theological idea expressed in this text is reiterated in 31:2.

This creates interpretive dissonance between the Epilogue and Dialogues. Apparently, the point is to underscore the security that Job and his family now enjoy. This is further underscored by the narrator's remark that after this Job lived long enough to see his children to the fourth generation, before dying in ripe old age. According to Ps 128:6 and Prov 17:6, it is a great blessing for parents to see their grandchildren. Joseph saw his children to the third generation (Gen 50:23). Job's lifespan appears to have been doubled.

In summary, my reading of the text proposes a number of points. First, the story of Job has also become that of his friends. Job's actions in the Epilogue are subsumed under the friends' actions when the friends do "as the Lord commanded them." On the other hand, the divine favor shown to Job also benefits the friends. Retribution and its suspension have been beautifully merged. Second, Job is ultimately consoled through the presence of his family members within the larger assembly. I have suggested that the ambiguity around the death of Job's children in the Prologue and the fact that they remain ten in the Epilogue creates a counter-theme to the death and loss of his children. This is similar to the experience of the binding of Isaac in Gen 22, where the theme of loss and death is developed alongside that of survival and restoration. And third, the inheritance of family property by Job's daughters is consonant with other instances in the ancient Near East and Israel. The use of the concept of inheritance in the Epilogue is, however, different than in the Dialogues. Whereas it is used in the Dialogues as a means of divine punishment, in the Epilogue inheritance is a tool of family and social security, survival, and justice; in fact, it is part of Job's blessing.

Chapter 4: Theological Reflections on the Epilogue

Significant work has been done to locate the book of Job within the history of Israelite religion. In the process, scholars have often focused on highlighting the ways in which the book is at resonance and/or dissonance with the rest of Israel's faith traditions.[371] At the same time, considerable work has been done to show how the book is at resonance with other ancient Near Eastern works. With its final editing generally placed within the context of the Babylonian exile,[372] the book can be partly seen as a resulting response to God[373] expressed in a manner that is at some resonance with the genre of Israelite laments. However, there is some variation in the manner of the laments, petitions, and protests in the book, as well as in the nature of the divine response.[374] Given the parallels between the book of Job and other ancient

---

371 Among the significant works, note especially Zuckerman, *Job the Silent*; Leo G. Perdue, *Wisdom in Revolt: Metaphorical Theology in the Book of Job* (ed. David J. A. Clines and Philip R. Davies; JSOTSup 112; Sheffield: Sheffield Academic Press, 1991); Frank M. Cross, *Canaanite Myth and Hebrew Epic: Essays in the History of the Religion of Israel* (Cambridge, Mass.: Harvard University Press, 1973), 343–345; Thorkild Jacobsen, *The Treasures of Darkness: History of Mesopotamian Religion* (New Haven: Yale University Press, 1976), 147–164; J. Gerald Janzen, "The Place of the Book of Job in the History of Israel's Religion," in *Ancient Israelite Religion: Essays in Honor of Frank Moore Cross* (ed. Patrick D. Miller et al.; Philadelphia: Fortress, 1987), 523–537; Ellen van Wolde, "Different Perspectives on Faith and Justice: The God of Jacob and the God of Job," in *The Many Voices of the Bible* (ed. Séan Freyne and Ellen van Wolde; London: SCM, 2002), 17–23; Katharine J. Dell, *The Book of Job as Sceptical Literature* (New York: Walter de Gruyter, 1991).
372 Dating the book of Job is complicated because different portions of the book were probably written at different times. Furthermore, there are no historical references in the text. Based on themes such as the divine council, the patriarchal setting of the Prologue and Epilogue, and other linguistic features within the text, different dates have been proposed, ranging from the 10th to the 5th century. See, Samuel Terrien, "The Book of Job: Introduction and Exegesis," *IB* (ed. George Arthur Buttrick; Nashville: Abingdon Press, 1982) 3: 884–888. On the linguistic evidence for dating the book to the postexilic period, see Hurvitz, "The Prose Tale," 31. Witte, »Die dritte Rede Bildads,« 355, dates the final stage of the redaction process around the 3rd CBCE.
373 In his Old Testament Theology, von Rad treated the Wisdom Literature in general and the book of Job in particular as Israel's response before God. See Gerhard von Rad, *The Theology of Israel's Historical Traditions* (vol. 1 of *Old Testament Theology*; trans. D. M. G. Stalker; London: John Knox, 1962), 383–459. Later on in a more developed work, von Rad treated Job within the context of Israel's trust and attack. See Gerhard von Rad, *Wisdom in Israel* (trans. James D. Martin; London: SCM, 1972), 207–239.
374 On the possibility of reading the book as a lament, see Claus Westermann, *The Structure of the Book of Job* (Philadelphia: Fortress, 1981); Müller, »Theodizee?,« 272; von Rad, *Wisdom in Israel*, 209; Patrick, "Job's Address to God," 269; Miller, *They Cried to the Lord: The Form and Theology of Biblical Prayer* (Minneapolis: Fortress, 1994), 168–170; idem, *Israelite Religion and Biblical Theology: Collected Essays* (ed.

Mesopotamian wisdom writings, the theological concerns of the book need not be limited to Israelite tradition or any particular date.[375] This allows for the continuity and discontinuity between Israelite religion and its ancient Near Eastern background. Accordingly, the book can be interpreted under broad theological categories that embrace not just Israel's prior cherished traditions, but also those generic ideas about the nature of the divine-human relationship expressed in the Old Testament and eventually in the Gospels.[376]

A number of such ideas are at the center of the book of Job, three of which will be the point of focus for my present purposes. First, there is the issue of retribution and the role that it plays in the evaluation of piety. Second, there is the issue of innocent suffering and its place in religious experience. And third, there is the issue of the nature of the divine-human in the context of its depiction in terms of the "master-servant" relationship. In many respects, given their broad scopes and multidimensional perspectives, these issues overlap and nourish one another in fruitful ways. However, the specificity of the contexts in which these issues are raised helps to restrict the sense in which they may be interpreted in those contexts; that is, the manner in which these issues are raised or posed in any given context helps to shape the kind of responses or expectations that one gets from the text.

The question at hand, therefore, is how the Epilogue contributes to our understanding of these issues raised in the book. What possible theological resources does the Epilogue provide for responding to the problems that arise within the context of such ideas? In the pages that follow, I intend to highlight a number of theological points that have grown out of my survey of the history of interpretation and reading of the text. I will argue that although the concept of restoration associated with the Epilogue is a broad one, it is nevertheless not a monolithic concept. That is, although the concept can be used to describe events of universal scope, it is also very closely related to the specific experience of the individual or community in pain, and is, in that sense, very contextual.

David J. A. Clines and Philip R. Davies; JSOTSup 267; Sheffield: Sheffield Academic Press, 2000), 445–469, especially 463–464. The oracle of salvation that usually comes at the end of laments is, to say the least, delayed in Job, since Job's protest is followed by divine rebuke.

375 See, J. J. M. Roberts, "Job and the Israelite Religious Tradition," *ZAW* 89 (1977): 107–114.

376 See, Samuel L. Terrien, *The Elusive Presence: Towards a New Biblical Theology* (San Francisco: Harper & Row, 1978); idem, "Presence in Absence," in *The Flowering of Old Testament Theology: A Reader in Twentieth-Century Old Testament Theology, 1930-1990* (ed. Ben C. Ollenburger et al.; Winona Lake, Ind.: Eisenbrauns, 1992), 254–269.

4.1 Re-posing the Problem of Job

In the development of his hermeneutics for biblical interpretation, Paul Ricoeur articulates three stages that comprised "spontaneous interpretation," "critical thought" associated with modern interpretation, and finally "appropriation." He then concludes that even though modern interpretation is very critical, the modern interpreter ultimately seeks "to go beyond criticism by means of criticism, by a criticism that is no longer reductive but restorative."[377] This idea of a restorative criticism allows Ricoeur to introduce his concept of a "second naïveté." He writes:

> "Does this mean that we could go back to a primitive naïveté? Not at all. In every way, something has been lost, irremediably lost: immediacy of belief. But if we can no longer live the great symbolisms of the sacred in accordance with the original belief in them, we can…aim at a second naïveté in and through criticism."[378]

For Ricoeur, this new reality associated with the second naïveté is fostered by the art of interpretation, which itself becomes a circle rotating between belief and understanding.[379] Although Ricoeur develops this hermeneutics in his treatment of the overall process of interpretation categorized under pre-modern, modern, and beyond, it is possible to apply his three-stage method, by analogy, to the book of Job within the context of its structure of Prologue-Dialogues-theophany/Epilogue. In this sense, the Epilogue will correspond to the third stage of second naïveté.[380] For my present purpose, I intend to focus on Ricoeur's idea of second naïveté as it explores the "relation between the text's parts and the whole," and "engenders a fusion between the world of the text and the world of the reader."[381]

4.1.1 The Nature of Retribution

The question that lies at the heart of the book of Job, it is fair to say, is posed at the very beginning by the Adversary: "does Job fear God for nothing?" The Adversary's question cuts across the fundamental issue of the nature of the master-servant relationship around which Job's piety is shaped, seeking to

---

377 Ricoeur, *Symbolism of Evil*, 350.
378 Ricoeur, *Symbolism of Evil*, 351.
379 Ricoeur, *Symbolism of Evil*, 350.
380 Ricoeur is situated within the general trend of historical developmentalism, and therefore does not attribute any critical value to the pre-modern period, even though there is a real sense in which pre-modern interpreters were critical of their texts, as we have seen in the history of interpretation. Nevertheless, Ricoeur's method is credible in its own right as an interpretive concept.
381 Mark I. Wallace, *The Second Naiveté: Barth, Ricoeur, and the New Yale Theology* rev. ed. (ed. Charles Mabee; StABH 6; Macon, Ga.: Mercer University Press, 1995), 52.

reveal whether the relationship is based on *quid pro quo*. To find out, God and the Adversary agree that Job the servant has to be "touched," and consequently that by being deprived of his material possessions and health, Job's true piety will be revealed. Part of the underlying assumption is that piety must be dematerialized if it is to be true. In 2:3, after the first round of attack, God restates God's approval of Job's piety and then, as though rebuking the Adversary, states that God has been incited "to swallow him for nothing." Job later on argues that he has been subjected to tremendous pain for nothing (9:17).

Although חנם (to be for naught, gratuitous) does not occur often in the book, it turns out to be a significant word here. In one sense, it constitutes God's argument against innocent or gratuitous suffering (Ezek 14:22). But given the nature of the second part of the Adversary's formulation, ("send your hand and touch him"), God's words in 2:3 take on another level of meaning. It is as though if Job had cursed God to God's face as the Adversary predicted, then Job's false piety would have been unmasked, and consequently there would be no reason for God to say that the suffering was for nothing. In other words, the suffering is problematic only because Job has not reacted as the Adversary predicted. The "test" and its specific objective appear to have the potential of depriving suffering of its morally outrageous character. This is the problem of the book: Job the servant is going to suffer, and the only question is whether he will suffer gratuitously or not. The outrage that readers may feel about Job's suffering will likely be muted if Job cursed God to God's face; we would tend to feel that he "deserved" the suffering. How does the Epilogue contribute toward a response to this problem?

4.1.2 The Nature of the Divine-Human Relationship

In his book on *The Ancient Orient*, Wolfram von Soden describes the regulating role that religion played in the face of the centralization of political power with the rise of the monarchy:

> "As a counterweight to the possibility that the central power, which had grown so strong, would be abused, there emerged a religiously grounded sense of the ruler's responsibility for the welfare of all subjects, especially the socially weak."[382]

This sense of responsibility for the welfare of the subjects was directly related to the idea that the divine powers were equally responsible for their subjects. It allowed an individual to come before the divine being,

> "expecting help and guidance in his personal life and personal affairs, expecting divine anger and punishment if he sins, but also profoundly trusting to divine compassion, forgiveness, and love for him if he sincerely repents."[383]

---

382 Wolfram von Soden, *The Ancient Orient: An Introduction to the Study of the Ancient Near East* (trans. Donald G. Schley; Grand Rapids, Mich.: Eerdmans, 1985), 65.

The sense of humility and self-abasement that one finds in penitential prayers comes to mind. But Thorkild Jacobsen argues that such prayers have "underlying presuppositions" that do not so much reveal humility but a sense of "unconscious human self-importance" that is almost "without limits."[384] Thus, the penitent "becomes so important that he can monopolize God's attention" and "God is in danger of becoming a mere instrument for relieving personal needs in one individual."[385]

On the one hand, there is a part of the religious experience that is intended to counteract the possibility of sheer political power, checking any unfortunate situation of oppression that may arise where sheer might is right. On the other hand, the personal component of religion with its personal needs and subjective assumptions problematizes the issue of what is right for an individual within a larger community. The result is a religious paradox that Jacobsen describes as consisting of

> "conspicuous humility curiously based on an almost limitless presumption of self-importance, its drawing the greatest cosmic powers into the little personal world of the individual, and its approach to the highest, the most awesome, and the terrifying in such an easy and familiar manner."[386]

Jacobsen's treatment of the problem of personal religion pushes the question of the book of Job beyond retributive religion; it raises the problem of the power dynamics of the divine-human relationship: can frail humanity (or should frail humanity attempt to) bring the awesome and terrifying God into the personal domain? Jacobsen finds a "significant step towards a solution" for this paradox in the theophany, where the imbalance is redressed and the personal egocentric view of the sufferer, however righteous, is rejected. The distance between the cosmic and the personal, between the infinite God and the single human individual, "is so great and so decisive that an individual has no rights, not even to justice."[387]

How does the Epilogue relate to this issue? How do the divine approval of Job, the rebuke of the friends, and the command to offer a sacrifice all contribute to our understanding of the dynamic between divine transcendence and human frailty? As I shall later argue, if one reads the Epilogue within the context of the theophany-epilogue continuum, then a framework emerges that constitutes a helpful interpretive medium where the experience of the transcendence and immanence of God meet in tension, and conversely where the individual experience of the frail petitioner interacts with the larger universal experience, and ceases to be purely individualistic.[388]

---

383 Jacobsen, *The Treasures of Darkness*, 147.
384 Jacobsen, *Treasures of Darkness*, 150.
385 Jacobsen, *Treasures of Darkness*, 150.
386 Jacobsen, *Treasures of Darkness*, 161.
387 Jacobsen, *Treasures of Darkness*, 163.
388 See, Miller, *They Cried to the Lord*, 3.

4.1.3 The Reality of Human Suffering

Through Job's outbursts in the soliloquy in chapter three and the ensuing debates, the human and experiential aspects of the "test" come into focus. It is simply impossible to bypass the religious, moral, psychological, and social implications of Job's suffering in search of the "test" objective or goal. The anthropological component of the experience becomes crucial and Job's suffering becomes not just a side issue in the process of seeking or achieving a predetermined objective. Rather, Job becomes the character that, through the "test" motif, is expected to participate in formulating and describing the dynamics of the divine-human relationship.[389]

Originally, the discussion about using suffering to test one's religious motives began in heaven and reached down to earth. But now, leading up to the theophany, the discussion begins from earth and ascends towards heaven, reaching its climax in the divine response from the whirlwind. At the end of the book, the question about Job's motives is neither raised nor is the Adversary still present. But the narrator mentions that the human gathering is in response to "the trouble/evil that the Lord brought upon Job" (42:11). These words carry an ominous character and tone that continue to resound in the background, as they play against the reality of God's sovereign ability to bring both good and evil as well as the moral and ethical challenge of suffering in general and suffering for nothing in particular. What possible theological resource does the Epilogue provide for dealing with the reality of human suffering?

In summary, three theological issues are discernible in the Epilogue. The first deals with the nature of the master-servant relationship within the context of a religious piety: is it based on rewards? Secondly, and related to the first, there is the issue of the nature of the general divine-human relationship (whether or not one is specifically referred to as God's servant). How does a finite and limited being relate in a meaningful way to the sovereign divine being? Conversely, how does the sovereign God freely interact with humankind in such a manner that God does not appear or become capricious and random in God's actions? And third, there is the issue of human suffering. Should suffering have any role in defining religious piety? If so, then what role does it have? And how does the Epilogue propose to deal with the reality of suffering?

---

389 In a general sense, one might assume that given the specific description of Job's probable reaction to being touched ("he will bless you to your face" – 1:11; 2:5), all of Job's laments and protests are theoretically within permissible range. By precisely spelling out what will constitute false piety, the narrator may have created enough room for legitimately exploring the multiple and complex reactions to suffering in general and innocent suffering in particular.

4.2 Defining the Restoration in the Epilogue

The concept of restoration is a broad and pervasive one, present in both Jewish and Christian interpretations and covering both the Old and New Testaments.[390] The Christian canon is anchored between two narratives in Gen 1 and Rev 21–22 that, assuming a situation of chaos and describing a post-conflict scenario respectively, can very well be perceived as "restoration" accounts. God is first encountered in the Torah within the context of a "reconstruction theology"[391] as God transforms the chaos, imposes order, and repeatedly describes the process as "good" (Gen 1:10, 12, 18, 21). At the end of the Christian canon, God's revelation to humankind is that of a new creation in which the righteous are comforted and restored (Rev 21–22).[392] Thus, although the underlying current is that of the reality and potency of chaos, the biblical accounts are persistent in maintaining and affirming an equally and more forceful testimony about the potency and reality of divine (and consequently human) triumph over these forces. Between these two mythical and trans-historical accounts, the historical experiences of humans are developed. Consequently, the concept of the restoration, serving as a large theological framework for the rest of the biblical material, becomes a kind of "purpose statement" of the lengthy path that God travels with God's people, pointing beyond the bitter experiences along the way.[393] As such, restoration should be understood against the background of the forces of chaos that must be overcome, not once but continually.[394] In a similar manner, the Epilogue can be read as a post-tragic

---

390 See the excellent essays in James M. Scott, ed., *Restoration: Old Testament, Jewish, and Christian Perspectives* (ed. John J. Collins and Florentino G. Martínez, Supplements to the Journal for the Study of the Old Testament 72; Leiden: Brill, 2001).

391 The expression "reconstruction theology" was coined in 1990, following the release of Nelson Mandela from prison, as a post-apartheid hermeneutical framework and theological challenge. See J. N. K. Magumba, foreword to *Theology of Reconstruction: Exploratory Essays* (ed. Mary N. Getui and Emmanuel A. Obeng; Nairobi: Acton Publishers, 1999), i; idem, "From Liberation to Reconstruction," in *African Theology Today* (ed. Emmanuel Katongole, African Theology Today Series 1; Scranton: University of Scranton Press, 2002), 189–206.

392 Janzen, *Job*, 4. Janzen identifies a similar thematic structure in the Old Testament, given its eschatological perceptions, for example, in Isaiah and Ezekiel.

393 See, Robert G. Boling, "Kings and Prophets: Cyrus and Servant – Reading Isaiah 40–55," in *Ki Baruch Hu: Ancient Near Eastern, Biblical, and Judaic Studies in Honor of Baruch A. Levine* (ed. Robert Chazan, William W. Hallo and Lawrence H. Schiffman; Winona Lake, Ind.: Eisenbrauns, 1999), 178; Carroll, "Postscript to Job," 163; Konrad Schmid and Odil Hannes Steck, "Restoration Expectations in the Prophetic Tradition of the Old Testament," in *Restoration: Old Testament, Jewish, and Christian Perspectives* (ed. James M. Scott in Supplements to the Journal for the Study of the Old Testament 72; ed. John J. Collins and Florentino G. Martínez; Leiden: Brill, 2001), 44–45.

394 See, Jon D. Levenson, *Creation and the Persistence of Evil: The Jewish Drama of Divine Omnipotence* (San Francisco: Harper & Row, 1988); Miller, *Israelite Religion*, 408–421.

theological articulation that uses the concept of restoration. But how might one understand the use of the concept of restoration in the Epilogue?

Only through a study of specific restoration accounts can the reader develop an idea of the specific nature and function of any particular restoration. That is, the nature and function of any restoration account partly depends on the nature of the "in-context" problem posed by the chaos. Accordingly, restoration accounts will differ from one another in detail and emphasis even though they overlap thematically. I will now present a possible trajectory that the concept takes within the book of Job itself.

4.2.1 Restoration Language in the Epilogue

The first expression that is used to describe the restoration is the idiom שׁב שְׁבִית ("to turn the fortunes of" – 42:10). In a number of instances, the expression does carry a sense of retribution, and the restoration is a consequence of Israel's repentance and obedience to God's commands (Deut 30:3; Hos 6:11; Jer 33:7). Therefore, when God restores Job's fortunes after the divine approval in 42:7, it is probable that the retributive character of restoration should be assumed. However, there are a number of other instances where the idiom is used without any explicit reference to some prior credible act by the beneficiary. Rather, the expression depicts an act of divine freedom intended to return nations to their land (Ezek 29:14 for Egypt; Ezek 16:53 for Sodom and Gomorrah; and Jer 48:47 for Moab), thereby reestablishing order as nations reclaim their positions of origin. For Israel specifically, the idiom is tied to God's prior promise of a land to the ancestors (Am 9:14; Jer 30:3), God's covenant with creation, precisely with day and night (Jer 33:26), God's compassion (Jer 30:18), or God's response to the gloating of other nations over Israel's misfortune (Zeph 2:7). In this sense, the restoration is largely, if not exclusively, a free sovereign act of God. This component of the idiom is suggested in the Epilogue by the divine response to Job's prayer, which is described in terms of divine favor. In the end, the retributive and non-retributive aspects of the expression stand together in the idiom.

The second point to note about the language of restoration is he comparison of "former" and "latter" times. As individual words, "first" and "last" may or may not be particularly relevant for constructing the idea of a restoration or anticipating one. There is, however, the use of "latter" in the context of a restoration account in Jer 48:47. More relevant and similar to what we have in the Epilogue is the comparison between "former" and "latter" in the work of Second-Isaiah, precisely within the context of restoration. In Is 46:10a we read about God: מַגִּיד מֵרֵאשִׁית אַחֲרִית וּמִקֶּדֶם אֲשֶׁר לֹא־נַעֲשׂוּ ("declaring/expounding the latter times more than the former; and more than ancient times, things not yet done.") Although the Hiphil of נגד means "to declare" or "to proclaim," the verb can also mean, "to expound" in the sense of revealing what is hidden or concealed (cf. Gen 41:25; 2 Sam 7:11; 1 Kg 10:3; Job 11:6). The idea is, therefore, not just one of distinguishing in a temporal sense the past and the future, but also of unveiling the content of God's new acts in such a way that they surpass those in the past. This is suggested by the prophet's call to his audience to remember God's actions in the past (Is 46:9), actions that had to do with God as Creator and Redeemer. The latter times will be even better; in fact, they will include such things as have never been done before. That is, מראשית // מקדם, and אחרית // אשר לא־נעשו. Accordingly, one can interpret the preposition מן in its comparative sense and translate as follows: "expounding the latter times more than the former; and more than ancient times, things not yet done." Therefore, the language of restoration includes not just the possibility of a return to the former state of things, but actually surpassing the former times. As I have argued in the preceding chapter, this is what we have in the Epilogue where Job's latter life was blessed "more than" the former.

The third linguistic feature that evokes the concept of a restoration is the lexeme נחם (to console, comfort, repent). Since it can be used in various senses, context is crucial for determining its meaning. The verb is used here in conjunction with the idea of God bringing trouble/evil upon someone who is referred to as God's servant. This cluster of ideas echoes similar expressions in the work of Second Isaiah, where God creates trouble/evil (45:7) and calls on the divine council to comfort God's people (40:1; Jer 48:17) who are repeatedly referred to as God's servant (42:1, 19; 44:1, 2). The language of restoration in the Epilogue is not limited to נחם, however. The narrator uses the verbs נחם and נוד, echoing the purpose of the friends who came "to console" and "to comfort" Job concerning "all the trouble/evil that the Lord had brought on him." (2:11) In Nah 3:7 and the restoration text of Is 51:19, both verbs are used, although they are framed in the form of questions: "Who will console?" and "Who will comfort?"/ "How shall I comfort you?" This suggests that the human council in Job takes up the responsibility of comforting and consoling Job, a responsibility that falls upon the divine council in Isaiah. Ultimately both the divine and human characters play a part in the restoration. The human assembly that gathers around Job does indeed comfort and console him (42:11).

In summary, the series of expressions on the restoration in the Epilogue and their underlying theological motifs, aspirations, and implications constitute the interpretive context and framework of the restoration. The first on the turning of Job's fortunes evokes the idea of both retributive and free divine action; the second about the former and latter times underscores the theological scope and open-endedness of the Epilogue as it incorporates but also transcends the preceding sections; and finally, the third which deals with comforting and consoling Job highlights the practical response to suffering. All these three aspects of the text together underscore the hermeneutical stance that I proposed in the last chapter, one that moves inwards in search of unity, outwards in search of diversity, and forwards in search of meaning. But what theological resource is there to sustain this interpretive proposal?

4.3 Theological Resource for Interpreting the Epilogue

It is fair to say that the task of the biblical theologian is increasingly complex and challenging.[395] Perhaps more than ever before, there is need for doing what one might call a *balanced biblical theology*, that is, a theology that seeks to incorporate and uphold the various ideas expressed in biblical narratives, and is sensitive to contextual and cultural needs and priorities. This is an endeavor that scholars have increasingly drawn attention to its value and demonstrated that value in their works; scholars have not only resisted attempts to suppress some of the voices in the biblical text but have tried to create broad frameworks and interpretive methodologies that accommodate the many and sometimes discordant voices expressed in the biblical text. Accordingly, we sometimes have a combination of opposite ideas that would otherwise seem incompatible.

In the Epilogue, there are instances of such combinations. I have argued that the Epilogue is both at resonance and dissonance with the preceding sections, and that the interpretive context in which the narrator describes the Epilogue as "more than" the former actually allows one to integrate these complex and diverse ideas in meaningful ways. For the present purpose, two such aspects are worth noting. First, divine transcendence and immanence are combined. Secondly, and closely related to the first, the retributive and non-retributive dimensions of the divine-human relationship are brought together.

4.3.1 Divine Transcendence and Immanence

The Epilogue follows God's address to Job from the whirlwind and Job's response. Repeatedly using cosmic and mythical language in the theophany, God questions Job about the creation of the world and its operations, the point of which is to bring Job to a heightened awareness of his limited capabilities. As Duck-Woo Nam states, God uses the rhetorical questions to challenge Job and demonstrate God's executive sovereignty over the world.[396] The storm from which God speaks also evokes the idea of unpredictability and mystery often associated with Israel's cultic experience at Sinai. Frank Cross notes that this older cultic material was reworked in the 6th century with focus on the themes of divine kingship and new creation,[397]

---

[395] See, Mark G. Brett, "The Future of Old Testament Theology," in *Congress Volume Olso 1998* (ed. André Lemaire and Magne Sæbø; VTSup 80; ed. H. M. Barstad et al.; Leiden: Brill, 2000), 465–488.
[396] Nam, *Talking about God*, 159.
[397] Cross, *Canaanite Myth and Hebrew Epic*, 170.

both of which themes are related to the idea of divine sovereignty. Job's two responses in 40:3–6 and 42:1–6 suggest that he has gotten the point of the rhetorical questions. He is of small account, with limited knowledge in contrast to God who can do all things (42:2). Like the nobles of his community who, in awe of Job's superior social and economic status, placed their hands on their mouths (29:7), Job now recognizes his small status in God's presence and must refrain from talking.[398]

Rhetorical questions of the kind that God uses to express the divine sovereignty to Job in 38: 5–11 also occur in Second Isaiah's oracles (Is 40:12–24), and appear to be part of a larger corpus associated with apocalyptic literature. In a detailed study of such rhetorical questions, Michael Stone shows that they often deal with meteorology, astronomy, and cosmology, and their central point is "to state the limitlessness and unknowability of the divine wonders."[399] In Second Isaiah as well as in Job, the sovereignty of God is demonstrated not only through such use of creation imagery, but also through the presence of the divine council.[400]

However, the concept of divine mystery and sovereignty is also used in Isaiah to address the needs of a people who had come to question not only the divine intentions but also divine ability to save them (Is 40:27; 49:14, 24).[401] Thus, in a stunning move, Second Isaiah uses the mysterious character of God as a resource to proclaim a restoration.[402] Israel does not know how the world was created and how it works, yet Israel knows that it was created and

---

398 James L. Crenshaw, "When Form and Content Clash: The Theology of Job 38: 1–40:5," in *Creation in the Biblical Traditions* (ed. Richard J. Clifford and John J. Collins; Washington: Catholic Biblical Association of America, 1992), 81–84, argues that part of the theological significance of the divine speeches is that they present a critique of wisdom's high anthropology and "convey the awareness of Wisdom's ultimate ineffectiveness." Crenshaw concludes: "The portrayal of the deity in the speeches increases the distance between human beings and their maker. This distancing takes place, paradoxically, despite a literary form that emphasizes incredible closeness. Here form and content clash, with the latter gaining supremacy."
399 Michael Stone, "Lists of Revealed Things in the Apocalyptic Literature," in *Magnalia Dei: The Mighty Acts of God: Studies on the Bible and Archaeology in Memory of G. Ernest Wright* (ed. Frank M. Cross et al.; New York: Doubleday, 1976), 422.
400 See, Frank M. Cross, "The Council of Yahweh in Second Isaiah," *JNES* 12 (1953): 274–277; Christopher Seitz, "The Divine Council: Temporal Transition and New Prophecy in the Book of Isaiah," *JBL* 109, no. 2 (1990): 229–247. Seitz sees the divine council not only as the place where communication between the divine and human beings takes place, but also as permitting flexibility in temporal points of view, where different periods of time centuries removed are brought together before a single divine horizon; the former things meet the new things.
401 Richard J. Clifford, *Fair Spoken and Persuading* (New York: Paulist, 1984), 14.
402 Edgar W. Conrad, "The 'Fear not' Oracles in Second Isaiah," *VT* 34, no. 2 (1984): 129–152, distinguishes "war oracles" in which Yahweh fights against the idols of the nations, and "patriarchal oracles" where Israel's role is not to fight but to be a witness to the new thing Yahweh does. See also, Dale Patrick, "Epiphanic Imagery in Second Isaiah's Portrayal of a New Exodus," *HAR* 8 (1984): 125–141. Using the tools of "intertextuality" and "inner biblical exegesis," Patricia Willey has explored the ways in which Second Isaiah addresses Israel's misfortune (especially through comfort) and points to a bright future. See Willey, *Remember the Former Things*, 105–208.

is sustained by God. From this knowledge, Israel can expect a restoration, even one that will be beyond their ability to comprehend. The transcendence of God plays a double role: it heightens the awareness about human limitations but it also translates into God's ability to do anything God wants, including a restoration of Israel.

The experience of God's sovereign power in the theophany continues into the Epilogue, as God begins to rebuke the friends. But in addition to the echoes of the theophanic background (see the references to God's sovereignty manifested in the divine anger in 40:11 and behemoth as God's eternal servant in 40:28), there is a significant change in the experience of the divine manifestation, as the transcendent God becomes accessible in the context of prayer (42:8–9). Job may be unable to control the stars and creatures of the world such as behemoth, but within the cultic setting Job can influence the actions that God takes. Within the theophany-epilogue continuum, divine sovereignty and lowliness, transcendence and immanence come together and become part of the theological basis or resource for the restoration. Like Second Isaiah who drew upon the mysterious and sovereign character of God to imagine and speak of a restoration for Israel, so now Job the servant must navigate the two divine attributes of transcendence and immanence in view of the restoration. In the theophanic encounter and the cult, the divine power that partly characterizes the transcendence of God becomes the divine ability to ensure restoration, even dramatic restoration of the sort expressed in the Epilogue.

The theological value of the Epilogue, therefore, is that it moves beyond perceiving the transcendence and immanence (the mysteriousness and accessibility) of God as abstract or mutually exclusive attributes to utilizing them as theological resources for describing the divine-human relationship and responding to situations of human need. In the Epilogue, the responsibility for order, deliverance, and justice that comes upon the divine council elsewhere is partly assumed by the human council that meets with Job. The mythical forces of chaos have a real historical and personal parallel in the problem of human suffering; mythical evil has become personal and social evil, and the two are not separable.[403] Through the medium of the cult, the human assembly now stands ready to respond to the threat. Within the overall context of the theophany-epilogue setting, Job and the friends stand before God as persons who know that they can and cannot influence God;

---

403 See, for example, Prov 1:9–11 where the wicked are compared with mythical evil, Sheol, that swallows the innocent. Bruggemann, "Theodicy in a Social Dimension," 18 writes: "The destiny of the righteous and the wicked is not simply a heavenly verdict, but a social practice. The verdict of God and the practice of the community hold together, and the debate is about both, never about one without the other." Similarly, Köhlmoos, *Das Auge Gottes*, 347, writes: »Der Himmel hat in der Gottesrede eine neue Dimension bekommen. Er ist nicht mehr der Ort des Thronsaals JHWHs, der Ort dem aus menschliches Geschick beobachtet und die Ereignisse auf der Erde beschlossen würden. Vielmehr ist der Himmel in das große Werk der Schöpfung einbezogen; er bildet mit der Erde eine räumlich Einheit.«

that is, they have experienced *both* the immanence and the transcendence of God.[404]

Although the story begins with decisions made at the sovereign level in heaven without any human involvement, and although the story is from the beginning a "test" in which human responsibility comes in only at the level of the nature of its response, the forceful and human character of the story expressed in the human discussion has worked its way into the center of the narrative. Furthermore, divine transcendence has been combined with divine immanence in a single instance. Therefore, the conclusion of the story becomes a joint endeavor between God and humans not only to bring this "test" to an end, but also to respond to the trouble that the "test" has created. The theological and moral value of reading the didactic story as a "test" and learning "lessons for life" has been combined with the theological and ethical responsibility of responding to, and interacting with the characters in their personal and varied experiences and expressions in the Dialogues. With regard to the divine character, the theological and hermeneutical value of divine transcendence as articulated in the theophany (possibly as a critique of wisdom's high anthropology)[405] and the theological and hermeneutical value of divine accessibility as articulated in the cultic scene of the Epilogue (possibly as a "critique" of divine arbitrariness and capriciousness) are brought together. This combination of the different manifestations of the divine and human characters in the story has implications on the doctrine of retribution and how it operates in the Epilogue.

4.3.2 Retribution and Beyond

A number of scholars have noted that the concept of retribution is used in the Epilogue, even after it has been challenged in the Dialogues. It is clearly the framework within which to interpret the divine rebuke of the friends and the approval of Job. Not only that, however; Job's protests in the Dialogues ultimately make sense only if he assumes the effectiveness of the law of retribution. As Crenshaw notes, "Job has no case at all against God apart from an operative principle of reward and retribution, for in a world devoid of such a principle good people have no basis for complaining that the creator has abandoned the helm."[406] Similarly, God's rebuke of the friends in the Epilogue has no moral or theological framework without a presumed

---

404 Miller, *Israelite Religion*, 464, writes that, "theology stands before God as both a discerning Joseph and a creaturely Job, interpreting God's work and knowing that it does not know."
405 See, Crenshaw, *Urgent Advice*, 464.
406 James L. Crenshaw, *A Whirlpool of Torment: Israelite Traditions of God as an Oppressive Presence* (Philadelphia: Fortress, 1984), 62.

principle of retribution. However, other scholars have noted that the restoration is an act of divine free will and mystery.[407]

My analysis of the text and survey of its history of interpretation suggest that the Epilogue is a combination of retributive and non-retributive action. In true retributive fashion, God rebukes the friends for their wrongs and threatens to punish them, but the punishment (although only hypothetical) is not retributive since it is described as a potential "outrageous" act. Moreover, the divine response to Job's prayer is expressed in terms of God's favor to Job (42:8–9; cf. 8:12). Finally, the expression, "to turn the fortunes" that is used to describe Job's restoration is sometimes used in retributive fashion and other times in a non-retributive manner. Both views are, therefore, expressed in the text.

4.4 Proposed Meanings of the Epilogue

How might the Epilogue of Job be meaningfully interpreted and appropriated within the overall structure and content of the book? Given the overall language of restoration that is used in the text and the theological resources that are discernible in it, there are three possible meanings that the Epilogue provides for understanding the book of Job.

4.4.1 The Master-Servant Relationship: Restoration As Retributive and Beyond-Retributive Justice

The survey of the history of interpretation showed that both Jewish and Christian interpreters have been drawn to the fact that Job is referred to as God's servant in the Epilogue. And it is tempting, given the nature of the personal relationship expressed in the phrase "my servant," to link the text back to the Prologue. However, the survey showed that ancient scholars focused on the reference to Job as "servant" not because they found it easy to connect with the Prologue, but because of its oddity given the nature of Job's words in the Dialogues. In other words, the reference to Job as God's servant in the Epilogue was perceived to be at some dissonance with the character of the Dialogues. Therefore, in order to fully understand the function of the restoration in the Epilogue, one has also to recognize and incorporate the way in which the word עבד is used in the Dialogues. Interestingly, this allows one to further understand the master-servant relationship that underlies the text, since Job emerges both as master and as servant. Even more, it will help foster the dynamic between the personal and generic dimensions of Job's

---

407 Murphy, *The Tree of Life*, 44; Janzen, *Job*, 267.

relationship with God, since עבד is used in a generic and personal sense in the Dialogues and in a personal sense in the Prologue and Epilogue.

The word עבד is used eight times in the Dialogues, referring to human beings (3:19; 7:2; 19:16; 21:15; 31:13), divine beings (4:18), and fierce animals (39:9; 40:28). In two instances, Job speaks from the perspective of a master who has lost his authority over his servants (19:16),[408] and one who used to treat his servant fairly, responding appropriately to their concerns (31:13). In the response from the theophany, God refers to the master-servant relationship, although mainly from the point of God's power and authority to control forces of the sea and land (39:9; 40:28).

In two other instances (3:19; 7:2), Job speaks from the perspective of a servant, and interprets the concept of servanthood in terms of forced labor that is so oppressive that the laborer has to long for the evening time of rest and daily pay. In fact, Job's words in 3:18–19 describe a situation of oppressed captives to whose voice the Lord listens (Ps 69:34; 102:21). And the voice of the taskmaster echoes the experience of suffering and hard labor prior to the Exodus (Exod 3:7; 5:6, 10, 13, 14). Therefore, Job's words here resonate with the aspirations of those who are oppressed and who want to be free from the dominion of their masters. The master-servant relationship as developed in the Dialogues, therefore, evokes the reality of power, possible power abuse and the influence of masters over their subjects. And within the context of the Dialogues, Job's response from the perspective of the servant puts the credibility of the master into focus. Henceforth, the image of the master cannot be taken for granted or held uncritically.

Incidentally, part of the reason why God liberated Israel from Egyptian servitude was so that Israel will worship (lit. "serve") God (Exod 4:23). This creates a potential paradox since liberation would mean changing from one master to another. In that sense, the credibility of the liberation depends on the character of the master. In the light of Job's experience, the liberating and positive force of the Exodus would be challenged by the experience of difficult service under God. That is, Job sees himself as God's servant, but the divine lordship is oppressive.[409] In 7:2, Job sees himself as a hireling who expects to be paid at the end of the day, as was the norm (Deut 24:15; Exod 22:14; Is 7:20; Jer 6:4; Matt 20:8, 12). Withholding such daily wages was prohibited (Lev 19:13; Mal 3:5; Jas 5:4; 1 Cor 3:8). And yet, it does appear that in spite of such expectations, masters sometimes did not fulfill their obligation. This possible failure on the part of the masters partly explains the question posed by the wicked rich people: "what is Shadday that we should serve him?" (Job 21:15). Evidently, therefore, the concept of

---

408 This text suggests to Whybray that the real nature of Job's loss was that of his relationship with God, since he still had a family, house, and servants at his disposal after the attacks. See R. Norman Whybray, *The Good Life in the Old Testament* (London: T&T Clark, 2002), 140–141.
409 Driver and Gray, *Job*, 39; Habel, *The Book of Job*, 111; Janzen, *Job*, 64.

servanthood in the Dialogues is construed within the context of the responsibility of the master to ensure the welfare of their servants. This understanding may, consequently, be perceived as part of the background against which the concept of the restoration is used in the Epilogue.[410]

When God refers to Job as "my servant" in the Epilogue, the reader may very well ponder the nature of the master-servant relationship developed in the Prologue and the Dialogues. In what way might the Epilogue be responding to the validity of the argument raised by Job the servant in the Dialogues? It is clear that as master, Job looks after the welfare of his servants and expects the same treatment as a servant of God. Therefore, although the Dialogues do raise significant questions about the concept of retribution, they do not repudiate the concept altogether. Perhaps the restoration of Job's health and property in the Epilogue is to be partly understood as God's response to this expectation.

From the Dialogues, it is clear that Job's laments and protests have implications on the different spheres of life (personal, social, cosmic). For those who control the political, social, economic, and religious dynamics of relationships that are framed as "master-servant" relationships, it is possible to sidestep their responsibilities towards the servants as von Soden notes in his description of the role of religion in the ancient Near East; it is possible to raise the question of "motives" and agree to a "test" whose consequences may result in social evil, that is, unjust power dynamics and human suffering in society.[411] Therefore, for those who (through the various structures of society) have no choice but to be servants, and especially those in forced labor, the question "Does Job worship God for nothing?" takes on a different perception, especially in the context of God's reference to Job as a servant and Job's understanding of the expectations and responsibilities associated with that relationship. For Israel who cries out under the oppressive yoke of servanthood in Pharaoh's land, and who is delivered to become (among other things) God's servant, the crucial question must be asked whether there is any real difference between the two lords, that is, between Pharaoh and YHWH, and consequently whether the Exodus motif has any real bearing and value.[412] For the servant, the Dialogues provide the context and hermeneutical force for a critique of oppressive and destructive power

---

410 For further discussion on the topic of servant of the Lord, see Roland de Vaux, *Ancient Israel: Its Life and Institutions* (trans. John McHugh; London: McGraw-Hill, 1961), 80–90.
411 See Brueggeman, "Theodicy in a Social Dimension," 4–5.
412 Jon D. Levenson, "The Resurrection of the Dead and the Construction of Personal Identity in Ancient Israel," in *Congress Volume: Basel 2001* (ed. André Lemaire; VTSup 92; Leiden: Brill, 2002), 307, writes: "The exodus has become a prototype of ultimate redemption, and historical liberation has become a partial but proleptic experience of eschatological experience, a token, perhaps *the* token of things to come. The full activation of God's potential in the foundational past has been transformed into a sign of a still greater activation of his potential in the future consummation – a consummation that moves the Jews not merely from slavery to freedom, but quite literally from death to life as well."

dynamics. The divine approval of Job in the Epilogue becomes a significant hermeneutical force. The Epilogue also provides alternative perceptions of the divine-human relationship, where Job and his friends can alter YHWH's actions, particularly destructive actions. The divine-human relationship is thus shaped by divine freedom and sovereignty as well as responsibility for the welfare of humankind. And although resulting from divine initiative, humans have the responsibility of formulating and enacting theologies that resist the use of the "master-servant" in destructive ways. This is what Job and his friends accomplish through their sacrifice and prayers.

4.4.2 The Divine-Human Relationship: Restoration as a New Beginning

The Epilogue is as much about Job's beginning as it is about the end. In fact, one may suggest that unlike Second Isaiah who speaks of "former things" which, in anticipation to his message about a new creation, should sometimes not be remembered (43:18–19), the narrator of Job still wants to talk about the first things (42:12; Is 46:9). More suggestive, perhaps, is the difference between the narrator of Job and John the Revelator for whom the first things had passed away and the chaos of the sea was no more (Rev 21:1). Perhaps the narrator of Job does not want the reader to forget the beginning of the story, and so to understand the latter part of Job's life (described in the Epilogue) not just as an end but also as an end that conceptually includes the first beginning. This is suggested by the enumeration of Job's material prosperity and the mention of God having brought trouble on him, which point back to the beginning of the story. A recollection or remembrance of Job's former days is clearly one of the narrator's strategies of speaking about a restoration that is largely a transcending of the past. The Epilogue is therefore a new beginning.

However, this new beginning is one with a difference; unlike the Prologue where there is no direct interaction between the decisions of heaven and the resulting human action on earth, the new beginning in the Epilogue emerges from the theophanic encounter. Originally, and in conjunction with the "test" motif, the response to suffering was to be Job's entirely. With the theophany, however, the divine presence introduces another factor. I have argued that the literary transition from the theophany to the Epilogue in 42:7 suggests that one can situate the Epilogue within the broader context of the divine speeches and the resulting human response. This theophany-epilogue continuum is significant because it provides an important component for examining not just the human response to the reality of chaos, but also the divine response; in fact, it allows one to explore not the human and divine responses in isolation but rather the divine-human response together. Within this framework of the theophany-epilogue continuum, the arguments expressing divine mystery and sovereignty in the theophany, especially the rhetorical questions relating to creation (38:5–11), now stand side by side with the activity and rhetoric of the cult and prayer.⁴¹³ In his treatment of the nature of the divine-human relationship in Deuteronomy and the Psalms, Patrick Miller finds that there is extensive use of what he refers to as *motivational* clauses. These clauses include *sanctions* and *promises* that urge and persuade the human community to obey the divine commands. Miller refers to this endeavor as the *rhetoric of persuasion*, where individuals and communities present reasons why the deity should respond to their prayers.⁴¹⁴ The theophany-epilogue continuum thus provides a meaningful context for exploring the paradoxical relationship between the transcendent God and frail humankind. And since the ultimate response to the reality of suffering is a joint responsibility that comes to the divine and human councils, this continuum also allows one to examine the role that the cult played in shaping that response.

That the temple represented the place of response to the reality of evil is part of Israelite thinking. A number of Psalms indicate that this was the case. In Ps 73, for example, we find that when the psalmist is perplexed and overwhelmed by the chaos caused by those who plan evil (Ps 73:8), he becomes hopeless but only until he enters the holy place of God where he comes to "understand" the fate of the evil doers, that is, their end (אחרית). In the temple, Israel is able to perceive an end to the threat of evil. Equally suggestive is the response to chaos presented in Ps 74. Particularly important is the fact that between the lament over the destruction of the temple and the oppression of the poor (Ps 74:1–11), and the imperatival/motivational appeal to God to act (74:18–23), we find a poem on God's creation and victory over the forces of chaos, including Leviathan (74:12–17).⁴¹⁵ The protest over the chaos and the plea for divine intervention are linked and nourished by a creation account.

---

413 Tryggve N. D. Mettinger has discussed the dynamic relationship between heaven and earth in the development of Israelite Temple Theology, and found that the temple was the interface between heaven and earth; in the sacred place of the sanctuary, heaven and earth became one. See, Mettinger, "The Dethronement of Sabaoth: Studies in the Shem and Kabod Theologies" (Coniectanea Biblica 18; Lund: Gleerup, 1982), 19–37. See also M. Metzger's, »Himmlische und irdische Wohnsttat Yahwes«" *UF* 2 (1970): 139–158, that explore the relationship between the cosmic rule of the deity in heaven and the rule of the earthly king depicted in the Nabu-aplu-iddina's relief in the Shamash temple. Elsewhere in Israelite literature, this dynamic is expressed in Solomon's dedication prayer (1 Kg 8:14–27) and Jacob's dream at Bethel in Gen 28:10–12, 22.
414 Miller, *Israelite Religion*, 325–327. Evidently, the motivational clauses and reasons that the petitioner brings before God to persuade God to act in one way or another are not present in the Epilogue. Rather, it is God who gives the reason for the prayer: "so that I will not do to you an outrage." Still, there is persuasion (through threat) in the command to make sacrifice and prayers.
415 One notes a number of literary and thematic echoes between this psalm and Job's experience within the context of the theophany-epilogue continuum. These include: (a) the problem of divine anger (Ps 74:1 // Job 42:7); (b) reference to God's actions in the past as a springboard for new action (Ps 74:2, 12 // Job 42:11); (c) the theme of inheritance redeemed or preserved (Ps 74:2 // Job 42:15); and (d) concern over the presence and threat of evil (Ps 74:3 // Job 42:11).

In an essay on *Creation in the Psalms*, Richard Clifford notes the frequent reference to God's actions in the past and concludes that these recitals of the past in the laments describe not just any period of the past, but the moment of the origin of Israel: the creation of Israel as God's people. Furthermore, the details of the past being referenced are tailored to address the current crisis.[416] Accordingly, this creation ideology is set in response to the threat and actuality of chaos in a world where history continues to transpire but may yet expire.[417] In this Psalm, as in the theophany-epilogue of Job, creation motif and cultic expression meet in response to the problem of chaos.[418]

The language of the Epilogue of Job is explicit about the presence of evil and the cultic activity; but it is less explicit about creation. However, the larger context of the theophany dealing with creation may allow one to include the use of creation ideology as part of the response to chaos. Furthermore, one can discern an underlying creation motif in the divine blessing and the resulting material prosperity mentioned in 42:11–17. That is, in 1:10 the Adversary argues that God hedges Job around and has "blessed the work of his hand" to the effect that his possession bursts forth in the whole earth. Although the verb שׂוּךְ (or סוּךְ – "to hedge" or "hedge in") may evoke either the idea of protection or obstruction, its use in 3:23 and 38:8 is set within the context of creation.[419] It is all this material prosperity along with Job's children that the Adversary refers to when he speaks of divine blessing. Accordingly, the divine blessing of Job in the Prologue may have the creation motif as an underlying current or sub-text.[420] Therefore, when God blesses Job in the Epilogue more than before, one is perhaps to discern echoes of the Prologue, with its underlying implications, since this is the only other instance in the text where the verb "to bless" is used with YHWH as subject. However, what we have in the theophany-epilogue setting is not uninterrupted blessing as in the Prologue. Rather, it is blessing that emerges out of chaos. Together with the divine blessing, echoes creation material elsewhere (Gen 1:28).[421]

---

416 Richard J. Clifford, "Creation in the Psalms," in *Creation in the Biblical Traditions* (ed. Richard J. Clifford and John J. Collins; Washington: Catholic Biblical Association of America, 1992), 61–62.
417 Miller, *Israelite Religion*, 486.
418 Note also that the Priestly creation account in Genesis 1 is worked into a cultic frame. Also, Job's lawsuit protest (ריב) is elsewhere part of the cultic terminology that urges God to act against chaos (Ps 74:22). For a discussion on the legal metaphor in Job and how it relates to the function of the gods as judges in the ancient Near East, see J. J. M. Roberts, "Job's Summons to Yahweh: The Exploitation of a Legal Metaphor," *ResQ* 16, no. 3 (1973): 159–165.
419 See, Pope, *Job*, 251.
420 Such a creation motif in the divine blessing in the Prologue may help explain Job's curse on creation in his opening soliloquy in chapter 3, following the loss of his possession, children, and health.
421 The broader implications of this blessing motif (for all of creation) as one that emerges from chaos would echo the divine blessing of humankind in the creation text of 1:28. Brueggemann describes this blessing as "a bold and overpowering affirmation" which asserts "God's radical intention to promote well being and prosperity. And that intent

Within the theophany-epilogue context, the narrator has re-posed the problem relating to the issue of suffering, but has also signaled possibilities of response through the use of creation imagery and blessing (which highlight divine sovereignty), and cultic prayer and sacrifice (which highlight divine accessibility to the sufferer). In re-posing the problem, God along with Job and his friends are all engaged in responding to the "evil/trouble that YHWH brought on Job." To accommodate the tension in the divine character as one who brings trouble, the narrator creates a literary and theological context referred to as "more than" before. Within this new context, the arguments based on the validity of new experience, religious tradition, and divine sovereignty and mystery are all viable options. In fact, these are no longer competing alternative responses but complementary possibilities that address the depth and complexity of suffering in general and innocent suffering in particular. Together, these various responses create the context of a new beginning– one in which God, Job and the friends all recognize the potency of chaos, but also affirm and work towards the ultimate possible triumph of the good. The Epilogue is a new beginning for God, Job, and the friends.

4.4.3 The Reality of Suffering: Restoration as Possible Triumph of the Good

Whether or not one reads the story as a test from the beginning, the forcefulness of the Dialogues makes the story as much a personal and social problem as it is a religious or spiritual "test." Therefore, the Epilogue takes on the responsibility of responding not only to the "test" aspect of the story but also to the moral and theological challenge that the story poses at the personal and social dimensions. I have suggested that within the theophany-epilogue continuum, creation imagery and cultic expression, along with the various rhetorical and religious traditions that underlie them, come together.

Jon Levenson has argued for the use of creation as part of the theological response to the threat of evil. In his analysis of the creation and flood accounts in Genesis, the *Enuma Elish*, and Ps 74, Levenson describes the creation myth as one "that speaks of God's total mastery not as something self evident, unthreatened and extant from all eternity, but as something won, as something dramatic and exciting."[422] Thus, chaos and evil are not

---

cannot be frustrated by any circumstance, not even such a circumstance as the traditionist's context of exile." See Walter Brueggemann, "The Kerygma of the Priestly Writers," in *Vitality of Old Testament Tradition* (ed. Walter Brueggemann and Hans W. Wolff; Atlanta: John Knox, 1975), 113. Evidence of such prosperity in exile has been described by Charles F. Pfeiffer, *Exile and Return* (Grand Rapids, Mich.: Baker Books House, 1962), 50–54.

422 Levenson, *Creation and the Persistence of Evil*, 9. For further readings on creation and chaos, see also Bunyan D. Napier, On Creation-Faith in the Old Testament: A Survey," *Int* 26 (1962): 21–42; R. B. Coote and D. R. Ord, *In the Beginning: Creation and the Priestly History* (Minneapolis: Fortress, 1991); Bernhard W. Anderson, *Contours of Old Testament Theology* (Minneapolis: Fortress, 1998), 87–97.

destroyed; rather, they must be persistently bridled and restrained.[423] This persistence of evil and the resulting need to respond to it is suggestive given that in the Epilogue of Job, the human assembly gathers to console and comfort Job for all the evil that the Lord had brought on him. Levenson rightly points out that it is in the post flood covenant with Noah that God compels the obedience of the adversity posed by the chaos,[424] although it should equally be noted that the post flood covenant is already anticipated in a pre-flood covenant in which God promises to preserve creation in the ark (Gen 6:17–19). That is, there is a certain portion of creation that is preserved in the ark, and that survives the presence of the chaos. Accordingly, one might argue that creation is as much, if not much more, about the persistence of the good as it is about the persistence of evil. In either case, Levenson clearly demonstrates that the primary guarantor of human survival and creation as a whole is God. This point is supported by the fact that in Ps 74:11 evil persists partly because of divine self-restraint. Should God begin to act, chaos will be overcome.

In Jer 32:42 God provides part of the moral and theological rationales for the concept of restoration by portraying it as the antithesis of the trouble/evil of the exile and chaos. God states:

כאשר הבאתי אל־העם הזה את כל־הרעה הגדולה הזאת
כן אנכי מביא עליהם את־כל־הטובה אשר אנכי דבר עליהם

(Just as I brought this great trouble/evil to this people, so I am bringing upon them all the good that I promised them.")

The theological basis for the coming restoration is set in terms of the opposition between good and evil. The restoration is God's undoing of God's prior actions. In the Epilogue of Job, it is maintained that God does bring trouble/evil (Job 42:11), and this can be understood in the background of the moral question about good and evil. In fact, Job had earlier maintained that God does indeed bring both good and evil; the only question was whether humans are able to receive both (Job 2:10). To a significant extent, the Prologue and Dialogues explore this dynamic between what God brings and what humans are able to receive, and one of the ways through which humans testify to having received evil/trouble is through protest and lament.[425] It is in response to such a lament over the destruction (Jer 32:36) that God promises to restore Israel.

Therefore, within the context of the Epilogue, the restoration may be perceived as the antithesis of the evil that came upon Job. In that sense, the

---

423 See Brueggemann, *Old Testament Theology*, 536.
424 Levenson, *Creation and the Persistence of Evil*, 17.
425 Robert Davidson, *The Courage to Doubt: Exploring an Old Testament Theme* (London: SCM, 1983), 183, writes: "Job's encounter with God was inseparable from his protests against an over-simplistic theology.... There was more faith in such deeply questioning protests and scepticism than in the pious affirmation of untroubled, but blind, certainty."

restoration is a divine initiative that may well resonate with 11QtgJob where God turns to Job in mercy. If so, then this may have broader theological implications because, as we have seen, the restoration language employed in the Epilogue is used elsewhere within the context of some of Israel's cherished traditions – the covenant with creation (Jer 33:26), the promise of land to the patriarchs (Amos 9:14), obedience to the Torah (Deut 30:3; Hos 6:11; Jer 33:7), and God's grace and compassion (Jer 30:18). That is, these traditions may underlie the restoration language of the Epilogue; through the restoration they survive, although not in any explicit form. What is explicit is the manner and context in which they do: not as theological clichés to be repeated but as theological resources in the service of the divine-human relationship in general and human need in particular. In this particular instance, what survives is the sense of God's favor to humans, retributive justice, and reconciliation. But also, these traditions survive not as the exclusive forms of theological articulation of what the divine-human relationship consists of, but as part of a larger repertoire that includes the mystery of God's sovereignty over, and accessibility to humankind. As Langdon Gilkey rightly notes, there is within Judaism and Christianity the conviction that God is also redeemer from evil as well as chastiser of evil. In Job, "God does not so much judge, repudiate, condemn, and destroy evil – God as moral law – as God transforms it, embraces it, participates in it, and overcomes it."[426]

As has been shown from the history of interpretation, both Jewish and Christian interpreters repeatedly argued that one of the ways through which evil and the trouble of this world are finally overcome is through the resurrection. The concept of the resurrection in itself is quite broad and complex, and full treatment of the topic lies beyond the limits of the present work. Of particular concern to me here is not the historical development of the general idea of resurrection, but its use within the context of retribution or rewards and punishment for the righteous and the wicked respectively. This is how the concept is used in LXX-Job and the *Testament of Job*. In this regard, the concept is variously used in Jewish and Christian understanding to describe bodily resurrection, revivification of the soul or spirit, eternal life, or assumption and exaltation to heaven. When used within the context of retribution, two things stand out. First, there is focus on bodily resurrection, the purpose of which is to maintain that the dead individual is identical to the resurrection person.[427] This appears to be one of the primary reasons for the

---

426 Langdon Gilkey, "Power, Order, Justice, and Redemption: Theological Comments on Job," in *Voice from the Whirlwind: Interpreting the Book of Job* (ed. Leo G. Perdue and W. Clark Gilpin; Nashville: Abingdon, 1992), 169.
427 In 2 Bar 21:12–26; 30:2–5, the souls of the dead are pictured as gathered in Sheol, but shall be raised in their original form so that the living may recognize them. Similarly, 1 En 29:6 mentions the bones of those to be raised, suggesting a bodily resurrection.

resurrection appearances in Luke and John.[428] Second, there is often the description and association of rewards from God, usually a life of glory and merriment (Dan 12:1–3; Lk 16:19–31).

One finds two views of the resurrection expressed in the *Testament of Job*, where resurrection is associated with Job's reward for his patient endurance of Satan's assault. On the one hand, the bones of Job's children are no longer in the rubble (T.Job 39:8–9) because the children have been taken up to heaven (T.Job 39:12); on the other hand, it is Job's soul that ascends to heaven while his body is prepared and buried (T.Job 42:10; 53: 7, 11).[429] The continued personal identity of the individual that is required for the belief in posthumous rewards and punishment appears to have been associated with some durable part of the human being such as human bones (Lk 24:39; Ezek 37).[430]

In the NT, two texts are important for my present purposes: Lk 24:36–43 and Jn 20:24–29. These texts portray a bodily, even "materialistic" view of the resurrection of Jesus. In his series of resurrection appearances, Jesus can go through closed doors (Jn 20:26) as well as appear and disappear at will (Lk 24:36; Jn 20:26). He can walk along with people and not be immediately recognized (Lk 24:27, 45); he is human enough to be confused with a gardener (Jn 20:15), and to eat (Lk 24:42–43), but he is equally different enough to be possibly confused with a ghost (Lk 24:37). This view of the resurrection stands in tension with other views, especially Paul's in 1 Cor 15:50, where he states that flesh and blood cannot inherit the kingdom of God.[431] These resurrection appearances, however, precede Jesus' exaltation to heaven. Therefore, they are "transitional," since they place Jesus after the resurrection but before the ascension.[432] Accordingly, they provide an important point of entry into an examination of the significance and implications of the resurrection for human life in this world.[433] Jesus'

---

428 See, Joseph A. Fitzmyer, *The Gospel According to Luke X-XXIV: Introduction, Translation, and Notes* (ed. William F. Albright and David N. Freedman; AB 28; New York: Doubleday, 1985), 1576; Fred B. Craddock, *Luke* (ed. James L. Mays, Patrick D. Miller, and Paul Achtemeier; IBC 42; Louisville: John Knox, 1990), 289–290.

429 For further analysis, see Spittler, "Testament of Job," 859; Émil Puech, *La Résurrection des Morts et le Contexte Scripturaire*, vol. 1 of *La Croyance des Esséniens en la Vie Future: Immortalité, Résurrection, Vie Éternelle? Histoire d'une Croyance dans le Judaïsme Ancien* (Paris: Librairie Lecoffre J. Gabalda, 1993), 166–168.

430 Anthony Harvey, "They Discussed among Themselves what this "Rising from the dead" Could Mean" (Mark 9:10)," in *Resurrection: Essays in Honour of Leslie Houlden* (ed. Stephen Barton and Graham Stanton; London: SPCK, 1994), 72; Rachel Wischnitzer-Bernstein, "The Concept of the Resurrection in the Ezekiel Panel of the Dura Synagogue," *JBL* 60, no. 1 (1941): 43–55.

431 Note, however, that even with Luke's own writing, the idea of a "spiritual" resurrection is possibly suggested where the righteous dead immediately go to be with God (Lk 16:25; 20:38).

432 Harvey, "'They Discussed Among Themselves,'" 75–76.

433 See, Robert Morgan, "Flesh is Precious: The Significance of Luke 24.36-43," in *Resurrection: Essays in Honour of Leslie Houlden* (ed. Stephen Barton and Graham Stanton; London: SPCK, 1994), 8–20; Paul Trudinger, "Two Lukan Gospel Stories: Key to the Significance of the Dominical Sacraments in the Life of the Early Church,"

appearances present a paradox since they combine qualities of the present life and the future life, qualities of a life that is subjected to death and that is beyond death. Jesus' resurrected body still has the scars of the crucifixion.

In the book of Job, this paradox is explored by Suzanne Boorer, who argues that unlike in the book of Proverbs where good and evil, order and chaos, life and death are treated as binary opposites, the book of Job resists such dualism; chaos is associated with death (Job 3:8) and life (38:8), and it is from Job's embracing of death and chaos, rather than from avoiding it that life emerges.[434] This double reality is equally expressed in a "letter to Job" published from the sixth conference of the Ecumenical Association of Third World Theologians in Switzerland. Elsa Tamez, the author of the letter, writes:

> "Now, Brother Job, you have really come to know God. You will never be the same after this experience of suffering. You'll never be again that rich gentleman who had all his wants and needs taken care of and who gave of his surplus to those who had nothing. You've had the intimate knowledge of being wretched and no one can erase this personal experience from your personal history. Now you know God better. You struggled with God until God blessed and restored you. What will you do now? God restored you, but what of us? Hoping to see you again here in the trash heap."[435]

The restoration is a scarred restoration because it never really takes away the experience of suffering and, for many within the community of faith, often does not materialize. The question, "what about us?" expresses both the hope for a restoration and possibly protest for not experiencing a restoration, as well as the realization that restoration may never occur, at least not in the present life. However, in an analysis of the corporate concept of human personality in the Old Testament, Levenson argues that the survival of individuals went beyond human parts and was perceived to be guaranteed through one's children or "seed." Accordingly, the "highly familial and collective concept" of personal identity that underlies the biblical texts suggests that, "birth is the reversal of death and thus the functional equivalent of the resurrection."[436] Job's new children, accordingly, reverse the loss of the first.

DRev 118, no. 410 (2000): 17–26; J. J. F. Durand, "Theology and Resurrection – Metaphors and Paradigms," *JTSA* 82 (1993): 3–20; Graeme Goldsworthy, "'With Flesh and Bones': A Biblical Theology of the Bodily Resurrection of Christ," *RTR* 57 (1998): 121–135.

434 Suzanne Boorer, "A Matter of Life and Death: A Comparison of Proverbs 1–9 and Job," in *Prophets and Paradigms: Essays in Honor of Gene M. Tucker* (ed. Stephen Breck Reid; JSOTSup 229; ed. David J. A. Clines and Philip R. Davies; Sheffield: Sheffield Academic Press, 1996), 187–204.

435 Elsa Tamez, "Letter to Job," in *Doing Theology in a Divided World: Papers from the 6th International Conference of the Ecumenical Association of Third World Theologians, Jan 5-13 1983, Geneva Switzerland* (ed. Virginia Fabella and Sergio Torres; New York: Orbis, 1985), 176.

436 Levenson, "The Resurrection of the Dead," 312.

In summary, there are three possible meanings that emerge from my reading of the text. First, the restoration can be understood as God's response to the aspirations of "servants" who expect to be rewarded for their service. If there is no real difference between God the master and Pharaoh, then the concept of liberation or deliverance becomes useless, since deliverance becomes simply a change from one master to another without any substantive change in the experience of the "servant." Accordingly, the theophany-epilogue context allows for critical self-evaluation that recognizes the crisis and suffering that can result from unequal power structures depicted in the moral framework of the Prologue. But more importantly, the Epilogue also provides an interpretive context that goes beyond a critique of the reality of suffering to proposing alternative models of the divine-human and human-human relationships that seek greater accountability, survival, success, and healing. Second, the Epilogue can be read as a new beginning in which Job, his friends, and God all unite to respond to the threat and reality of evil in the world. As a new beginning, God along with Job and his friends all recognize not only the potency of evil and its destructive power, but also embark on preventing such destruction. And third, the Epilogue can be seen as the reversal of chaos and the ultimate (though scarred) triumph of the good. For both Jewish and Christian interpreter over the centuries, this triumph and restoration begins with this world but does not end with it.

Conclusion

Scholars are unanimous that the Epilogue of the book of Job is at some dissonance with the rest of the book, especially with the poetic section, although scholars differ on how to deal with the dissonance, or even whether the dissonance is substantive or just apparent. I have argued that the dissonance is both literary and theological, and that it is substantive. Of particular concern to me has been the tension between the divine rebuke of Job in the theophany and the approval in the Epilogue (42:7). How "true" are Job's words in the Prologue and Dialogues? And how is it that the friends are rebuked for not speaking rightly? Equally important has been the apparent return to the concept of retribution in the Epilogue, after its limitations have been clearly demonstrated in the Dialogues. This return to retribution places the Epilogue at some resonance with the Prologue.

Scholarly interpretations have largely focused on highlighting these resonances or dissonances in isolation from one another. I have argued that it is not enough to immediately associate the Epilogue with the Prologue simply on the basis of their prosaic form and their similar literary and thematic features. Neither is it enough to simply highlight the dissonances between the Epilogue and the Dialogues. Rather, I have suggested that one should move beyond simply arguing for resonances or dissonances in the text, and try to incorporate both in the interpretation of the Epilogue. When one reads the Epilogue carefully, there are a number of resonances and dissonances that emerge between the Epilogue and the Prologue as well as between the Epilogue and the Dialogues. These resonances and dissonances are what constitute the form and content of the Epilogue. They contribute towards the interpretation and understanding of the text. Accordingly, the proper interpretation of the Epilogue has to take these factors into consideration.[437]

The narrator uses both literary and thematic concepts that, as a cluster, resonate quite significantly with each of the preceding sections. Thus, for example, the divine approval of Job, his intercession for his friends at the time of sacrifice, and the doubling of his possessions all combine to resonate with his depiction in the Prologue. On the other hand, the rebuke of the friends for not speaking rightly, the gathering of a human council (including Job's brothers, sisters, and former acquaintances) around him, and the idea of God lifting Job's face all combine to resonate with the Prologue and the Dialogues. But precisely because of such resonances, I have argued that the differences in meaning and the specific nuances that these concepts suggest

---

437 D. Cox, *Man's Anger and God's Silence*, 137.

and portray in the Epilogue become significant for understanding the Epilogue. The resonances and dissonances together create the form and content of the Epilogue. The narrator places these differences and similarities within a literary and theological context that he refers to as "more than" before. Accordingly, a *both-and* model of interpretation largely replaces the *either-or*, confrontational model that is sometimes used to interpret the text. Only through such a hermeneutic is one able to do justice to the elements of constancy, change, diversity, and unity within the text. It is such a hermeneutic that equally allows for holding together the elements of dialogue and monologue, as well as the personal and the broader social dimensions of faith that contribute in articulating and nurturing the divine-human relationship.

The survey of the history of interpretation of the text reveals, as one would expect, that there has been considerable diversity in the interpretation of the Epilogue. However, a number of persistent concerns appear to underlie these diverse interpretations. For example, does the divine approval of Job at the end indicate that Job was a perfectly righteous person? What is the nature of the restoration? Is it divine providence acting out in freedom and mercy, or is the restoration in accordance with the doctrine of retribution? Through my analysis of the versions (particularly LXX-Job and 11QtgJob), it is argued that there was clearly, on the one hand, an attempt to see Job as a righteous person who interceded for his friends so that God spared them from destruction. On the other hand, underlying this perception of Job as a righteous person, there was also the view that he was not altogether right. Accordingly, there is some tension between divine rebuke and divine approval within the witness of the versions.

This tension continues into later Rabbinic and Christian writing. An examination of the rabbinic/patristic and the medieval periods showed that the Epilogue served to portray Job both as a literary character within the structure of the book and as a paradigm for Israel and the church. As a literary character, the divine approval of Job and the restoration were understood within the context of God's sovereign providence and mercy towards God's people. Accordingly, Job's troubles were intended to bring him to a greater knowledge of God's will, and the Epilogue is a demonstration of that new phase of divine-human relationship that transcends material blessing. And yet, there was also the view that Job was rewarded because of his endurance (an idea strongly developed in the *Testament of Job*). When the Epilogue was interpreted as a paradigm, two things happened. First, there was much more use of allegorical interpretations. Second, the focus was not so much on Job's qualities as on God's actions to restore Job. Accordingly, Job was interpreted not just in conjunction with the rest of the text, but primarily in conjunction with the real life experiences of the audience. For Jewish interpreters, Job was related to national experiences of liberation and restoration. During moments of national hardship, the

Epilogue served to draw the attention of the audience to God's ability to mercifully restore the people. For Christian interpreters who saw Job as a non-Israelite, Job was a pre-figuration of Christ and God's redemptive purposes for the world. For both Jewish and Christian interpreters, the restoration signaled that suffering is a temporary experience, and the threat of chaos does not have the final word; rather, evil is eventually overcome either in this world or in the next.

A number of theological reflections emerged from my reading of the text. The Epilogue raises three fundamental issues relating to the nature of the master-servant relation, the nature of the broader divine-human relationship, and finally the reality of suffering. And since the Epilogue is closely associated with God's address to Job from the whirlwind, these issues can be dealt with within the theophany-epilogue continuum. Accordingly, three conclusions emerged. First, the Epilogue re-poses the question of religious motives that emerge in the master-servant relationship as well as the concept of retributive justice. Within a post-tragic and post-dialogue context, the concept of justice in retribution is no longer framed from the perspective of the "master" alone but also from the perspective of Job the servant. For those who have no choice but to be servants, the question whether Job feared God for nothing takes another dimension. My analysis of the use of "servant" in the Dialogues led me to conclude that the Epilogue can be understood as a response to the desire for liberation and reward that servants had. Part of this liberation involves recognition of the credibility of Job's critique in the Dialogues, credibility that receives divine approval in the Epilogue. But the restoration also transcends the retributive component of the text as defined in material terms to include a sense of greater knowledge and experience of God. This new experience is expressed in the fact that God shows favor to Job, that is, lifts Job's face in contradistinction from the traditional understanding of retribution.

Second, I proposed that the Epilogue is as much a new beginning as it is an end to the narrative. The language of the Epilogue points back to the beginning of the story and its development in the Dialogues, and thereby invites the reader to re-read the entire narrative. The result of this process is that the reader interacts with the text both as an "insider" (who participates in the Dialogues) and an "outsider" (who is situated outside the literary context of the Dialogues). Accordingly, the various responses to the problems that are developed in the narrative become not just competing alternatives but complementary possibilities for describing the nature of the divine-human relationship. Within this framework, retribution is both affirmed and surpassed. This is demonstrated in the Epilogue by the divine rebuke of the friends and the divine favor shown to Job in answer to the prayers that he offered for his friends. Both Job and his friends come together and experience the transcendence and immanence of God at the altar, and this constitutes part of their new beginning.

Finally, because the Epilogue mentions that the human gathering was in order to console Job for his trouble, the reality of suffering is not undermined. With the absence of the Adversary, it is likely that if trouble should touch Job (or any other person), there is no reason to assume that it is necessarily a test. The reader may decide to interpret the event as a "test" and come up with some exterior cause for it or, like the friends argued all along in accordance with much of Israelite tradition, interpret it as a result of some sin, or place it at God's feet as partly a mysterious act. The theophany-epilogue continuum, which allows one to bring together the elements of divine transcendence and immanence expressed through the language of creation and the cult respectively, provides a context in which all these possibilities become theological resources for responding to the reality of suffering. In this context, the response to the threat of trouble is not just Job's or just that of the human community but also the responsibility of the deity. On the one hand, the divine transcendence expresses the component of divine freedom not to restore (at least in material terms) those who suffer loss. On the other hand, the divine transcendence (in conjunction with the experience if divine accessibility at the altar) allows the reader to envisage the possibility and even the reality of the restoration as victory over chaos. In this sense, the Epilogue becomes an illustration of what such a restoration means, namely, the reversal of chaos as well as a new beginning for Job, his friends, and God.

Bibliography

Al-Fayyūmī, Saadiah Ben Joseph. *The Book of Beliefs and Opinions.* Translated by Samuel Rosenbalt. New Haven: Yale University Press, 1948.
⎯⎯⎯. *The Book of Theodicy: Translation and Commentary on the Book of Job.* Edited by Leon Nemoy, Judah Goldin, and Isadore Twersky. Translated by L. E. Goodman. Yale Judaica Series 25. New Haven: Yale University Press, 1988.
Alt, Albrecht. »Zur Vorgeschichte des Buches Hiob.« *Zeitschrift für die alttestamentliche Wissenschaft* 55 (1937): 265–268.
Alter, Robert. *The Art of Biblical Narrative.* New York: Basic Books, 1981.
Ambrose, Saint. *Seven Exegetical Works.* Translated by Michael P. McHugh. Washington: Catholic University of America Press, 1972.
Anderson, Bernhard W. *Contours of Old Testament Theology.* Minneapolis: Fortress, 1998.
Anderson, Francis I. *Job: An Introduction and Commentary.* Downers: Intervarsity, 1977.
Aquinas, Thomas. *The Literal Exposition on Job: A Scriptural Commentary Concerning Providence.* Translated by Anthony Damico with Interpretive Essay and Notes by Martin D. Yaffe. Atlanta: Scholars Press, 1989.
⎯⎯⎯. *Summa Contra Gentiles.* Vol. 3, bk. 1. Translated by the English Dominican Fathers from the Latest Leonine Edition. London: Burns Oates & Washbourne, 1928.
Averintsev, Sergei. "Bakhtin, Laughter, and Christian Culture." Pages 79–95 in *Bakhtin and Religion: A Feeling for Faith.* Edited by Susan M. Felch and Paul J. Contino. Evanston, Ill.: Northwestern University Press, 2001.
Ayedze, Kossi A. "Tertullian, Cyprain and Augustine on Patience: A Comparative and Critical Study of Three Treatises on a Stoic-Christian Virtue in Early North African Christianity." Ph.D. diss., Princeton Theological Seminary, 2000.

Bakhtin, Mikhail. *Problems of Dostoevsky's Poetics.* Translated and edited by Caryl Emerson. Theory and History of Literature 8. Minneapolis: University of Minnesota Press, 1984.
Balentine, Samuel E. "My Servant Job Shall Pray for You." *Theology Today* 58, no. 4 (2002): 502–518.
Barton, John. "Intertextuality and the 'Final Form' of the Text." Pages 33–37 in *Congress Volume Olso 1998.* Edited by André Lemaire and Magne Sæbø. Supplements to Vetus Testamentum 80. Leiden: Brill, 2000.
⎯⎯⎯. "The Significance of a Fixed Canon of the Hebrew Bible." Pages 67–83 in *Antiquity.* Part 1 of *From the Beginnings to the Middle Ages (until 1300).* Vol. 1 of *The Hebrew Bible, Old Testament: The History of*

its Interpretation. Edited by Magne Sæbø. Göttingen: Vandenhoeck & Ruprecht, 1996.

Baskin, Judith R. "Job as Moral Exemplar in Ambrose." *Vigiliae Christianae* 5, no. 3 (1981): 222–231.

_____. *Pharaoh's Counsellors: Job, Jethro, and Balaam in Rabbinic and Patristic Tradition*. Edited by Jacob Neusner, Wendell S. Dietrich, and Alan Zuckerman. Brown Judaica Studies 47. Chico, Calif.: Scholars Press, 1983.

Baumann, Eberhard. "שבו שתוב: Eine Exegetische Untersuchung." *Zeitschrift für die alttestamentliche Wissenschaft* 47 (1929): 17–44.

Begg, C. T. "Comparing Characters: The Book of Job and the Testament of Job." Pages 435–445 in *The Book of Job*. Edited by W. A. M. Beuken. Bibliotheca Ephemeridum Theologicarum Lovaniensium 114. Leuven: Leuven University Press,1994.

Ben Maimon, Moses. *The Guide for the Perplexed*. Translated by M. Friedländer. 2nd ed. New York: George Routledge, 1919.

Ben-Barak, Zafrira. "Inheritance by Daughters in the ANE." *Journal of Semitic Studies* 25 (1980): 28–31.

Benin, Stephen D. "The Search for Truth in Sacred Scripture: Jews, Christians, and the Authority to Interpret." Pages 13–32 in *With Reverence for the Word: Medieval Scriptural Exegesis in Judaism, Christianity, and Islam*. Edited by Jane Dammen McAuliffe, Barry D. Walfish, and Joseph W. Goering. Oxford: Oxford University Press, 2003.

Ben-Shammai, Haggai. "The Tension Between Literal Interpretation and Exegetical Freedom: Comparative Observations on Saadia's Method." Pages 33–50 in *With Reverence for the Word: Medieval Scriptural Exegesis in Judaism, Christianity, and Islam*. Edited by Jane Dammen McAuliffe, Barry D. Walfish, and Joseph W. Goering. Oxford: Oxford University Press, 2003.

Boling, Robert G. "Kings and Prophets: Cyrus and Servant – Reading Isaiah 40–55." Pages 171–188 in *Ki Baruch Hu: Ancient Near Eastern, Biblical, and Judaic Studies in Honor of Baruch A. Levine*. Edited by Robert Chazan, William W. Hallo, and Lawrence H. Schiffman. Indiana: Eisenbrauns, 1999.

Boorer, Suzanne. "The Dark Side of God? A Dialogue with Jung's Interpretation of the Book of Job." *Pacifica* 10 (1997): 277–297.

_____. "A Matter of Life and Death: A Comparison of Proverbs 1-9 and Job." Pages 187–204 in *Prophets and Paradigms: Essays in Honor of Gene M. Tucker*. Edited by Stephen Breck Reid. Journal for the Study of the Old Testament: Supplement Series 229. Edited by David J. A. Clines and Philip R. Davies. Sheffield: Sheffield Academic Press, 1996.

Borger, R. "Zu שבו שוב/תי." *Zeitschrift für die alttestamentliche Wissenschaft* 66 (1954): 315–316.

Bracke, John M. "Šûb šĕbût: A Reappraisal." *Zeitschrift für die alttestamentliche Wissenschaft* 97 (1985): 233–244.

Brenner, Athalya. "Job the Pious? The Characterization of Job in the Narrative Framework of the Book." *Journal for the Study of the Old Testament* 43 (1989): 37–52.
Brett, Mark G. "The Future of Old Testament Theology." Pages 465–488 in *Congress Volume: Olso 1998*. Edited by André Lemaire and Magne Sæbø. Supplements to Vetus Testamentum 80. Edited by H. M. Barstad et al. Leiden: Brill, 2000.
Brockelmann, Carl. *Hebräische Syntax*. Neukirchen: Moers, 1956.
Brottier, Laurence. "L'Actualisation de la Figure de Job chez Jean Chrysostome." Pages 63–110 in *Le Livre de Job Chez les Pères*. Cahiers de Biblia Patristica 5. Strasbourg: Centre d'Analyse et de Documentation Patristique, 1996.
Brown, David. *Discipleship and Imagination: Christian Tradition and Truth*. Oxford: Oxford University Press, 2000.
Brown, Francis, Samuel R. Driver, and Charles A. Briggs, eds. *The Brown-Driver-Briggs Hebrew and English Lexicon with an Appendix Containing the Biblical Aramaic Coded with the Numbering System from Strong's Exhaustive Concordance of the Bible*. Peabody, Mass.: Hendrickson, 1997.
Brueggemann, Walter. "The Kerygma of the Priestly Writers." Pages 101–118 in *Vitality of Old Testament Tradition*. Edited by Walter Brueggemann and Hans W. Wolff. Atlanta: John Knox, 1975.
_____. "Texts That Linger, Not Yet Overcome." Pages 21–41 in *Shall Not the Judge of All the Earth Do What is Right? Studies on the Nature of God in Tribute to James L. Crenshaw*. Edited by David Penchansky and Paul L. Redditt. Winona Lake, Ind.: Eisenbrauns, 2000.
_____. "Theodicy in a Social Dimension." *Journal for the Study of the Old Testament* 33 (1985): 3–25.
_____. *Theology of the Old Testament: Testimony, Dispute, Advocacy*. Minneapolis: Fortress, 1997.
Budde, Karl F. R. *Das Buch Hiob*. Göttingen: Vandenhoeck & Ruprecht, 1913.
Buttenwieser, Moses. *The Book of Job*. New York: McMillan, 1922.

Calvin, John. *Institutes of the Christian Religion*. Edited by John T. McNell. Translated by Ford Lewis Battles. 2 vols. The Library of Christian Classics 20–21. Philadelphia: Westminster, 1960.
_____. *Sermons on Job*. Translated by Arthur Golding. London: Banner of Truth, 1574.
Carroll, Noël. "On the Narrative Connection." In *New Perspectives on Narrative Perspective*. Edited by Willie van Peer and Seymour Chatman. New York: State University of New York Press, 2001.
Carroll, Robert P. "Postscript to Job." *Modern Churchman* 19 (1976): 161–166.
Cazier, Pierre. "Lectures du Livre de Job Chez Ambrose, Augustin et Grégoire le Grand." Pages 82–111 in *Le Livre de Job*. Lectures de

l'Écriture, Graphè 6. Paris: Presses de l'Université Charles-de-Gaulle, 1997.

Cheney, Michael. *Dust, Wind and Agony: Character, Speech and Genre in Job*. Coniectanea Biblica 36; Lund: Almqvist and Wiksell, 1994.

Chrysostom, John. *Commentaire sur Job*. Translated by Henri Sorlin. 2 vols. Paris: Cerf, 1988.

———. "Homilies on the Gospel of Saint Matthew." In *A Select Library of Nicene and Post-Nicene Fathers of the Christian Church*. Vol. 10. Edited by Philip Schaff in Connection with a Number of Patristic Scholars of Europe and America. Reprint of 1903. Michigan: Eerdmans, 1986.

Clifford, Richard J. "Creation in the Psalms." Pages 57–69 in *Creation in the Biblical Traditions*. Edited by Richard J. Clifford and John J. Collins. Washington: Catholic Biblical Association of America, 1992.

———. *Fair Spoken and Persuading*. New York: Paulist, 1984.

Clines, David J. A. "Deconstructing the Book of Job." Pages 65–80 in *The Bible as Rhetoric: Studies in Biblical Persuasion and Credibility*. Edited by Martin Warner. London: Routledge 1990.

———. "False Naivety in the Prologue of Job." *Hebrew Annual Review* 9 (1985): 127–136.

———. *Job 1-20*. Word Biblical Commentary 17. Texas: Wordbooks, 1989.

———. "Job and the Spirituality of the Reformation." Pages 49–72 in *The Bible, The Reformation and the Church: Essays in Honour of James Atkinson*. Edited by W. P. Stephens. Sheffield: Sheffield Academic Press, 1995.

Collins, John J. "Structure and Meaning in the Testament of Job." Pages 35–52 in vol. 1 of the *SBL Seminar Papers*. Edited by George MacRae. Cambridge, Mass.: Society of Biblical Literature, 1974.

Conrad, Edgar W. "The 'Fear not' Oracles in Second Isaiah." *Vetus Testamentum* 34, no. 2 (1984): 129–152.

Cooper, Alan. "Narrative Theory and the Book of Job." *Studies in Religion* 11 (1982): 35–44.

———. "Reading and Misreading the Prologue to Job." *Journal for the Study of the Old Testament* 46 (1990): 69–79.

Coote, R. B., and D. R. Ord. *In the Beginning: Creation and the Priestly History*. Minneapolis: Fortress, 1991.

Cowley, A. *Jewish Documents of the Time of Ezra*. New York: MacMillan, 1919.

Cox, Claude E. "Methodological Issues in the Exegesis of LXX Job." Pages 79–89 in *Sixth Congress of the International Organization for Septuagint and Cognate Studies*. BLSCS 23. Edited by Claude E. Cox. Atlanta: Scholars Press, 1987.

———. "Origen's Use of Theodotion in the Elihu Speeches." *Second Century: A Journal of Early Christian Studies* 3 (1983): 89–98.

Cox, Dermot. *Man's Anger and God's Silence: The Book of Job*. Middlegreen: St Paul Publications, 1990.

Craddock, Fred B. *Luke*. Edited by James L. Mays, Patrick D. Miller, and Paul J. Achtemeier. Interpretation: A Bible Commentary for Teaching and Preaching 42. Louisville: John Knox, 1990.

Crenshaw, James L. "Popular Questioning of the Justice of God in Ancient Israel." *Zeitschrift für die alttestamentliche Wissenschaft* 83, no. 3 (1970): 180–195.

_____. "When Form and Content Clash: The Theology of Job 38:1– 40:5." Pages 70–84 in *Creation in the Biblical Traditions*. Edited by Richard J. Clifford and John J. Collins. Washington: Catholic Biblical Association of America, 1992.

_____. *A Whirlpool of Torment: Israelite Traditions of God as an Oppressive Presence*. Philadelphia: Fortress, 1984.

Cross, Frank M. *Canaanite Myth and Hebrew Epic: Essays in the History of the Religion of Israel*. Cambridge, Mass.: Harvard University Press, 1973.

_____. "The Council of Yahweh in Second Isaiah." *Journal of the Ancient Near Eastern Studies* 12 (1953): 274–277.

Dailey, Thomas F. *The Repentant Job: A Ricoeurian Icon for Biblical Theology*. New York: University Press of America, 1994.

Davidson, Robert. *The Courage to Doubt: Exploring an Old Testament Theme*. London: SCM, 1983.

De Troyer, Kristin. *Rewriting the Sacred Text: What the Old Greek Texts Tell us About the Literary Growth of the Bible*. Edited by James R. Adair. Society of Biblical Literature Text-Critical Studies 4. Atlanta: Society of Biblical Literature, 2003.

Delitzsch, Friedrich. *Das Buch Hiob: Neu Übersetzt und Kurz Erklärt: Ausgabe mit Sprachlichem Kommentar*. Leipzig: Hinrichs, 1902.

Dell, Katharine J. *The Book of Job as Sceptical Literature*. New York: Walter de Gruyter, 1991.

Delmaire, Jean-Marie. "Les Principaux Courants de l'Exégèse Juive sur Job." Pages 59–79 in *Le Livre de Job*. Lectures de l'Écriture: Graphè 6. Paris: Presses de l'Université Charles-de-Gaulle, 1997.

Dhorme, Edouard. *A Commentary on the Book of Job*. Translated by Harold Knight. New York: Thomas Nelson, 1967.

Di Cella, Alexander. "An Existential Interpretation of Job." *Biblical Theology Bulletin* 15 (1985): 49–55.

Dietrich, Ernst L. שׁוּב שְׁבוּת: *Die endzeitliche Wiederherstellung bei den Propheten*. Beihefte zur Zeitschrift für die alttestamentliche Wissenschaft 40. Giessen: Töpelmann,1925.

Driver, Samuel R., and George B. Gray. *A Critical and Exegetical Commentary on the Book of Job Together with a New Translation*. International Critical Commentary 18. Edinburgh: T&T Clark, 1958.

Duhm, Bernhard. *Das Buch Hiob: Erklärt*. Freiburg: Mohr, 1897.

Durand, J. J. F. "Theology and Resurrection– Metaphors and Paradigms." *Journal of Theology for Southern Africa* 82 (1993): 3–20.

Eaton, J. H. *Job*. Sheffield: JSOT Press, 1985.
Ebach, Jürgen. »Hiob/Hiobbuch.« *Theologische Realenzyklopädie* 15 (1986): 360–380.
Emerson, Caryl. *The First Hundred Years of Mikhail Bakhtin*. Princeton: Princeton University Press, 1997.
Evans, G. R. *Fifty Key Medieval Thinkers*. London: Routledge, 2002.

Fishbane, Michael. "Inner Biblical Exegesis." Pages 33–48 in *Antiquity*. Part 1 of *From the Beginnings to the Middle Ages (until 1300)*. Vol. 1 of *The Hebrew Bible, Old Testament: The History of its Interpretation*. Edited by Magne Sæbø. Göttingen: Vandenhoeck & Ruprecht, 1996.
_____. "Types of Intertextuality." Pages 39–44 in *Congress Volume: Olso 1998*. Edited by André Lemaire and Magne Sæbø. Supplements to Vetus Testamentum 80. Leiden: Brill, 2000.
Fitzmyer Joseph A. *The Aramaic Inscriptions of Sefire*. Rev. ed. Rome: Editrice Pontificio Instituto Biblico, 1995.
_____. *The Gospel According to Luke X-XXIV: Introduction, Translation, and Notes*. Edited by William F. Albright and David N. Freedman. Anchor Bible 28. New York: Doubleday, 1985.
Forrest, Robert W. E. "An Inquiry into Yahweh's Commendation of Job." *Studies in Religion* 8, no. 2 (1979): 159–166.
Freedman, N. David, "The Book of Job." Pages 33–51 in *The Hebrew Bible and Its Interpreters*. Edited by William H. Propp, Baruch Halpern, and David N. Freedman. Biblical and Judaic Studies 1. Winona Lake, Ind.: Eisenbrauns, 1990.
_____. "The Orthographic Peculiarities in the Book of Job." Pages 44–60 in *Poetry and Orthography*. Edited by John R. Huddlestan. Vol 2 of *Divine Commitment and Human Obligation: Selected Writings of David Noel Freedman*. Michigan: Eerdmans, 1997.
Frei, Hans W. *The Eclipse of Biblical Narrative: A Study in Eighteenth and Nineteenth Century Hermeneutics*. New Haven: Yale University Press, 1974.
Fullerton, Kember. "The Original Conclusion to the Book of Job." *Zeitschrift für die alttestamentliche Wissenschaft* 42 (1924): 116–136.

Gamble, Harry Y. *Books and Readers in the Early Church: A History of Early Christian Texts*. New Haven: Yale University Press, 1995.
Gard, Donald H. "The Concept of Job's Character According to the Greek Translator of the Hebrew Text." *Journal of Biblical Literature* (1953): 182–186.
Gehman, Henry S. "The Theological Approach of the Greek Translator of Job 1–15." *Journal of Biblical Literature* 68 (1949): 231–240.
Gentry, Peter John. *The Asterisked Materials in the Greek Job*. Edited by Leonard J. Greenspoon. Society of Biblical Literature Septuagint and Cognate Studies 38. Atlanta: Scholars, 1995.

Gesenius-Kautzsch, *Hebrew Grammar*. Second Edition Revised in Accordance with the Twenty-eighth German Edition, 1909 by A. E. Cowley. Oxford: Clarendon Press, 1983.

Gibson, John C. L. *Job*. Philadelphia: Westminster, 1985.

Gilkey, Langdon. "Power, Order, Justice, and Redemption: Theological Comments on Job." Pages 159–171 in *Voice from the Whirlwind: Interpreting the Book of Job*. Edited by Leo G. Perdue and W. Clark Gilpin. Nashville: Abingdon, 1992.

Gillespie, Michael P. *The Aesthetics of Chaos: Nonlinear Thinking and Contemporary Literary Criticism*. Florida: University of Florida Press, 2003.

Ginsberg, H. L. "Job the Patient and Job the Impatient." *Conservative Judaism* 21, no. 3 (1967): 12–28.

Ginzberg, Louis. *The Legends of the Jews*. Vol. 2. *From Joseph to the Exodus*. Translated by Henrietta Szold. London: John Hopkins, 1948.

Glatzer, Nahum N. *The Dimensions of Job: A Study and Selected Readings*. New York: Schocken, 1969.

Goering, Joseph W. "An Introduction to Medieval Christian Biblical Interpretation." Pages 197–203 in *With Reverence for the Word: Medieval Scriptural Exegesis in Judaism, Christianity, and Islam*. Edited by Jane Dammen McAuliffe, Barry D. Walfish, and Joseph W. Goering. Oxford: Oxford University Press, 2003.

Goldsworthy, Graeme. "'With Flesh and Bones': A Biblical Theology of the Bodily Resurrection of Christ." *Reformed Theological Review* 57 (1998): 121–135.

Good, Edwin. *In Turns of Tempest: A Reading of Job*. California: Stanford University Press, 1996.

Gordis, Robert. *The Book of God and Man: A Study of Job*. Chicago: University of Chicago Press, 1965.

⎯⎯⎯⎯. *The Book of Job: Commentary, New Translation, and Special Studies*. New York: Jewish Theological Seminary of America, 1978.

Gordon, Cyrus H. "Homer and Bible: The Origin and Character of East Mediterranean Literature." *Hebrew Union College Annual* 26 (1955): 43–108.

⎯⎯⎯⎯. *Textbook of Ugaritic Grammar*. Rome: Editrice Pontificio Instituto Biblico, 1998.

Gray, G. Buchanan. "The Additions in the Ancient Greek Version of Job." *Expositor* 19 (1931): 422–438.

Gray, John. "The Book of Job in the Context of Near Eastern Literature." *Zeitschrift für die alttestamentliche Wissenschaft* 82 (1950): 251–269.

⎯⎯⎯⎯. "The Massoretic Text of the Book of Job, the Targum and the Septuagint Version in the Light of the Qumran Targum." *Zeitschrift für die alttestamentliche Wissenschaft* 86 (1974): 331–350.

Green, Barbara. *Mikhail Bakhtin and Biblical Scholarship: An Introduction*. Edited by Danna Nolan Fewell. The Society of Biblical Literature Semeia Studies 38. Atlanta: Society of Biblical Literature, 2000.

Greenberg, M. "Job." Pages 283–304 in *The Literary Guide to the Bible*. Edited by Robert Alter and Frank Kermode. Cambridge, Mass.: Harvard University Press, 1987.

Gregory the Great, Saint. *Morals on the Book of Job*. A Library of Fathers of the Holy Catholic Church Anterior to the Division of East and West 1, parts 1 and 2. Translated by Members of the English Church. Oxford: John Henry Parker, 1844.

_____. *Morals on the Book of Job*. A Library of Fathers of the Holy Catholic Church Anterior to the Division of East and West 3, part 2. Translated by Members of the English Church. Oxford: John Henry Parker, 1850.

Grosz, Katarzyna. "Bridewealth and Dowry in Nuzi." Pages 193–206 in *Images of Women in Antiquity*. Edited by Averil Cameron and Amélie Kuhrt. Rev. ed. Detroit: Wayne State University Press, 1993.

Gruber, Mayer I. "The Many Faces of Hebrew נשא פנים ›lift up the face‹" *Zeitschrift für die alttestamentliche Wissenschaft* 95 (1983): 252–260.

Gutiérrez, Gustavo. *On Job: God-talk and the Suffering of the Innocent*. Translated by Matthew J. O'Connell. New York: Orbis, 1987.

Haas, Cees. "Job's Perseverance in the Testament of Job." Pages 117–154 in *Studies on The Testament of Job*. Edited by Michael A. Knibb and Pieter W. van der Horst. Cambridge: Cambridge University Press, 1989.

Habel, Norman C. *The Book of Job: A Commentary*. Old Testament Library. Philadelphia: Westminster, 1985.

_____. "Literary Features and the Message of the Book of Job." Pages 97–123 in *Sitting with Job: Selected Studies on the Book of Job*. Edited by Roy B. Zuck. Grand Rapids, Mich.: Baker, 1992.

Hall, Christopher A. *Reading Scripture with the Church Fathers*. Downers Grove, Ill.: Inter Varsity, 1998.

Harl, M., and N. De Lange, eds. *Origène, Philocalie, 1–20 sur les Écritures et la Lettre à Africanus sur l'Histoire de Suzanne*. Sources Chrétiennes 302. Paris: Cerf, 1983.

Hartley, John E. *The Book of Job*. Michigan: Eerdmans, 1988.

Harvey, Anthony. "'They Discussed among Themselves what this "Rising from the dead" Could Mean' (Mark 9:10)." Pages 69–78 in *Resurrection: Essays in Honour of Leslie Houlden*. Edited by Stephen Barton and Graham Stanton. London: SPCK, 1994.

Heater, Homer. *A Septuagint Translation Technique in the Book of Job*. Washington: Catholic Biblical Association, 1982.

Hoffman, Yair. "Ancient Near Eastern Literary Conventions and the Restoration of the Book of Job." *Zeitschrift für die alttestamentliche Wissenschaft* 103, no. 3 (1991): 399–411.

_____. *A Blemished Perfection: The Book of Job in Context*. Edited by David J. A. Clines and Philip R. Davies. Journal for the Study of the Old Testament Supplement Series 213. Sheffield: Sheffield Academic Press, 1996.

Hoftijzer, J., and K. Jongeling. *Dictionary of North-West Semitic Inscriptions with Appendices by R. C. Steiner, A. Mosak Moshavi, and B. Porten.* Edited by H. Altenmüller et al. Handbook of Oriental Studies 2. Leiden: Brill, 1995.
Holladay, William L. *The Root Šûbh in the Old Testament, with Particular Reference to the Usage in Covenantal Contexts.* Leiden: Brill, 1958.
Hölscher, G. *Das Buch Hiob.* HAT; Tübingen: Mohr, 1952.
Horst, Friedrich. *Hiob 1–19.* BKAT 16/1 (Neukirchen-Vluyn: Neukirchener Verlag, 1968.
Horst, J. "μακροθυμία." Pages 374-387 in *TDNT* 4. Edited by G. Kittel and G. Friedrich. Translated by Geoffrey W. Bromiley. Grand Rapids, Mich.: Eerdmans, 1985.
Horst, Pieter W. van der. "The Role of Women in the Testament of Job." *Nederlands Theologisch Tijdschrift* 40, no. 4 (1986): 273–289.
Hübner, Hans. "New Testament Interpretation of the Old Testament." Pages 332–372 in Antiquity. Part 1 of *From the Beginning to the Middle Ages (until 1300).* Vol. 1 of *The Hebrew Bible, Old Testament: The History of Its Interpretation.* Edited by Magne Sæbø. Göttingen: Vandenhoeck & Ruprecht, 1996.
Hurvitz, Avi. "The Date of the Prose-Tale of Job Linguistically Reconsidered." *Harvard Theological Review* 67 (1974): 17–34.
Hyers, Conrad. *Comic Vision of the Christian Faith: A Celebration of Life and Laughter.* New York: Pilgrim Press, 1981.
_____. "The Dialectic of the Sacred and the Comic." Pages 208–240 in *Holy Laughter: Essays on Religion in the Comic Perspective.* Edited by M. Conrad Hyers. New York: Seabury, 1969.
Hyman, Arthur. "Demonstrative, Dialectical and Sophistic Arguments in the Philosophy of Moses Maimonides." Pages 35–51 in *Maimonides and His Time.* Edited by Eric C. Ormsby. Washington: Catholic University of America Press, 1989.

Jackson, Timothy P. "Must Job Live Forever? A Reply to Aquinas on Providence and Freedom, Evil and Immortality." Pages 217–252 in *Human and Divine Agency: Anglican, Catholic, and Lutheran Perspectives.* Edited by F. Michael McLain and W. Mark Richardson. New York: University Press of America, 1999.
Jacobs, Irving. "Literary Motifs in the Testament of Job." *Journal of Jewish Studies* 21 (1970): 1–10.
Jacobsen, Thorkild. *The Treasures of Darkness: History of Mesopotamian Religion.* New Haven: Yale University Press, 1976.
Janowski, Bernd. »Sündenvergebung 'um Hiobs willen': Fürbitte und Vergebung in 11QTgJob 38:2f und Hiob 42:9f LXX.« *Zeitschrift für die neutestamentliche Wissenschaft* 73, no. 4 (1982): 251–280.
Janzen, J. Gerald. *Job.* Edited by James Luther Mays, Patrick D. Miller, and J. Achtemeier. Interpretation: A Bible Commentary for Teaching and Preaching 18. Atlanta: John Knox, 1985.

_____. "The Place of the Book of Job in the History of Israel's Religion." Pages 523–537 in *Ancient Israelite Religion: Essays in Honor of Frank Moore Cross*. Edited by Patrick D. Miller, Paul D. Hanson, and S. Dean McBride. Philadelphia: Fortress, 1987.

Jongeling, B., C. J. Labuschagne, and A. S. van der Woude. *Aramaic Texts from Qumran*. Leiden: Brill, 1976.

Jung, Carl G. *Answer to Job*. Translated by R. F. Hull. Princeton: Princeton University Press, 1973.

Kallen, Horrace. *The Book of Job as a Greek Tragedy*. New York: Hill & Wang, 1959.

Kaufman, Stephen A. "The Job Targum from Qumran." *Journal of the American Oriental Society* 93 (1973): 317–327.

Kautzsch, K. *Das sogannante Volksbuch von Hiob und der Ursprung von Hiob cap. I. II. XLII, 7 –17: ein Beitrag zur Frage nach der Integrität des Buches Hiob*. Tübingen: Mohr, 1900.

Kermode, Frank. *The Sense of an Ending*. Oxford: Oxford University Press, 1966.

Kissane, E. J. *The Book of Job Translated from a Critically Revised Hebrew Text with Commentary*. New York: Sheed & Ward, 1946.

Kittel, G., and G. Friedrich, eds. *Theological Dictionary of the New Testament*. Translated by G. W. Bromiley. 10 vols. Grand Rapids: Eerdmans, 1964–1976.

Köhlmoos, Melanie. *Das Auge Gottes: Textstrategie im Hiobbuch*. FAT 25. Tübingen: Mohr, 1999.

Kraeling, Emil G. *The Book of the Ways of God*. New York: Charles Scribner's Sons, 1938.

Kraft, Robert A., Harold Attridge, Russell Spittler, and Janet Timbie, eds. *The Testament of Job According to the SV Text: Greek Text and English Translation*. Missoula, Mont.: Scholars, 1974.

Kretzmann, Norman. "The Metaphysics of Providence: Aquinas's Natural Theology in Summa Gentiles III." *Medieval Philosophy and Theology* 9, no. 2 (2000): 191–213.

Kuhl, C. »Neuere Literarkritik des Buches Hiob.« *Theologische Rundschau* 21, no. 4 (1953): 257–317.

Kutsch, Ernst. »Die Textgliederung im hebräischen Ijobbuch sowie in 4QtgJob und in 11QtgJob.« *BZNF* (1983): 221–228.

_____. »Hiob und seine Freunde: Zu Problemen der Rahmenerzählung des Hiobbuches.« in *Zur Aktualität des Alten Testaments. Festschrift für Georg Sauer zum 65*. Edited by Siegfried Kreuzer and Kurt Lüthi. Frankfurt: Peter Lang, 1992.

Leaman, Oliver. *Evil and Suffering in Jewish Philosophy*. Cambridge: Cambridge University Press, 1995.

Levenson, Jon D. *Creation and the Persistence of Evil: The Jewish Drama of Divine Omnipotence*. San Francisco: Harper & Row, 1988.

_____. "The Resurrection of the Dead and the Construction of Personal Identity in Ancient Israel." Pages 305–322 in *Congress Volume: Basel 2001*. Edited by André Lemaire. Supplements to Vetus Testamentum 92. Leiden: Brill, 2002.

Lévêque, Jean. "L'Épilogue du Livre de Job: Essai d'Interprétation." Pages 37–55 in *Toute la Sagesse du Monde: Hommage à Maurice Gilbert s. j.* Edited by François Mies. Namur: Presses Universitaires de Namur, 2000.

_____. *Job et Son Dieu: Essai D'Exégèse et de Théologie Biblique*. Vol. 1. Paris: Lecoffre, 1970.

_____. "Le Thème du Juste Souffrant en Mésopotamie et la Problématique du Livre de Job." Pages 11–33 in *Le Livre de Job*. Lectures de L'Écriture, Graphè 6. Paris: Presses de l'Université Charles-de-Gaulle, 1997.

Levine, Baruch A. *Numbers 21-26: A New Translation with Introduction and Commentary*. Edited by William F. Albright and David N. Freedman. Anchor Bible 4A. New York: Doubleday, 2000.

Lewy, Hans, Alexander Altmann, and Isaak Heinemann, eds. *Three Jewish Philosophers*. New York: Temple Book, 1974.

Liddell, Henry G. *An Intermediate Greek-English Lexicon Founded Upon the 7th edition of Liddell and Scott's Greek-English Lexicon*. Oxford: Clarendon, 2000.

Lübbe, John C. "Describing the Translation Process of 11QtgJob: A Question of Method." *Revue de Qumran* 13 (1988): 583–593.

MacDonald, Duncan B. "The Original Form of the Legend of Job." *Journal of Biblical Literature* 14 (1895): 63–71.

_____. "Some External Evidence on the Original Form of the Legend of Job." *American Journal of Semitic Languages and Literatures* 14, no. 3 (1898): 137–164.

Machinist, Peter. "Job's Daughters and their Inheritance in the Testament of Job and its Biblical Congeners." Pages 67–80 in *The Echoes of Many Texts: Reflections on Jewish and Christian Traditions: Essays in Honor of Lou H. Silberman*. Edited by William G. Dever and J. Edward Wright. Atlanta: Scholars Press, 1997.

Magumba, J. N. K. Foreword to *Theology of Reconstruction: Exploratory Essays*. Edited by Mary N. Getui and Emmanuel A. Obeng. Nairobi: Acton Publishers, 1999.

_____. "From Liberation to Reconstruction." Pages 189–206 in *African Theology Today*. Edited by Emmanuel Katongole. African Theology Today Series 1. Scranton: University of Scranton Press, 2002.

Mangan, Céline. "The Targum of Job Translated with a Critical Introduction, Apparatus, and Notes." Pages 1–98 in *The Aramaic Bible: The Targums*. Edited by Kevin Cathcart, Michael Maher, and Martin MacNamara. 18 vols. Collegeville, Minn.: Liturgical Press, 1991.

Marcos, N. Fernández. "The Septuagint Reading of the Book of Job." Pages 251–266 in *The Book of Job*. Edited by W. A. M. Beuken. Bibliotheca

Ephemeridum Theologicarum Lovaniensium 14. Leuven: Leuven University Press, 1994.

Margain, Jean. "11QtgJob et la langue Targumique: À Propos de la Particule BDYL." *Revue de Qumran* 13 (1988): 525–528.

Marrow, Francis J. "11Q Targum and the Massoretic Text." *Revue de Qumran* 8, no. 2 (1973): 253–256.

Marsman, Hennie J. *Women in Ugarit and Israel: Their Social and Religious Position in the Context of the Ancient Near East*. Leiden: Brill, 2003.

Mathew, Geevarughese. "The Role of the Epilogue in the Book of Job." Ph.D. diss., Drew University, 1995.

Mathew, Susan F. "All for Nought: My Servant Job." Pages 51–71 in *The Bible on Suffering: Social and Political Implications*. Edited by Anthony J. Tambasco. New York: Paulist, 2001.

McCarthy, Dennis J. "The Wrath of YHWH and the Structural Unity of the Deuteronomistic History." Pages 97–110 in *Essays in Old Testament Ethics*. Edited by James L. Crenshaw and John T. Willis. New York: Ktav, 1974.

McEvoy, James. "The Patristic Hermeneutic of Spiritual Freedom and its Biblical Origins." Pages 1–25 in *Scriptural Interpretation in the Fathers: Letter and Spirit*. Edited by Thomas Finan and Vincent Twomey. Cambridge: Cambridge University Press, 1995.

McIntyre, John. *Theology After the Storm: The Humanity of Christ, Theology of Prayer, The Cliché as a Theological Medium*. Cambridge: Eerdmans, 1997.

Mettinger, Tryggve N. D. "The Dethronement of Sabaoth: Studies in the Shem and Kabod Theologies." Pages 19–37 in *Coniectanea Biblica* 18. Lund: Gleerup, 1982.

Metzger, M. »Himmlische und irdische Wohnsttat Yahwes.« *Ugaritische Forschungen* 2 (1970):139–158.

Michel, Andreas. »Ijob und Abraham.« Pages 73–98 in *Gott Mensch Sprache: Schülerfestschrift für Walter Groß zum 60*. Edited by Andreas Michel and Hermann-Josef Stipp. Ottilien: Verlag Erzabtei, 2001.

Miller, Patrick D. *Israelite Religion and Biblical Theology: Collected Essays*. Edited by David J. A. Clines and Philip R. Davies. Journal for the Study of the Old Testament Supplement Series 267. Sheffield: Sheffield Academic Press, 2000.

──────. *They Cried to the Lord: The Form and Theology of Biblical Prayer*. Minneapolis: Fortress, 1994.

Møller-Christensen, V., and K. E. Jordt Jørgensen. *Encyclopedia of Bible Creatures*. Philadelphia: Fortress, 1965.

Moore, Rickie D. "The Integrity of Job." *Catholic Biblical Quarterly* 45 (1983):17–31.

──────. "Raw Prayer and Refined Theology: 'You have not Spoken Straight to Me as My Servant Job Has.'" Pages 35–48 in *The Spirit and the Mind: Essays in Informed Pentecostalism to Honor Dr. Donald N. Bowdie Presented on his 65th Birthday*. Edited by Terry L. Cross and Emerson B. Powery. New York: University Press of America, 2000.

Moorhead, John. *Ambrose: Church and Society in the Late Roman World*. Edited by David Bates. The Medieval World. London: Longman, 1999.

Morgan, Robert. "Flesh is Precious: The Significance of Luke 24.36–43." Pages 8–20 in *Resurrection: Essays in Honour of Leslie Houlden*. Edited by Stephen Barton and Graham Stanton. London: SPCK, 1994.

Morreal, John. *Comedy, Tragedy, and Religion*. New York: State University of New York, 1999.

Morson, Gary Saul., and Caryl Emerson, eds. *Mikhail Bakhtin: Creation of a Prosaics*. Stanford, Calif.: Stanford University Press, 1990.

Moster, Julius B. "The Punishment of Job's Friends." *Jewish Bible Quarterly* 25, no. 4(1997): 211–219.

Müller, Hans-Peter. »Theodizee? Anschlußerörterungen zum Buch Hiob.« *Zeitschrift für Theologie und Kirche* 89 (1992): 249–279.

Muraoka, Takamitsu. "Notes on the Old Targum of Job from Qumran Cave XI." *Revue de Qumran* 9, no. 1 (1977): 117–125.

Murphy, Roland E. *The Tree of Life: An Exploration of Biblical Wisdom Literature*. 2nd ed. Grand Rapids, Mich.: Eerdmans, 1990.

Nam, Duck-Woo. *Talking about God: Job 42:7 – 9 and the Nature of God in the Book of Job*. Edited by Hemchand Gossai. Studies in Biblical Literature 49. New York: Peter Lang, 2003.

Napier, Bunyan D. "On Creation-Faith in the Old Testament: A Survey." *Interpretation* 26 (1962): 21–42.

Neusner, Jacob. *The Presence of the Past, The Pastness of the Present: History, Time, and Paradigm in Rabbinic Judaism*. Bethseda, Md.: CDL, 1996.

_____. *Texts Without Boundaries: Protocols of Non-Documentary Writing in the Rabbinic Canon*. Edited by Jacob Neusner. Studies in Judaism 3. New York: UniversityPress of America, 2002.

_____. *A Theological Commentary to the Midrash*. Edited by Jacob Neusner. Studies in Ancient Judaism 1: Pesiqta deRab kahana. New York: University Press of America, 2001.

_____. *The Tosefta Translated from the Hebrew with a New Introduction*. Peabody, Mass.: Hendrickson, 2002.

Newsom, Carol A. "Bakhtin, the Bible, and Dialogic Truth." *Journal of Religion* 76, no. 2 (1996): 290–306.

_____. *The Book of Job: A Contest of Moral Imaginations*. Oxford: Oxford University Press, 2003.

_____. "The Book of Job: Introduction, Commentary, and Reflections." Pages 317–637 in *1 & 2 Maccabees, Introduction to Hebrew Poetry, Job, Psalms*. Vol. 4 of *The New Interpreter's Bible: General Articles and Introduction, Commentary, and Reflections for each Book of the Bible*

Including the Apocrypha/Deuterocanonical Books in Twelve Volumes. Edited by Leander E. Keck et al. Nashville: Abingdon, 1996.

_____. "Cultural Politics in the Book of Job." *Biblical Interpretation* 1 (1993): 119–134.

_____. "Job and His Friends: A Conflict of Moral Imaginations." *Interpretation* 53 (1999): 239–253.

_____."Narrative Ethics, Character, and the Prose Tale of Job." Pages 121–124 in *Character and Scripture: Moral Formation, Community, and Biblical Interpretation*. Edited by William P. Brown. Grand Rapids, Mich.: Eerdmans, 2002.

Nicole, Jules-Marcel. *Le Livre de Job*. Vol. 2. Cherbourg: EDIFAC, 1987.

Nielsen, Kirsten. "Intertextuality and Hebrew Bible." Pages 17–31 in *Congress Volume Olso 1998*. Edited by André Lemaire and Magne Sæbø. Supplements to Vetus Testamentum 80. Leiden: Brill, 2000.

Noth, Martin. »Noah, Daniel und Hiob in Ezechiel xiv.« *Vetus Testamentum* 1 (1951): 251–260.

O'Connor, Daniel J. "The Cunning Hand: Repetitions in Job 42:7, 8." *Irish Theological Quarterly* 57, no. 1 (1991): 14–25.

Oeming, Manfred. »Ihr habt nitch Recht vom mir geredet wie mein Knecht Hiob: Gottes Schlusswort als Schlüssel zur Interpretation des Hiobbuchs und als kritische Anfrage an die moderne Theologie.« *Evangelische Theologie* 60, no. 2 (2000): 103–116.

Olson, Dennis T. *Deuteronomy and the Death of Moses: A Theological Reading*. Minneapolis: Fortress, 1994.

_____. *Numbers*. Edited by James L. Mays, Patrick D. Miller, and Paul J. Achtemeier. Interpretation: A Bible Commentary for Teaching and Preaching 4. Louisville: John Knox Press, 1996.

_____. "Biblical Theology as Provisional Monologization: A Dialogue with Childs, Brueggemann and Bakhtin." *Biblical Interpretation* 6 (1998): 162–180.

Oostendorp, Herre van. "Holding onto Established Viewpoints during Processing News Reports." Pages 173–188 in *New Perspectives on Narrative Perspective*. Edited by Willie van Peer and Seymour Chatman. New York: State University of New York Press, 2001.

Orlinsky, Harry M. "Studies in the Septuagint of the Book of Job." *Hebrew Union College Annual* 28 (1957): 53–74; 29 (1958): 229–271; 30 (1959): 153–167; 32 (1961): 239–268; 33 (1962): 119–151; 35 (1964): 57–78; 36 (1965): 37–47.

Osgood, S. Joy. "Women and Inheritance of Land in Early Israel." Pages 29–52 in *Women in the Biblical Tradition*. Edited by George J. Brooke. Lewiston: Edwin Mellen, 1992.

Paget, J. N. B. Carleton. "Christian Exegesis of the Old Testament in the Alexandrian Tradition." Pages 478–542 in *Antiquity*. Part 1 of *From the Beginning to the Middle Ages (until 1300)*. Vol 1 of *The Hebrew Bible,*

Old Testament: The History of Its Interpretation. Edited by Magne Sæbø. Göttingen: Vandenhoeck & Ruprecht, 1996.

Paradise, Jonathan. "A Daughter and Her Father's Property at Nuzi." *Journal of Cuneiform Studies* 32 (1980): 190–198.

Pardee, Dennis G. "More on the Preposition in Ugaritic." *Ugaritische Forschungen* 11 (1980): 685–692.

_____. "The Preposition in Ugaritic." *Ugaritische Forschungen* 8 (1976): 251–252.

Patrick, Dale. "Epiphanic Imagery in Second Isaiah's Portrayal of a New Exodus." *Hebrew Annual Review* 8 (1984): 125–141.

_____. "Job's Address to God." *Zeitschrift für die alttestamentliche Wissenschaft* 91 (1979): 268–282.

Penchansky, David. *The Betrayal of God: Ideological Conflict in Job*. Louisville: John Knox, 1990.

Perdue. Leo G. *Wisdom in Revolt: Metaphorical Theology in the Book of Job*. Edited by David J. A. Clines and Philip R. Davies. Journal for the Study of the Old Testament Supplement Series 112. Sheffield: Sheffield Academic Press, 1991.

Pestman, P. W. "The Law of Succession in Ancient Egypt." Pages 58–78 in *Essays on Oriental Laws of Succession*. Edited by J. Brugman, M. David, F. R. Kraus, and P. W. Pestman. Studia et Documenta 9. Leiden: Brill, 1969.

Pfeiffer, Charles F. *Exile and Return*. Grand Rapids, Mich.: Baker Books House, 1962.

Phillips, Anthony. "NEBALAH: A Term for Serious Disorderly and Unruly Conduct." *Vetus Testamentum* 25, no. 2 (1975): 237–242.

Ploeg, J. P. M. van der., and A. S. van der Woude. *Le Targum de Job de la Grotte XI de Qumran*. Leiden: Brill, 1971.

Polzin, Robert M. *Biblical Structuralism: Method and Subjectivity in the Study of Ancient Texts*. Philadelphia: Fortress, 1977.

_____. "The Framework of the Book of Job." *Interpretation* 28 (1974): 182–200.

Pope, Marvin H. *Job: Text, Translation and Notes*. Edited by William F. Albright and David N. Freedman. Anchor Bible 15. New York: Doubleday & Company, 1965.

Porter, Stanley E. "The Message of the Book of Job: Job 42:7b as Key to Interpretation?"*Evangelical Quarterly* 63 (1991): 305–312.

Preuschen, Erwin. »Die Bedeutung von שבו שתוב im Alten Testamente: Eine alte Controverse.« *Zeitschrift für die alttestamentliche Wissenschaft* 15 (1895): 1–74.

Procopé, J. F. "Greek Philosophy, Hermeneutics and Alexandrian Understanding of the Old Testament." Pages 451–477 in *Antiquity*. Part 1 of *From the Beginning to the Middle Ages (until 1300)*. Vol 1 of *The Hebrew Bible, Old Testament: The History of Its Interpretation*. Edited by Magne Sæbø. Göttingen: Vandenhoeck & Ruprecht, 1996.

Puckett, David L. *John Calvin's Exegesis of the Old Testament.* Louisville: Westminster, 1995.
Puech, Émil. *La Croyance des Esséniens en la Vie Future: Immortalité, Résurrection, Vie Éternelle? Histoire d'une Croyance dans le Judaïsme Ancien. Vol. 1. La Résurrection des Morts et le Contexte Scripturaire.* Paris: Librairie Lecoffre J. Gabalda,1993.
Puech, Émil, and Florentino García-Martínez. "Remarques sur la Colonne 38 de 11Q Tg Job." *Revue de Qumran* 9, no. 3 (1978): 401–407.
Pyeong, Yohan. *You Have Not Spoken What is Right About Me: Intertextuality and the Book of Job.* Edited by Hemchand Gossai. Studies in Biblical Literature 45. New York: Peter Lang, 2003.
Pyper, Hugh. "The Reader in Pain: Job as Text and Pretext." Pages 234–255 in *Text as Pretext: Essays in Honor of Robert Davidson.* Edited by Robert P. Carroll. Journal for the Study of the Old Testament Supplement Series 138. Edited by David J. A. Clines and Philip R. Davies. Sheffield: Sheffield Academic Press, 1992.

Rad, Gerhard von. *The Theology of Israel's Historical Traditions.* Vol. 1 of *Old Testament Theology.* Translated by D. M. G. Stalker. London: John Knox, 1962.
———. *Wisdom in Israel.* Translated by James D. Martin. London: SCM, 1972.
Rahnenführer, D. »Das Testament des Hiob und das Neue Testament.« *Zeitschrift für die neutestamentliche Wissenschaft* 62 (1971): 68–93.
Ranston, Harry. *The Old Testament Wisdom Books and their Teachings.* London: Epworth, 1930.
Rashi. *The Book of Job.* Translated and Edited with Commentary by A. J. Rosenberg. Judaica Books of the Hagiographa: The Holy Writings. New York: Judaica, 1989.
Reed, Annette Y. "Job as Jobab: The Interpretation of Job in LXX Job 42:17b–e." *Journal of Biblical Literature* 120, no. 1 (2001): 31–55.
Reines, A. "Maimonides' Concepts of Providence and Theodicy." *Hebrew Union College Annual* 42 (1972): 169–206.
Ricoeur, Paul. *The Symbolism of Evil.* Translated by Emerson Buchanan. Boston: Beacon Press, 1967.
Roberts, J. J. M. "Job and the Israelite Religious Tradition." *Zeitschrift für die alttestamentliche Wissenschaft* (1977): 107–114.
———. "Job's Summons to Yahweh: The Exploitation of a Legal Metaphor." *Restoration Quarterly* 16, no. 3 (1973): 159–165.
Rosenthal, Franz. *A Grammar of Biblical Aramaic.* Edited by Werner Diem and Franz Rosenthal. New rev. ed. Porta Linguarum Orientalium, Neue Serie, 5. Wiesbaden: Harrassowitz, 1995.
Roth, Martha T. "The Neo-Babylonian Widow." *Journal of Cuneiform Studies* 43–45 (1991–1993): 1–26.

Roth, Wolfgang M. W. "NBL." *Vetus Testamentum* 10 (1960): 394–409.
Rowley, H. H. *From Moses to Qumran: Studies in the Old Testament*. New York: Association, 1963.

Sakenfeld, Katharine Doob. "Zelophehad's Daughters." *Perspectives in Religious Studies* 15 (1988): 37–47.
Samuel, Sandmel. *The Hebrew Scriptures: An Introduction to their Literature and Religious Ideas*. New York: Knopt, 1963.
Sanders, James A. "Stability and Fluidity in Text and Canon." Pages 203–217 in *Tradition of the Text: Studies Offered to Dominique Barthélemy in Celebration of his 70th Birthday*. Edited by Gerald J. Norton and Stephen Pisano. Göttingen: Vandenhoeck & Ruprecht, 1991.
Sarna, N. "Epic Substratum in the Prose of Job." *Journal of Biblical Literature* 76 (1957): 13–25.
Schaller, B. »Das Testament Hiobs und die Septuaginta-Übersetzung des Buches Hiob.« *Biblica* 61 (1980): 377–406.
Schmid, Konrad, and Odil Hannes Steck. "Restoration Expectations in the Prophetic Tradition of the Old Testament." Pages 41–81 in *Restoration: Old Testament, Jewish, and Christian Perspectives*. Edited by James M. Scott. Supplements to the Journal for the Study of the Old Testament 72. Edited by John J. Collins and Florentino G. Martinez. Leiden: Brill, 2001.
Schneider, Wolfgang. *Grammatik des Biblischen Hebräisch*. Munich: Claudius, 1974.
Schoors, Antoon. "(Mis)use of Intertextuality in Qoheleth Exegesis." Pages 45–59 in *Congress Volume: Olso 1998*. Edited by André Lemaire and Magne Sæbø. Supplements to Vetus Testamentum 80. Leiden: Brill, 2000.
Schreiner, Susan E. "Exegesis and Double Justice in Calvin's Sermons on Job." *Church History* 58 (1989): 322–338.
_____. "'Through a Mirror Dimly': Calvin's Sermons on Job." *Calvin Theological Journal* 21, no. 2 (1986): 175–192.
_____. *Where Shall Wisdom be Found?: Calvin's Exegesis of Job from Medieval and Modern Perspectives*. Chicago: University of Chicago Press, 1994.
Scott, James M., ed. *Restoration: Old Testament, Jewish, and Christian Perspectives*. Edited by John J. Collins and Florentino G. Martinez. Supplements to the Journal for the Study of the Old Testament 72. Leiden: Brill, 2001.
Seder Olam: The Rabbinic View of Biblical Chronology. Translation and commentary by Heinrich W. Guggenheimer. Northvale, N. J.: Jason Aronson, 1998.
Seitz, Christopher. "The Divine Council: Temporal Transition and New Prophecy in the Book of Isaiah." *Journal of Biblical Literature* 109, no. 2 (1990): 229–247.
Shen, Dan. "Breaking Conventional Barriers." Pages 159–172 in *New Perspectives on Narrative Perspective*. Edited by Willie van Peer and Seymour Chatman. New York: State University of New York Press, 2001.

Shepherd, David. "Before Bomberg: The Case of the Targum of Job in the Rabbinic Bible and the Solger Codex (MS Nürnberg)." *Biblica* 79 (1998): 360–380.

————. *Targum and Translation: A Reconsideration of the Qumran Aramaic Version of Job*. Edited by W. J. van Bekkum et al., Studia Semitica Neerlandica 45. Assen: Royal van Gorcum, 2004.

————. "Will the Real Targum Please Stand Up? Translation and Coordination in the Ancient Aramaic Versions of Job." *Journal of Jewish Studies* 51 (2000): 88–116.

Signer, Michael A. "Restoring the Narrative: Jewish and Christian Exegesis in the Twelfth Century." Pages 70–82 in *With Reverence for the Word: Medieval Scriptural Exegesis in Judaism, Christianity, and Islam*. Edited by Jane Dammen McAuliffe, Barry D. Walfish, and Joseph W. Goering. Oxford: Oxford University Press, 2003.

Simon, Richard. *Histoire Critique du Vieux Testament*. Rotterdam: Leers, 1685.

Ska, Jean Louis. "Genèse XVIII 6 – Intertextualité et Interprétation: 'Tout Fait Farine au bon Moulin.'" Pages 61–70 in *Congress Volume: Olso 1998*. Edited by André Lemaire and Magne Sæbø. Supplements to Vetus Testamentum 80. Leiden: Brill, 2000.

Smith, R. Payne. *A Compendium Syriac Dictionary*. Oregon: Wipf and Stock, 1999.

Snaith, Norman H. *The Book of Job: Its Origin and Purpose*. Studies in Biblical Theology, Second Series 11. London: SCM, 1968.

Soden, Wolfram von. *The Ancient Orient: An Introduction to the Study of the Ancient Near East*. Translated by Donald G. Schley. Grand Rapids, Mich.: Eerdmans, 1985.

Sokoloff, Michael A. *A Dictionary of Jewish Babylonian Aramaic of the Talmudic and Geonic Periods*. Baltimore: John Hopkins University Press, 2002.

————. *The Targum to Job From Qumran Cave XI*. Jerusalem: Bar-Ilan University Press, 1974.

Sperber, Daniel. "Notes on the Kesitah." *Révue des Études Juives* 127 (1968): 265–268.

Spiegel, Shalom. "Noah, Danel, and Job: Touching on Canaanite Relics in the Legends of the Jews." Pages 305–355 in *Louis Ginzberg Jubilee Volume on the Occasion of his Seventieth Birthday*. New York: American Academy for Jewish Research, 1945.

Spittler, Russell P. "Job, The Testament of." Pages 869–871 in vol. 3 of *The Anchor Bible Dictionary*. Edited by David Noel Freedman; 6 vols. New York: Doubleday,1992.

————. "Testament of Job: A New Translation and Introduction." Pages 829–868 in vol. 1 of *The Old Testament Pseudepigrapha*. 2 vols. Edited by James H. Charlesworth. New York: Doubleday, 1983.

Spronk, Klaas. "The Legend of Kirtu (KTU 1.14–16): A Study of the Structure and Its Consequences for Interpretation." Pages 62–82 in *The*

Structural Analysis of Biblical and Canaanite Poetry. Edited by Willem van der Meer and Johannes C. der Moor. Journal for the Study of the Old Testament Supplement Series 74. Edited by David J. A. Clines and Philip R. Davies. Sheffield: JSOT Press, 1988.

Stec, David M, ed. *The Text of the Targum of Job: An Introduction and Critical Edition.* Arbeiten zur Geschichte des antiken Judentums und des Urchristentums 20. Edited by Martin Hengel, Peter Schäfer, Pieter W. van Horst, Martin Goodman, Daniël R. Schwartz. Leiden: Brill, 1994.

Steible, H. *Die Neusumerischen Bau-und Weihinschriften.* Stuttgart: Steiner, 1991.

Sternberg, Meir. *The Poetics of Biblical Narrative: Ideological Literature and the Drama of Reading.* Edited by Hebert Marks and Robert Polzin. Indiana Studies in Biblical Literature. Bloomington, Ind.: Indiana University Press, 1985.

Stone, Michael. "Lists of Revealed Things in the Apocalyptic Literature." Pages 414–452 in *Magnalia Dei: The Mighty Acts of God: Essays on the Bible and Archaeology in Memory of G. Ernest Wright.* Edited by Frank M. Cross, Werner E. Lemke, and Patrick D. Miller. New York: Doubleday, 1976.

Strauss, Hans. *Hiob 19:1– 42:7.* BKAT 16/2 (Neukirchen Vluyn: Neukirchener Verlag, 2000.

Stump, Eleonore. "Aquinas on the Suffering of Job." In *Human and Divine Agency: Anglican, Catholic, and Lutheran Perspectives.* Edited by F. Michael McLain and W. Mark Richardson. New York: University Press of America, 1999.

Swete, Henry B. *An Introduction to the Old Testament in Greek.* Cambridge: Cambridge University Press, 1914.

Synan, Edward. "The Four 'Senses' and Four Exegetes." Pages 225–236 in *With Reverence for the Word: Medieval Scriptural Exegesis in Judaism, Christianity, and Islam.* Edited by Jane Dammen McAuliffe, Barry D. Walfish, and Joseph W. Goering. Oxford: Oxford University Press, 2003.

Syring, Wolf-Dieter. *Hiob und sein Anwalt: Die Prosatexte des Hiobbuches und ihre Rolle in seiner Redaktions- und Rezeptionsgeschichte.* BZAW 336. Berlin: Walter de Gruyter, 2004.

Szpek, Heidi M. *Translation Technique in the Peshitta to Job: A Model for Evaluating a Text with Documentation from the Peshitta to Job.* Edited by Michael V. Fox and E. Elizabeth Johnson. Society of Biblical Literature Dissertation Series 137. Atlanta: Scholars Press, 1993.

Tamez, Elsa. "Letter to Job." Pages 174–176 in *Doing Theology in a Divided World: Papers from the 6th International Conference of the Ecumenical Association of Third World Theologians, Jan 5-13 1983, Geneva Switzerland.* Edited by Virginia Fabella and Sergio Torres. New York: Orbis, 1985.

Taylor, Mark C. *Erring: A Postmodern A/Theology.* Chicago: University of Chicago Press, 1984.

Terrien, Samuel. "The Book of Job: Introduction and Exegesis." Pages 875–1198 in vol. 3 of *The Interpreter's Bible*. Vol. III of XII volumes. Edited by George Arthur Buttrick et al. Nashville: Abingdon Press 1982.

⎯⎯⎯⎯⎯⎯⎯. *The Elusive Presence: Towards a New Biblical Theology*. San Francisco: Harper & Row, 1978.

⎯⎯⎯⎯⎯⎯⎯. *Job*. Commentaire de l'Ancien Testament 13. Paris: Delachaux et Niestlé,1963.

⎯⎯⎯⎯⎯⎯⎯. "Presence in Absence." Pages 254–269 in *The Flowering of Old Testament Theology: A Reader in Twentieth-Century Old Testament Theology, 1930-1990*. Edited by Ben C. Ollenburger, Elmer A. Martens, and Gerhard F. Hasel. Sources for Biblical and Theological Study. Edited by David W. Baker. Winona Lake, Ind.: Eisenbrauns, 1992.

Thickstun, William R. *Visionary Closure in the Modern Novel*. London: MacMillan, 1988.

Tilley, Terrence W. "God and the Silencing of Job." *Modern Theology* 5, no. 3 (1989): 257–270.

Toivari-Viitala, Jaana. *Women at Deir El-Medina: A Study of the Status and Role of the Female Inhabitants in the Workmen's Community during the Ramesside Period*. Edited by J. F. Borghouts, R. J. Demarée, J. de Roos, R. van Walsem, and H. O. Willems. Egyptologische Uitgaren 15. Leiden: Nederlands Instituut voor het Nabije Oosten, 2001.

Tov, Emanuel. "History and Significance of a Standard Text of the Hebrew Bible." Pages 49–66 in Antiquity. Part 1 of *From the Beginning to the Middle Ages (until 1300). Vol 1 of The Hebrew Bible, Old Testament: The History of Its Interpretation*. Edited by Magne Sæbø. Göttingen: Vandenhoeck & Ruprecht, 1996.

Tremblay, P. Hervé. *Job 19, 25–27 Dans la Septante et Chez les Pères Grecs: Unanimité d'une Tradition*. Etudes Bibliques, Nouvelle Série 47. Paris: Gabalda, 2002.

Tropper, Josef. *Ugaritische Grammatik*. Münster: Ugarit-Verlag, 2000.

Trudinger, Paul. "Two Lukan Gospel Stories: Key to the Significance of the Dominical Sacraments in the Life of the Early Church." *Downside Review* 118, no. 410 (2000): 17–26.

Tsevat, Matitiahu. "The Meaning of the Book of Job." Pages 189–218 in *Sitting with Job: Selected Studies on the Book of Job*. Edited by Roy B. Zuck. Grand Rapids, Mich.: Baker, 1992.

Tur-Sinai, Naphtali H. *The Book of Job: A New Commentary*. Jerusalem: Kiryath Sepher, 1957.

Urbach, Ephraim E. *The Sages: Their Concepts and Beliefs*. Translated by Israel Abrahams. Jerusalem: Magnes, 1987.

Urbrock, William J. "Job As Drama: Tragedy or Comedy?" *Currents in Theology and Mission* 8 (1981): 35–40.

Vaux, Roland de. *Ancient Israel: Its Life and Institutions*. Translated by John McHugh. London: McGraw-Hill, 1961.

Walfish, Barry D. "An Introduction to Medieval Jewish Biblical Interpretation." Pages 1–12 in *With Reverence for the Word: Medieval Scriptural Exegesis in Judaism, Christianity, and Islam.* Edited by Jane Dammen McAuliffe, Barry D. Walfish, and Joseph W. Goering. Oxford: Oxford University Press, 2003.

Wallace, Mark I. *The Second Naiveté: Barth, Ricouer, and the New Yale Theology.* Edited by Charles Mabee. Rev. ed. Studies in American Biblical Hermeneutics 6. Macon, Ga.: Mercer University Press, 1995.

Waltke, Bruce K., and Michael O'Connor. *An Introduction to Biblical Hebrew Syntax.* Winona Lake, Ind.: Eisenbrauns, 1990.

Wawrykow, Joseph P. "New Directions in Research on Thomas Aquinas." *Religious Studies Review* 27, no. 1 (2001): 32–38.

Weinberg, J. "Job Versus Abraham: The Quest for the Perfect God-Fearer in Rabbinic Tradition." Pages 281–296 in *The Book of Job.* Edited by W. A. M. Beuken. Bibliotheca Ephemeridum Theologicarum Lovaniensium 114. Leuven: Leuven University Press, 1994.

Weiss, Meir. *The Story of Job's Beginning: Job 1-2: A Literary Analysis.* Jerusalem: Magnes, 1983.

Weiss, R. "Further Notes on the Qumran Targum to Job." *Journal of Semitic Studies* 19 (1974): 13–18.

Westermann, Claus. *The Structure of the Book of Job.* Philadelphia: Fortress, 1981.

Whedbee, William. *The Bible and the Comic Vision.* Cambridge: Cambridge University Press, 1998.

⸺⸺⸺. "The Comedy of Job." *Semeia* 7 (1977): 1–39.

Whybray, Norman R. *The Good Life in the Old Testament.* London: T&T Clark, 2002.

⸺⸺⸺. "'Shall Not the Judge of All the Earth Do What is Just?' God's Oppression of the Innocent in the Old Testament." Pages 1–19 in *Shall Not the Judge of All the Earth Do What is Right? Studies on the Nature of God in Tribute to James L. Crenshaw.* Edited by David Penchansky and Paul L. Redditt. Winona Lake, Ind.: Eisenbrauns, 2000.

Willey, Patricia T. *Remember the Former Things: The Recollection of Previous Texts in Second Isaiah.* Edited by Michael V. Fox and E. Elizabeth Johnson. Society of Biblical Literature: Dissertation Series 161. Atlanta: Scholars, 1997.

⸺⸺⸺. "The Rhetoric of Recollection." Pages 71–78 in *Congress Volume Olso 1998.* Edited by André Lemaire and Magne Sæbø. Supplements to Vetus Testamentum 80. Leiden: Brill, 2000.

Wischnitzer-Bernstein, Rache. "The Concept of the Resurrection in the Ezekiel Panel of the Dura Synagogue." *Journal of Biblical Literature* 60, no. 1 (1941): 43–55.

Witte, Markus. »Die dritte Rede Bildads (Hiob 25) und die Redaktionsgescgichte des Hiobbuches.« Pages 349–355 in *The Book of*

Job. Bibliotheca Ephemeridum theologicarum Lovaniensium 114. Edited by William A. Beuken. Leuven: Leuven University Press, 1994.

———. *Vom Leiden zur Lehre. Der dritte Redegang (Hiob 21–27) und die Redaktionsgeschichte des Hiobbuches*. BZAW 230. Berlin: Walter de Gruyter, 1994.

Wolde, Ellen van. "Different Perspectives on Faith and Justice: The God of Jacob and the God of Job." Pages 17–23 in *The Many Voices of the Bible*. Edited by Séan Freyne and Ellen van Wolde. London: SCM, 2002.

Yaffe, Martin D. "Providence in Medieval Aristotelianism: Moses Maimonides and Thomas Aquinas on the Book of Job." Pages 111–128 in *The Voice From the Whirlwind: Interpreting the Book of Job*. Edited by Leo G. Perdue and W. Clark Gilpin. Nashville: Abingdon, 1992.

Zerafa, Peter P. *The Wisdom of God in the Book of Job*. Rome: Herder, 1978.

Zöckler, Otto. *The Book of Job: A Commentary*. New York: Scribner, 1874.

Zuckerman, Bruce. "The Date of 11Q Targum Job: A Palaeographic Consideration of its Vorlage." *Journal for the Study of the Pseudepigrapha* 10 (1987): 57–78.

———. "Two examples of editorial Modification in 11QtgJob." Pages 269–273 in *Biblical and Near Eastern Studies: Essays in Honor of William Sanford LaSor*. Edited by Gary A. Tuttle. Michigan: Eerdmans, 1978.

———. *Job the Silent: A Study in Historical Counterpoint*. New York: Oxford University Press, 1991.

Index of Scriptural and Ancient Sources

MT

Genesis
1 124
1:10 124
1:12 124
1:18 124
1:21 124
1:28 136
6:17-19 138
15:1 101
15:4 15
15:13 46
18:25 45
19:21 16
20:2 12
20:7 14
20:13 17
21:12 46
21:23 17
22:1 101
22:1-19 .... 107, 112
22:2 .... 45, 107, 113
22:3 107
22:5 113
22:6 107
22:6-7 113
22:7 107
22:8 .... 107, 113
22:9 113
22:10 107
22:11 14
22:12 .... 107, 109, 113
22:13 107
22:15 .... 109, 113
22:16-17 107
24:12 17
24:14 .... 14, 17
26:24 14
27:19 18
28:10-12 135
28:17 15
28:22 135
32:21 16
33:19 .... 22, 23
34:7 17
36 37
37:9 10
39:7 101
40:1 .... 10, 101
40:14 17
41:25 126
41:32 13
42:36 23
47:9 46
50:23 117

Exodus
1:17 18
3:7 132
4:23 132
5:6 132
5:10 132
5:13 132
5:14 132
9:3-6 112
9:20 46
20:5-6 106
21:4 78
22:14 132
24:5-6 44
30:24 24

Leviticus
19:13 132
19:15 .... 16, 33

Numbers
6:26 16
12:7 14
21:7 14
21:29 .... 18, 19
23:1 107
23:3 107
23:4 107
23:6 107
23:14 107
23:29 107
27:1-11 115
27:4 115
27:7 115
27:10 115
27:11 115
36 115
36:1-12 115

Deuteronomy
6:15 11
7:4 11
9:20 14
10:17 .... 16, 33
10:21 82
11:17 11
13:15 13
17:4 13
22:21 17
24:15 132
28:50 33
29:26 11
29:27 20
30:3 .... 19, 20, 125, 139
31:14 11

Joshua
1:2 14
2:12 17
7:1 11
7:15 17
23:16 11
24:32 22

Judges
1:24 17
2:14 11
2:20 11
3:8 11
6:39 11
8:35 17
10:7 11
19:23 17
20:6 17

1 Samuel
3:12 12
4:19 12
7:5 14
12:19 14
12:23 14
15:6 17
20:8 17
23:23 12
25:25 17
25:35 16
30:26 21

2 Samuel
2:5 17
2:6 17
2:22 16
3:8 17
7:5 14
7:11 126
7:19 12
9:1 17
9:2 17
9:7 17
10:2 17
13:12 17
15:20 17
24:1 11

1 Kings
2:7 17
7:37 23
8:14-27 135
8:28 16
8:29 16
8:34 33
8:36 33
8:39 33
8:45 16
8:49 16
8:49-50 33
8:50 33
10:3 126
16:12 12
17:17 101
21:1 101
21:3 115
21:4 115

2 Kings
9:30 24
9:32 16
13:3 11
19:34 14
20:6 14

1 Chronicles
21:1 86
25:5 23
29:2 24

2 Chronicles
6:35 16
6:39 16
6:40 16

Ezra
7:1 101
19:4 12

Nehemiah
1:6 16
1:11 16

Esther
6:9 23

Job
1:1 .... 84, 107
1 .... 73, 74
1-2 74
1:2 84
1:1-3 .... 4, 24
1:1-5 74
1-2 74
1:2-3 98
1:3 .... 85, 92
1:5 .... 4, 10, 14, 38,
   85, 86, 91, 92,
   96, 107, 109, 113
1:6 97
1:8 .... 2, 12, 13, 85,
   86, 95, 96, 107
1:9 107
1:10 .... 19, 21, 91, 92, 98
1:11 .... 2, 4, 12, 80,
   84, 86, 92, 123
1:12 .... 22, 95
1:13 .... 97, 107
1:15 112
1:16 .... 46, 112
1:17 .... 46, 112
1:18 .... 97, 112
1:19 107
1:20 40
1:20-21 65
1:21 .... 5, 7, 20, 92, 111
1:22 .... 5, 36, 91
2:1 97
2 73
2:2 95
2:3 .... 12, 13, 85, 86
   95, 96, 100,
   106, 107, 121
2:4 .... 21, 84
2:5 .... 2, 4, 12, 86
   92, 123
2:6 .... 95, 99
2:7 106
2:7-11 65
2:8 46
2:9 .... 17, 86, 92
2:10 .... 5, 36, 86,
   91, 96, 98,
   105, 106, 138
2:11 .... 20, 22, 36, 37,
   85, 97, 101,
   106, 111, 126
2:11-13 .... 1, 74, 103
2:12 106
2:13 .... 12, 46, 105
3 .... 75, 136
3:1 .... 10, 75, 102
3-31 74
3:2 101
3:3 75
3:4 75
3:8 .... 75, 141
3:18-19 132
3:19 132
3:23 .... 75, 136
3-31 74
4:1 106
4:2 12
4:8-9 106
4:12-19 77
4:18 .... 68, 132
5:1 .... 96, 109
5:8 .... 12, 96, 109
5:8-11 106
6:1 101
6:10 111
6:22 98

Index of Scriptural and Ancient Sources 171

6:29 .... 20, 111	15:1 101	27:1 .... 22, 84, 101
7:2 132	15:11 111	27:4 .... 103, 105
7:4 40	15:22 .... 20, 111	27:7 40
7:7 .... 20, 111	15:23 .... 13, 87, 95, 96	27:11 116
7:9b 40	15:35 .... 13, 87	27:12 116
7:10 .... 20, 111	16:1 101	27:13 87
8:1 101	16:2 111	27:14 116
8:3 91	16:8 40	27:15 116
8:5 .... 96, 109	16:15 46	27:16 .... 13, 87
8:5-6 91	16:21 21	27:16-17 116
8:7 .... 87, 91, 98	17:5 116	27:17 .... 13, 87
8:8 .... 13, 29, 87	17:10 .... 20, 111	28 87
8:9 91	18:1 101	28:27 13
8:11-13 106	18:12 .... 13, 87, 95, 96	29 22
8:12 131	19:1 101	29:1 .... 22, 84, 101
8:20 91	19:13 .... 87, 97	29:5 107
9:1 101	19:13-14 22	29:7 128
9:2-11 53	19:16 132	29:13 92
9:5 38	19:17 112	29:25 111
9:12 .... 20, 111	19:18 40	30:8 98
9:13 .... 20, 38, 111	19:21 46	31:2 .... 87, 116
9:14-20 106	19:25/6 40	31:3 116
9:17 121	20 116	31:13 132
9:18 .... 20, 111	20:1 101	31:14 .... 20, 111
9:22 45	20:2 .... 20, 111	31:15 .... 13, 87
9:22-23 61	20:7 116	31:40 105
9:24 106	20:9 116	32-42 74
10:9 .... 20, 111	20:10 .... 20, 111, 116	32:1 105
10:15 16	20:18 116	32:1-6 84
10:16 .... 20, 111	20:20-21 116	32:2 .... 87, 95
10:19 106	20:23 38	32:3 .... 21, 75, 87, 95
10:21 .... 20, 111	20:29 .... 87, 116	32:5 87
11:1 101	21:1 101	32:6 101
11:6 .... 106, 126	21:3 10	32:14 .... 20, 111
11:10 .... 20, 111	21:8 .... 13, 87, 95, 96	33:5 .... 20, 111
11:13 .... 13, 87, 96, 109	21:15 132	33:25 .... 20, 111
11:13-15a 109	21:17 116	33:26 ... 20, 96, 109, 111
11:15 .... 15, 16, 87, 96	21:34 111	33:29 62
12:1 101	22:1 101	33:32 .... 20, 111
12:4 21	22:8 .... 16, 38, 87, 96	34:1 101
12:5 .... 13, 87, 95, 96	22:23 .... 20, 111	34:15 .... 20, 111
13:3 12	22:26 15	34:19 .... 16, 38, 87,
13:4 65	22:26-27a 109	88, 96, 108
13:7 .... 103, 105	22:27 .... 96, 109	35:1 101
13:7-8 .... 16, 96	23:1 101	35:4 .... 20, 111
13:8 87	23:13 .... 20, 111	36:1 101
13:9-10 106	24:1-2 116	36:4 .... 103, 105
13:10 .... 16, 36	24:18 116	36:33 41
13:22 .... 20, 111	24:22 40	38 75
14:12 40	25:1 101	38:1 101
14:13 38	26:1 101	38:2 10
14:14 40	27 .... 30, 116	38:3 75

38:5-11 .... 128, 134	42:9 .... 10, 12, 18, 22, 82, 85, 87, 91, 94	74:12-17 135
38:8 .... 75, 136, 141	42:9b-11 31	74:18-23 135
38:12 75	42:10 .... 5, 14, 18, 19, 20, 21, 46, 73, 84, 97, 111, 112, 125	74:22 136
38:15 75		82:2 16
38:16 75		86:17 17
38:17 75	42:10-12 94	90:7-10 100
38:19 75	42:10-17 .... 77, 111	102:18 16
38:41 .... 13, 87	42:11 .... 22, 31, 32, 73, 85, 87, 97, 101, 102, 106, 123, 126, 135, 138	102:21 132
38-41 1		103:7-13 44
39:4 .... 20, 111		109:13 21
39:9 132		126:1 19
39:12 .... 20, 111		126:4 19
40:1 101	42:11-17 ...... 73, 94, 136	126:5 18
40:3 101	42:12a 91	128:6 117
40:3-5 73	42:12 .... 1, 5, 6, 7, 23, 31, 85, 87, 91, 92, 107, 112, 134	136:4 82
40:3-6 128		145:3 82
40:4 .... 20, 111		145:9 59
40:5 105	42:12-13 97	
40:6 101	42:12-17 31	Proverbs
40:6-42:7 73	42:12b-17 92	1:9-11 129
40:7 48	42:13 .... 107, 111	3:12 59
40:8 88	42:13-15 31	6:17 103
40:11 129	42:14 24	6:35 16
40:28 .... 129, 132	42:15 .... 24, 91, 116, 135	12:19 103
42 76	42:16 .... 10, 46	17:6 117
42:1 101	42:16-17 31	17:17 21
42:1-6 .... 1, 70, 76, 102, 104, 128	42:16b-17 35	18:5 16
	42:17 24	21:6 103
42:2 128		26:28 103
42:3 .... 10, 82	Psalms	31:29 23
42:5 .... 14, 104, 107	2:7 12	
42:5-6 63	6:10 16	Ecclesiastes
42:6 .... 5, 34, 55, 61, 76, 101	14:7 .... 19, 20	6:12 91
	40:5 67	7:8 91
42:7 ..... 1, 5, 7, 9, 11-13, 36, 39, 43, 55-58, 60, 63, 70, 75, 78, 85, 87, 88, 92, 94, 100-102, 105, 107, 125, 134, 135, 143	41 52	7:14 91
	45:9 24	
	46:2 21	Song of Solomon
	53:7 .... 19, 20	2:14 24
	61:2 16	
	66:19 16	Isaiah
42:7-8 .... 87, 94	69:27 12	3:3 16
42:7-9a 31	69:34 132	7:20 132
42:7-9 .... 1, 37, 60, 76, 94, 102, 113	71:19 82	9:14 16
	73 135	20:3 14
42:7-10 .... 73, 74	73:8 135	23:11 12
42:7-17 .... 1, 4, 5, 6	74:1 135	29:22 12
42:8 .... 11, 13, 14, 15, 16, 17, 33, 73, 85, 87, 91, 92, 95, 98, 104, 107, 108, 109	74:1-11 135	32:7 103
	74 .... 135, 137	37:21 12
	74:2 135	37:33 12
	74:3 135	40:1 126
42:8b 35	74:11 138	40:1-2 47
42:8-9 ..... 8, 85, 107, 129	74:12 135	40:2 47

40:10 60	Lamentations	Malachi
40:12-24 128	1:13 46	1:8 16
40:27 128	2:10 .... 46, 47	1:9 16
40:28 82	4:2 46	2:9 16
42:1 .... 14, 126		3:5 132
42:19 .... 14, 126	Ezekiel	
43:18-19 134	14 73	**LXX**
44:1 .... 14, 126	14:13 18	
44:2 126	14:15 111	Genesis
45:7 .... 106, 126	14:18 111	36:32-35 37
46:9 .... 126, 134	14:20 111	36:33 41
46:10a 125	14:22 .... 86, 111, 121	
49:14 128	16:53 .... 19, 125	Exodus
49:24 128	18:1-3 106	34:6 49
51:19 126	23:19 24	
54:11 24	28:25 14	2 Samuel
54:17 60	29:14 .... 19, 125	16:5-13 49
	37 140	
Jeremiah	37:25 14	Job
4:30 24	46:16 115	1:4 22
6:4 132		1:5 38
7:17 14	Daniel	1:20 .... 36, 40
11:14 14	2:22 23	1:22a 36
14:11 14	7:8 23	2:10d 36
16:13 47	7:12 23	2:11 .... 22, 36, 37
25:29a 68	12:1-3 140	3:9 49
26:15 15		4:2 41
29:7 14	Hosea	6:11 49
29:14 20	6:8 17	7:3 49
29:23 17	6:11 .... 19, 125, 139	7:4 40
30:3 .... 19, 125	7:11 24	7:9b 40
30:17-18 21		8:15 49
30:18 .... 18, 19,	Amos	9:4 49
125, 139	9:14 .... 19, 125, 139	9:5 38
32:24 46		9:13 38
32:36 138	Micah	13:10 38
32:42 138	6:12 103	14:12 40
32:44 19		14:12-14 40
33:7 .... 18, 125, 139	Nahum	14:13 38
33:11 18	3:7 126	14:13-17 53
33:26 .... 19, 125, 139		14:14 .... 40, 49
42:2 14	Zephaniah	15:31 49
42:20 14	2:7 .... 19, 20, 125	16:8 40
48:17 125	3:20 19	17:13 49
48:46 20		19:18 40
48:47 .... 19, 20,	Zechariah	19:25-26 40
125, 126	1:16 21	19:26 40
		20:23 38
		20:26 49
		22:8 38
		22:21 49

24:22 40	John	Genesis Rabbah
27:7 40	9:3 67	49:9 45
31:31 41	20:15 140	
32:4 49	20:24-29 140	Jerusalem Talmud
32:16 49	20:26 140	Sota 5:8 46
33:5 49		
33:22 41	Romans	KTU
34:19 38	8:18 52	1.14-16 114
38:12 41	8:28 64	1.15:III.16 114
41:3 49	15:5 49	
42:6 39	15:13 49	Pesiqta deRab Kahana
42:7 .... 18, 36, 39		16:6 46
42:7-9 37	1 Corinthians	
42:8 39	3:8 132	Sefire
42:8e 35	15:50 140	3:24 19
42:9 10		
42:11 36	Hebrews	Sirach (Hebrew)
42:14 41	13:20 49	49:9 73
42:16 .... 36, 37		
42:16-17 39	1 Peter	Testament of Job
42:16b-17 17	4:17 68	1:3-5 48
42:16c-e 35		1:5 50
42:17 40	James	2:1 48
42:17b 36	5:4 132	4:5-9 50
42:17b-e 35	5:7-11 49	4:6 50
	5:11 .... 49, 50	4:9 48
Psalms		19-26 50
25:3 49	Revelation	26:5 50
37:9 49	21:1 134	27:7 50
	21-22 124	28:8 48
New Testament		29:3 48
	Others	30:1 48
Matthew		31:3 48
6:33 66	Baba Bathra	33:5-9 48
20:8 132	16a 40, 45, 61, 63	38:2-4 48
20:12 132		39:8-9 140
	Baba Kama	39:12 140
Luke	9:29 44	40:5-6 48
16:19-31 140		42:10 140
16:25 140	2 Baruch	43:1-13 48
20:38 140	21:12-26 139	45:1-5 48
24:27 140	30:2-5 139	53:7 140
24:36 140		53:11 140
24:36-43 140	CTU	
24:37 140	1.14 23	11QtgJob
24:39 140		42:9b 33
24:42-43 140	1 Enoch	Col 6.8 (MT, 22:8) 33
24:45 140	29:6 139	

Index of Authors

Abrahams, I., ... 45, 166
Achtemeier, A., ... 17, 116, 140, 151, 155, 160
Adair, J. R., ... 35, 151
Albright, W. F., ... 24, 116, 140, 152, 157, 161
Alt, A., ... 73, 103, 147
Alter, R., ... 74, 84, 89, 147, 154
Altmann, A., ... 59, 157
Ambrose 52, 53, 54, 69, 147, 148, 149, 159
Anderson, B., ... 137, 147
Anderson, F. I., ... 78, 147
Aquinas 64, 65, 66, 147, 155, 156, 165, 167, 168
Attridge, H., ... 156
Averintsev, S., ... 4, 147
Ayedze, K. A., ... 49, 147

Baker, W. D., ... 162, 167
Bakhtin, M., ... 4, 6, 93, 147, 152, 153, 159, 160
Balentine, S. E., ... 3, 91, 147
Barstad, H. M., ... 127, 149
Barton, J., ... 6, 27, 140, 147
Barton, S., ... 140, 159
Baskin, J. R., ... 41, 43, 46, 47, 53, 148
Bates, D., ... 52, 159
Battles, F. L., ... 66, 149
Baumann, E., ... 19, 148
Begg, C. T., ... 48, 148
Bekkum, W. J. van, ... 32, 164
Ben-Barak, Z., ... 114, 148
Benin, S. D., ... 58, 148
Ben-Shammai, H., ... 59, 148
Beuken, W. A. M., ... 30, 35, 43, 48, 148, 157, 167, 168
Boling, R. G., ... 124, 148
Boorer, S., ... 76, 141, 148
Borger, R., ... 19, 148
Borghouts, J. F., ... 114, 166
Bracke, J. M., ... 20, 148
Brenner, A., ... 79, 149

Brett M. G., ... 127, 149
Briggs, C. A., ... 10, 24, 149
Brockelmann, C., ... 10, 149
Bromiley, G. W., ... 155, 156
Brooke, G. J., ... 116, 160
Brottier, L., ... 54, 149
Brown, D., ... 28, 149
Brown, F., ... 10, 24, 149
Brown, W. P., ... 74, 160
Brueggemann, W., ... 3, 4, 81, 91, 136, 138, 149, 160
Brugman, J., ... 114, 161
Buchanan, E., ... 99, 162
Budde, K. F. R., ... 12, 102, 149
Buttenwieser, M., ... 73, 149
Buttrick, G. A., ... 118, 166

Calvin, John 66, 67, 68, 69, 70, 71, 149, 162, 163
Cameron, A., ... 115, 154
Carroll, N., ... 98, 149
Carroll, R. P., ... 93, 99, 124, 149, 162
Cathcart, K., ... 23, 157
Cazier, P., ... 53, 149
Cella, A. di, ... 3, 151
Charlesworth, J. H., ... 164
Chatman, S., ... 85, 86, 98, 149, 160, 163
Chazan, R., ... 124, 148
Cheney, M., ... 5, 150
Chrysostom 52, 54, 55, 57, 63, 150
Clifford, R. J., ... 128, 136, 150, 151
Clines, D. J. A, ... 67, 74, 75, 77, 78, 82, 93, 94, 99, 112, 114, 118, 119, 141, 148, 150, 154, 158, 161, 162, 165
Collins, J. J., ... 47, 48, 124, 128, 136, 150, 151, 163
Conrad, E. W., ... 99, 113, 128, 150, 155
Contino, P. J., ... 4, 147
Cooper, A., ... 93, 150
Coote, R. B., ... 137, 150
Cowley, A., ... 116, 150
Cox, C. E., ... 28, 34, 150

Cox, D., ... 2, 143, 150
Craddock, F. B., ... 140, 151
Crenshaw, J. L., ... 2, 11, 72, 76, 128,
      130, 149, 151, 158, 167
Cross, F. M., ... 118, 127, 128, 151,
      156, 159, 165
Cross, T., ... 12, 159

Dailey, T. F., ... 94, 100, 151
Damico, A., ... 64, 147
David W. Baker 166
Davidson, R., ... 99, 138, 151, 162
Davies, P. R., ... 94, 99, 114, 118,
      119, 141, 148, 154,
      158, 161, 162, 165
Delitzsch, F., ... 73, 151
Dell, K. J., ... 118, 151
Delmaire, J., ... 28, 44, 151
Demarée, R. J., ... 166
Dever, W. G., ... 48, 157
Dhorme, E., ... 10, 12, 15, 19, 20,
      21, 23, 24, 34, 35,
      36, 40, 41, 74, 98, 151
Diem, W., ... 23, 162
Dietrich, E. L., ... 19, 151
Dietrich, W. S., ... 148
Driver, S. R., ... 10, 12, 19, 24, 72,
      73, 132, 149, 151
Duhm, B., ... 15, 151
Durand, J. J. F., ... 141, 151

Eaton, J. H., ... 77, 152
Ebach, J., ... 42, 152
Emerson, C., ... 4, 147, 152
Evans, G. R., ... 52, 152

Fabella, V., ... 141, 165
Felch, S. F., ... 4, 147
Fewell, D. N., ... 4, 153
Finan, T., ... 51, 158
Fishbane, M., ... 6, 27, 152
Fitzmyer, J. A., ... 19, 140, 152
Forrest, R. W. E., ... 103, 105, 152
Fox, M. V., ... 6, 11, 165, 167
Freedman, D. N., ... 2, 21, 24, 116, 140,
      152, 157, 161, 164
Frei, H., ... 71, 152
Freyne, S., ... 118, 168
Friedländer, M., ... 62, 148
Friedrich, G., ... 156
Fullerton, K., ... 73, 79, 152

Gamble, H. Y., ... 31, 152
García-Martínez, F., .. 29, 30, 31, 124, 162
Gard, D. H., ... 35, 39, 40, 152
Gehman, H. S., ... 35, 40, 152
Gentry, P. J., ... 34, 37, 152
Gesenius-Kautzsch 153
Getui, M. N., ... 124, 157
Gibson, J. C. L., ... 83, 153
Gilkey, L., ... 139, 153
Gillespie, M. P., ... 78, 90, 153
Gilpin, W. C., ... 65, 139, 153, 168
Ginsberg, H. L., ... 75, 153
Ginzberg, L., ... 14, 45, 153, 164
Glatzer, N. N., ... 55, 153
Goering, J. W., ... 58, 59, 64, 148,
      153, 164, 165, 167
Goldin, J., ... 12, 147
Golding, A., ... 66, 149
Goldsworthy, G., ... 141, 153
Good, E., ... 102, 153
Goodman, M., ... 12, 147
Gordis, R., ... 43, 73, 75, 107, 153
Gordon, C. H., ... 23, 24, 73, 153
Gossai, H., ... 10, 87, 159, 162
Gray, G. B., ... 10, 12, 19, 24, 34, 37;
      40, 72, 73, 132, 151, 153
Gray, J., ... 29, 31, 71, 153
Green, B., ... 4, 153
Greenberg, M., ... 89, 154
Greenspoon, L. J., ... 34, 152
Gregory the Great 52, 55, 56, 57,
      64, 70, 154
Grosz, K., ... 115, 154
Gruber, M. I., ... 15, 154
Guggenheimer, H. W., ... 46, 163
Gutíerrez, G., ... 17, 77, 154

Haas, C., ... 50, 154
Habel, N. C., ... 74, 89, 107, 112,
      116, 132, 154
Hall, C. A., ... 52, 154
Hallo, W. W., ... 124, 148
Halpern, B., ... 2, 152
Hanson, P. D., ... 156
Harl, M., ... 34, 35, 154
Hartley, J. E., ... 17, 154
Harvey, A., ... 140, 154
Hasel, G. F., ... 166
Heater, H., ... 22, 34, 35, 36, 37, 154
Heinemann, I., ... 59, 157
Hengel, M., ... 165
Hoffman, Y., ... 94, 154

Index of Authors

Hoftijzer, J., ... 155
Holladay, W. L., ... 20, 155
Hölscher, G., ... 103, 155
Horst, F., ... 103, 155
Horst, J., ... 49, 155
Horst, P. W. van der, ... 48, 50, 154, 155, 165
Hübner, H., ... 51, 155
Huddlestan, J. R., ... 21, 152
Hull, R. F., ... 76, 156
Hurvitz, A., ... 14, 73, 85, 118, 155
Hyers, C., ... 99, 113, 155
Hyman, A., ... 62, 155

Jackson, T. P., ... 64, 155
Jacobs, I., ... 47, 155
Jacobsen, T., ... 118, 122, 155
Janowski, B., ... 11, 155
Janzen, G., ... 17, 77, 118, 124, 131, 132, 155
Johnson, E. E., ... 6, 11, 165, 167
Jongeling, B., ... 30, 155, 156
Jørgensen, K. E. J., ... 24, 158
Jung, C. G., ... 76, 148, 156

Kallen, H., ... 99, 156
Katongole, E., ... 124, 157
Kaufman, S. A., ... 29, 156
Kautzsch, K., ... 14, 73, 153, 156
Keck, L. E., ... 71, 160
Kermode, F., ... 83, 89, 154, 156
Kissane, E. J., ... 103, 156
Kittel, G., ... 155, 156
Knibb, M. A., ... 50, 154
Knight, H., ... 10, 151
Köhlmoos, M., ... 105, 129, 156
Kraeling, E. G., ... 73, 156
Kraft, R. A., ... 47, 156
Kraus, F. R., ... 161
Kretzmann, N., ... 65, 156
Kreuzer, S., ... 103, 156
Kuhl, C., ... 103, 156
Kuhrt, A., ... 115, 154
Kutsch, E., ... 30, 31, 32, 103, 156

Labuschagne, C. J., ... 30, 156
Lange, M. de, ... 34, 35, 154
Leaman, O., ... 64, 156
Lemaire, A., ... 6, 127, 133, 147, 149, 152, 157, 160, 163, 164, 167
Lemke, W. E., ... 165

Levenson, J. D., ... 124, 133, 137, 138, 141, 156
Lévêque, J., ... 3, 103, 157
Levine, B. A., ... 116, 124, 148, 157
Lewy, H., ... 59, 157
Liddell, H. G., ... 39, 157
Lübbe, J. C., ... 30, 157
Lüthi, K., ... 103, 156

Mabee, C., ... 120, 167
MacDonald, D. B., ... 72, 73, 157
Machinist, P., ... 48, 157
MacNamara, M., ... 23, 157
MacRae, G., ... 47, 150
Magumba, J. N. K., ... 124, 157
Maher, M., ... 23, 157
Maimonides........... 61, 62, 63, 64, 65, 66, 69, 70, 71, 155, 162, 168
Mangan, C., ... 23, 157
Marcos, N. F., ... 35, 40, 41, 157
Margain, J., ... 29, 158
Marks, H., ... 89, 165
Marrow, F. J., ... 29, 158
Marsman, H. J., ... 114, 116, 158
Martens, E. A., ... 166
Martin, J. D., ... 118, 162
Mathew, G., ... 3, 158
Mathew, S. F., ... 85, 158
Mays, J. L., ... 17, 116, 140, 151, 155, 160
McAuliffe, J. D., ... 58, 59, 64, 148, 153, 164, 165, 167
McBride, S. D., ... 156
McCarthy, D. J., ... 11, 158
McEvoy, J., ... 51, 158
McHugh, M. P., ... 52, 133, 147, 166
McIntyre, J., ... 91, 158
McLain, F. M., ... 64, 65, 155, 165
McNell, J. T., ... 66, 149
Meer, W. van der, ... 114, 165
Mettinger, T. N. D., ... 135, 158
Metzger, M., ... 135, 158
Michel, A., ... 107, 158
Mies, F., ... 3, 157
Miller, P. D., ... 17, 109, 116, 118, 122, 124, 130, 135, 136, 140, 151, 155, 156, 158, 160, 165
Møller-Christensen, V., ... 24, 158
Moor, J. C. der, ... 114, 165
Moore, R. D., ... 12, 89, 91, 102, 104, 118, 156, 158
Moorhead, J., ... 52, 159
Morgan, R., ... 140, 159

Morreal, J., ... 99, 159
Morson, G. S., ... 4, 159
Moster, J. B., ... 3, 107, 159
Müller, H., ... 3, 118, 159
Muraoka, T., ... 29, 159
Murphy, R. E., ... 81, 131, 159

Nam, D., ... 10, 11, 12, 107, 127, 159
Napier, B. D., ... 137, 159
Nemoy, L., ... 12, 147
Neusner, J., ... 28, 41, 44, 45, 47, 148, 159
Newsom, C. A., ... 1, 4, 71, 74, 78, 81,
86, 89, 92, 93, 103, 159
Nicole, J., ... 105, 160
Nielsen, K., ... 6, 160
Norton, G. J., ... 27, 163
Noth, M., ... 73, 160

Obeng, E. A., ... 124, 157
O'Connell, M. J., ... 17, 154
O'Connor, D. J., ... 105, 160
O'Connor, M., ... 10, 167
Oeming, M., ... 104, 160
Ollenburger, B., ... 119, 166
Olson, D. T., ... 4, 83, 93, 115, 116, 160
Oostendorp, H. van, ... 85, 160
Ord, D. R., ... 137, 150
Orlinski, H. M., ... 34, 35, 38, 40, 160
Ormsby, E. C., ... 62, 155
Osgood, S. J., ... 116, 160

Paget, J. N. B., ... 51, 160
Paradise, J., ... 114, 161
Pardee, D. G., ... 10, 161
Patrick, D., ... 104, 118, 128, 161
Peer, W. van der, ... 85, 86, 98,
149, 160, 163
Penchansky, D.,.. 3, 76, 77, 149, 161, 167
Perdue, L. G., ... 65, 76, 118, 139,
153, 161, 168
Pestman, P. W., ... 114, 161
Pfeiffer, C. F., ... 137, 161
Phillips, A., ... 17, 161
Pisano, S., ... 27, 163
Ploeg, J. P. van der, ... 29, 30, 31, 32, 161
Polzin, R., ... 77, 89, 100, 161, 165
Pope, M. H., ... 24, 34, 71, 72, 73,
75, 103, 116, 136, 161
Porter, S. E., ... 3, 102, 103, 106, 161
Powery, E. B., ... 12, 159
Preuschen, E., ... 19, 161
Procopé, J. F., ... 51, 58, 161

Propp, W. H., ... 2, 152
Puckett, D. L., ... 66, 162
Puech, E., ... 29, 30, 31, 140, 162
Pyeong, Y., ... 87, 162
Pyper, H., ... 99, 162

Rad, G. von, ... 118, 162
Rahnenführer, D., ... 47, 162
Ranston, H., ... 74, 162
Rashi 16, 23, 61, 71, 91, 162
Reed, Y. A., ... 30, 31, 37, 41, 162
Reid, S. B., ... 141, 148
Reines, A., ... 62, 162
Richardson, W. M., ... 64, 65, 155, 165
Ricoeur, P., ... 99, 120, 162
Roberts, J. J. M., ... 119, 136, 162
Roos, J. de, ... 166
Rosenbalt, S., ... 147
Rosenberg, A. J., ... 16, 162
Rosenthal, F., ... 23, 162
Roth, M. T., ... 115, 162
Roth, W. M., ... 17, 163
Rowley, H. H., ... 72, 74, 163

Saadiah 12, 59, 60, 61, 62, 63, 70, 147
Sæbo, M., ... 6, 27, 51, 128, 148,
149, 150, 153, 156, 161,
162, 163, 164, 165, 168, 169
Sakenfeld, K. D., ... 115, 163
Samuel, S., ... 76, 163
Sanders, J. A., ... 27, 163
Sarna, N., ... 23, 24, 73, 163
Schäfer, P., ... 165
Schaff, P., ... 150
Schaller, B., ... 48, 163
Schiffman, L. H., ... 124, 148
Schley, D., ... 121, 164
Schmid, K., ... 124, 163
Schneider, W., ... 14, 163
Schoors, A., ... 6, 163
Schreiner, S. E., ... 67, 68, 163
Schwartz, D. R., ... 165
Scott, J. M., ... 39, 124, 157, 163
Seitz, C., ... 128, 163
Shen, D., ... 86, 163
Shepherd, D., ... 29, 32, 164
Signer, M. A., ... 59, 61, 164
Simon, R., ... 72, 73, 164
Ska, J. L., ... 6, 164
Smith, P. R., ... 164
Snaith, N. H., ... 72, 73, 164
Soden, W. von, ... 121, 133, 164

Sokoloff, M., 32, 164
Sorlin, H., 54, 150
Sperber, D., 23, 164
Spiegel, S., 14, 28, 44, 73, 164
Spittler, R. P., ... 47, 48, 50, 140, 156, 164
Spronk, K., 114, 164
Stalker, D. M. G., 118, 162
Stanton, G., 140, 154, 159
Stec, D. M., 165
Steck, O. H., 124, 163
Steible, H., 165
Stephens, W. P., 67, 150
Sternberg, M., 88, 89, 165
Stipp, H. J., 107, 158
Stone, M., 128, 165
Strauss, H., 10, 165
Stump, E., 64, 165
Swete, H. B., 41, 165
Synan, E., 64, 165
Syring, W., 29, 45, 85, 95, 103, 165
Szold, H., 45, 153
Szpek, H. M., 11, 165

Tambasco, A. J., 85, 158
Tamez, E., 141, 165
Taylor, M. C., 87, 110, 165
Terrien, S., 102, 118, 119, 166
Thickstun, W. R., 82, 166
Tilley, T. W., 106, 166
Timbie, J., 156
Toivari-Viitala, J., 114, 115, 166
Tov, E., 27, 166
Tremblay, P. H., 40, 41, 166
Tropper, J., 23, 166
Troyer, K. de, 35, 151
Trudinger, P., 140, 166
Tsevat, M., 84, 166
Tur-Sinai, N. H., 17, 23, 166
Tuttle, G. A., 29, 168

Twersky, I., 12, 147
Twomey, V., 51, 158

Urbach, E., 44, 45, 166
Urbrock, W. J., 99, 166

Vaux, R. de, 133, 166

Walfish, B. D., 58, 59, 64, 148, 153, 164, 165, 167
Wallace, M. I., 120, 167
Walsem, R. van, 166
Waltke, B. K., 10, 167
Warner, M., 78, 150
Wawrykow, J. P., 65, 167
Weinberg, J., 43, 46, 167
Weiss, M., 92, 167
Weiss, R., 29, 167
Westermann, C., 118, 167
Whedbee, W., 99, 167
Whybray, R. N., 3, 132, 167
Willems, H. O., 166
Willey, P. T., 6, 128, 167
Willis, J. T., 11, 158
Wischnitzer-Bernstein, R., 140, 167
Witte, M., 30, 118, 167
Wolde, E. van, 118, 168
Wolff, H. W., 137, 149
Woude, A. S. van der, 29, 30, 31, 32, 156, 161
Wright, J. E., 48, 128, 157, 165

Yaffe, M. D., 64, 65, 147, 168

Zerafa, P. P., 78, 168
Zöckler, O., 10, 168
Zuck, R. B., 84, 90, 154, 166
Zuckerman, A., 148
Zuckerman, B., 29, 30, 31, 50, 73, 75, 86, 98, 118, 168